THE AKHMATOVA JOURNALS

VOLUME I 1938–41

Lydia Chukovskaya

Translated from the Russian by
Milena Michalski and Sylva Rubashova
Poetry translated by Peter Norman

FARRAR, STRAUS & GIROUX
NEW YORK

Library of Congress catalog card number: 93-27286

This book has been translated from
Zapiski ob Anne Akhmatovoy (1938–1941),
Vol. 1 (Moscow, 1989), which the author has subsequently revised
and extended for the present edition.
First edition: Paris: YMCA-Press, 1976
Second edition: Paris: YMCA-Press, 1984

CONTENTS

LIST OF ILLUSTRATIONS

NOTE ON TRANSLITERATION

Russian names and other words have been transliterated according to
System 1 as defined by J. T. Shaw in *The Transliteration of Modern
Russian for English-Language Publications*, Madison and London, 1967.

Our one consistent variation is that we have transliterated "кс" as
"ks" rather than as "x". A few names already familiar in a certain
English spelling are given in that spelling; these include Lydia
(Chukovskaya), Mandelstam and Meyerhold.

Note to English-readers

a) the letter e can represent either of two sounds: "e" (as in "egg")
and "Ye" (as in "yes"), so that for example, Elena and Ezhov are
pronounced with an initial sound of "ye", while Erenburg has an initial
sound of "e".

b) "Ya", "Yu", "Ts" and "Ch" sometimes appear as initial letters –
this is because each represents a single letter of the Russian alphabet.

From beneath what ruins I speak!
From beneath what crumbling landslip I cry!
[. . .]
Nevertheless, they will recognize my voice,
Nevertheless, once more they will believe it.

ANNA AKHMATOVA
Rough draft

The Akhmatova Journals
1938–41

Instead of a Foreword

In my time I have had to flee Leningrad twice: in February 1938 and in May 1941.

The first flight saved me from the camps. As I fled, I knew what I was running from and why. The second flight, as it later turned out, saved me from two deaths at one and the same time: the camps and one that no one yet knew about, one still unborn – Leningrad, the blockade.

. . . February 1938. A little wooden window on Shpalernaya Street – where, doubled up, I said: "Bronshteyn, Matvey Petrovich," and held out some money – replied to me from above in a deep voice: "Gone!" and a man, whose face was too high for the visitor to see, pushed my hand with the money away with his elbow and stomach.

"Gone!" I immediately went to queue at the Prosecutor's Office on Liteyny Prospekt. Some two or three days and nights on the steps, and there I was already in the Prosecutor's Office. To my question he replied that I could find out what decision had been made at the Military Prosecutor's Office in Moscow. That same night I took the Red Arrow to Moscow. Next morning, one of my Leningrad friends phoned to tell me that Lyusha and nanny Ida were being moved to Kirochnaya Street, to Korney Ivanovich's . . . I understood the information to mean: they had come for me to the flat at Five Corners, my flat, Mitya's, where Lyusha and nanny Ida and I had carried on living after Mitya's arrest. I was not wrong: they had come, it turned out, at one in the morning, by which time I was standing at the corridor window of the train watching the Leningrad platform sail past me.

At the Military Prosecutor's Office in Moscow, in Pushkin Street, I heard the sentence, quite standard in those days: "Bronshteyn, Matvey Petrovich? Ten years without right of correspondence and confiscation of property."

By that time we already knew that such a sentence for a husband meant arrest and the camps for his wife. That is why the morning's friendly telephone call with information about Lyusha and insistent advice not to return to Leningrad had not surprised me. We were also convinced by then, because of numerous examples, that if a wife left immediately after her husband had been sentenced, she would not be pursued. But something we did not even guess at then: "Ten years without right of correspondence" – this was the euphemism for being shot. On hearing the sentence at the Military Prosecutor's Office, I did not understand that Matvey Petrovich was no longer of this world. I felt I had to stay alive, avoid arrest, not only for Lyusha's sake, but also for Mitya's, because if I were to land in prison, who on earth would organize the rescue work?*

All the same, I did return to Leningrad from Moscow, but not to my flat, nor to the one on Kirochnaya Street. I stayed with friends for two days and met Lyusha,† Ida and Korney Ivanovich in a little park. I said goodbye, took some money from Korney Ivanovich and left.

Such were the circumstances of my first flight.

First I lived with Mitya's parents in Kiev. Then in Vorzel near Kiev. Then in Yalta. No one looked for me. After receiving information from Korney Ivanovich that Pyotr Ivanych (our code name for the NKVD) had settled down, come to his senses and no longer had his eye on other men's wives, I returned to Leningrad, to my home. The flat had been looted: Mitya's library of one and a half thousand volumes had been transferred to the cellars of the Peter and Paul Fortress, large pieces of furniture and winter clothes had been taken to an unknown destination, little things like sheets, children's toys, overshoes and clocks had been sold on the cheap to someone for the benefit of the confiscators. They put some Vasya Katyshev in Mitya's room, one of "theirs", who inherited from the crushed enemy of the people, not only the room, but also the bookcase, the writing desk and the clock. I didn't take Lyushenka home for some time, for fear that they would arrest me after all, but week after week passed, and they still didn't touch me. So, when I stopped expecting the doorbell to ring every night, I brought Lyusha and nanny Ida home, and once again resumed my efforts on behalf of Mitya.

It is to the time of my return to Leningrad, following my first escape, that the first entries in my diary relate. For that was the time I started seeing Anna Andreevna Akhmatova.

On 15 May 1941, that is, one month before the war, I was forced to leave Leningrad for the second time. This time the reason was that

---

* On the theoretical physicist Matvey Petrovich Bronshteyn and his books, his fate and our attempts to save him, see the section headed ". . . But strong are the bolts of prison gates" (p. 244).

† Lyusha (Elena) – my daughter by my first marriage.

rumours had reached Pyotr Ivanovich concerning the existence of some "document about '37", as Ida's interrogators called the unknown document. (In fact this was *Sofia Petrovna*, a novella about '37, which I wrote in the winter of 1939–40.)

But I shall come to my second escape later. The same goes for my last, final departure from Leningrad in 1944, which was also not of my own free will.

My entries on the Terror, incidentally, are notable in that the only things which are fully reproduced are dreams. Reality was beyond my powers of description; moreover, I did not even attempt to describe it in my diary. It could not have been captured in a diary, and anyway could one even conceive of keeping a real diary in those days? The content of our conversations, whispers, guesses, silences of that time is scrupulously absent from these notes. The content of my days – which I sometimes spent doing occasional work (I had been sacked from my full-time job in '37), but most often in queues to various representatives of Pyotr Ivanych, in Leningrad or Moscow, or writing letters and petitions, or meeting Mitya's colleagues, scholars and writers, who tried to intercede for him – in other words, real life, my daily life, has been omitted from my notes, or almost omitted; just faint glimmers of it, here and there. The main content of my conversations with old friends and with Anna Andreevna has also been omitted. Occasionally some sign, some initials, some hint for a future which was never to be, and that's all. In those days, Anna Andreevna lived under the spell of the torture chamber, demanding from herself and others constant memory of it, despising those who behaved as though it didn't exist. To write down our conversations – wouldn't that mean risking her life? Not to write anything about her? This would also be criminal. In my confusion I wrote sometimes more openly, sometimes more secretively, kept my notes sometimes at home, sometimes at a friend's, wherever I felt was safer. But invariably, whilst re-creating our talks with the greatest possible accuracy, I omitted or veiled their main content: my efforts on behalf of Mitya, hers on behalf of Lyova; news from these two fronts; information "about those who perished in the night".

The literary conversations in my diary illicitly crept into the foreground: in reality the names Ezhov, Stalin, Vyshinsky and words such as "died", "shot", "banished", "queue", "search", and so on, came up in our conversations no less frequently than discussions about books and paintings. Whereas I assiduously omitted the names of the masters of the torture chambers, I recorded Anna Andreevna's stories about Rozanov,

Modigliani or even just about Larisa Reysner, or Zinaida Gippius. The torture chamber, which had swallowed up, physically, whole quarters of the city, and spiritually all our conscious and unconscious thoughts, the torture chamber, crying out its own clumsily crafted lies from every newspaper column, from every radio set, at the same time demanded of us that we should not take its name in vain, even within four walls, tête-à-tête. We were disobedient, we mentioned it continually, vaguely suspecting while doing so that, even when we were alone, we were not alone, that someone never took his eyes off us, or rather his ears. Surrounded by muteness, the torture chamber wished to remain at once all-powerful and nonexistent; it would not let anyone's word call it out of its almighty nonexistence; it was next door, a stone's throw away, and at the same time it was as if it wasn't there; women stood in the queues in silence, or whispering, used only indefinite forms of speech: "they came", "they took"; Anna Andreevna, when visiting me, recited parts of "Requiem" also in a whisper, but at home in Fontanny House did not even dare to whisper it; suddenly, in mid-conversation, she would fall silent and, signalling to me with her eyes at the ceiling and walls, she would get a scrap of paper and a pencil; then she would loudly say something very mundane: "Would you like some tea?" or "You're very tanned", then she would cover the scrap in hurried handwriting and pass it to me. I would read the poems and, having memorized them, would hand them back to her in silence. "How early autumn came this year," Anna Andreevna would say loudly and, striking a match, would burn the paper over an ashtray.

It was a ritual: hands, match, ashtray – a beautiful and mournful ritual.

Day by day, month by month, my fragmentary notes became less and less a re-creation of my own life, turning into episodes in the life of Anna Akhmatova. In the ghostly, fantastical, troubled world that surrounded me, she alone appeared not as a dream, but as a reality, even though she was writing about ghosts at the time. She was a fact, a certainty amidst all those wavering uncertainties. In the mental state in which I existed during those years – stunned, deadened – I seemed to myself less and less truly alive, and my non-life unworthy of description. ("It's a good thing that it is over.") By 1940 I had virtually ceased making notes about myself, whereas I wrote about Anna Andreevna more and more often. I was drawn to writing about her because she herself, her words, her deeds, her head, shoulders and the movements of her hands were possessed of such perfection, which, in this world, usually belongs only to great works of art. Before my very eyes, Akhmatova's fate –

something greater even than her own person – was chiselling out of this famous and neglected, strong and helpless woman, a statue of grief, loneliness, pride, courage. I had known Akhmatova's earlier poems by heart since childhood, and the new ones, together with the movement of hands burning paper over an ashtray, and the aquiline profile, sharply defined as a blue shadow on the white wall of the transit prison, were now entering my life with the same inescapable naturalness as the bridges, St Isaac's, the Summer Garden or the embankment had already entered it long ago.

June–July 1966
Moscow

1938

10 November 1938

Yesterday I was at Anna Andreevna's on business.

I had known her poems by heart since childhood, had collected pictures of her, but I never imagined that someday I would go to see her "on business".

When I was about 13, Korney Ivanovich once took me to see her and she signed a copy of "By the Seashore" for me. I didn't dare to look at her because on entering K.I. remarked: "Lida says that it's a line shorter than the journal version." That "Lida says" killed me.

After that – or before? – I saw her in the House of Writers at the Blok memorial evening. She recited "Our Lady of Smolensk has her name day today"* and left straight away. I was struck by her bearing, her azure shawl, her walk, her distracted look, her voice. It was impossible to believe that she was the same kind of human being as the rest of us. After she had left I felt very keenly "the secret pain of parting". But nobody could have forced me to go and make her acquaintance.

Then, in Olgino, I met her on a straight avenue leading from the station to the sea. (Or maybe it was in Lakhta?) She was walking with a lady with luxuriant hair (only later did I guess that this was Sudeykina). I greeted Anna Andreevna, even more ashamed of myself than usual: of my awkwardness, my round shoulders. The avenue was straight, like a music string, and watching them go, I thought how much easier it would be to express their harmonious appearance on that avenue by some musical, not verbal, phrase.

Yesterday I was at Anna Andreevna's on business.†

---

* See: *Anno Domini* MCMXXI. Petrograd: Petropolis, 1922.
† Rumours were circulating implying that when N. N. Punin and Lyova were arrested A.A. wrote a letter to Stalin and handed it in at the Kremlin's Kutafya tower, and both were released.

   I went to find out what she had written. Lyova had already been rearrested then, but Nikolay Nikolaevich was free.

   Lyova: son of Anna Andreevna and Nikolay Stepanovich Gumilyov. See "... But strong

I walked through the House of Entertaining Science (what a stupid name!) into the garden. The branches of the trees seemed to grow out of her poems or Pushkin's. I climbed the tricky back staircase that belonged to another century, each step as deep as three. There was still some connection between this staircase and her, but then! When I rang the bell a woman opened the door, wiping soapsuds from her hands. Those suds and the shabby entrance hall, with its scraps of peeling wallpaper, were somehow quite unexpected. The woman walked ahead of me. The kitchen; washing on lines, its wetness slapping one's face. The wet washing was just like the ending of a nasty story, like something out of Dostoevsky, perhaps. Beyond the kitchen, a little corridor, and to the left, a door leading to her room.

She was wearing a black silk dressing gown with a silver dragon on the back.

I asked. I thought she would look for a rough draft or a copy. No. In an even voice, looking lucidly and directly at me, she recited it all to me by heart.

I remembered one phrase: "We all live for the future, and I do not want to be left with such a filthy stain."*

The general appearance of the room was one of neglect, chaos. By the stove an armchair, missing a leg, ragged, springs protruding. The floor unswept. The beautiful things – the carved chair, the mirror in its smooth bronze frame, the lubok prints on the walls – did not adorn the room; on the contrary, they only emphasized its squalor further.

The only thing that was genuinely beautiful was the window onto the garden, and a tree gazing right in at the window. Black branches.

And, of course, she herself.

I was struck by her arms: youthful, delicate, the hands tiny like Anna Karenina's.

"I wonder, should I hang pictures on the wall, or is it no longer worth the trouble?"

"On 19 September, I left Nikolay Nikolaevich.[1] We lived together for 16 years. But I didn't even notice against *this* background."

---

are the bolts of prison gates" for details of his fate (p. 243).

    Nikolay Nikolaevich Punin: art historian, Anna Andreevna's husband. See the section headed "Behind the Scenes", note 1.

* Amongst the charges brought against Lyova was this too: his mother had allegedly incited him to murder Zhdanov, to avenge his father who had been shot. But the phrase I had remembered proves that Anna Andreevna had quoted her second letter to Stalin, not the letter of 1935, but the one from 1938, which had had no effect on this occasion. And the rumours about the Kutafya tower and the magical rescue of the prisoners were nothing but belated reports about her letter of 1935. (*Journals*, vol. 2.)

"One good thing: I am so ill that I'll probably die soon."

"Knyazev has died. Svyatopolk-Mirsky is hoarding crusts."[2]

"A woman behind me in the queue began to cry when she heard my name."

I asked her to recite some of her poems. In the same, even, almost colourless voice she recited:

> Some gaze into affectionate eyes,
> The others drink till the morn's sunrays,
> But all night I try to compromise
> With my inextinguishable conscience.

"Gaze" [vzory] – "compromise" [peregovory] for some reason sounds just as piercing here as Pushkin's "strange" [stranen] – "shot" [ranen].

> Quite motionless he lay, and strange [stranen]
> Was his lifeless brow as if he swooned.
> He was shot [ranen] right through beneath his breast –
> And blood flew smoking from his wound.

The "strange . . . shot" always made me feel more pain than the flow of blood . . . And in the same way "gaze . . . compromise" pounds my heart with God knows what.*

Then she told me that Boris Leonidovich was not happy with the following line from her poem dedicated to him:

> So as not to disturb the fragile sleep of the frog.

He didn't like the frog.†

I left her late. Walked in darkness trying to recall the poems. I had to remember them there and then, from start to finish, because already I could not let them go even for a second. Where words had slipped my mind, I put in my own to keep the metre and, in response, from somewhere deep in the recesses of memory, those unworthy words lured out the real ones. I remembered everything word for word. But later, while getting washed and ready for bed, I could not recall a single step down

---

* See: *The Flight of Time* [*Beg vremeni*]. Moscow and Leningrad: Sovetskiy pisatel, 1965 (hereafter referred to as *FT* for short [followed by the section title in English and also, at the first occurrence, in Russian in square brackets; for other abbreviations used in this edition see the section "Behind the Scenes"]; "Some gaze into affectionate eyes" see *FT*, *Reed* [*Trostnik*]).

† I refer the reader to the section called "The Poems of Anna Akhmatova" which follows these journal entries, **no. 1**. Included there are all those poems without which my notes may seem unclear. [The poems which appear in this section are numbered from 1 to 54 and these numbers appear in bold type in the footnotes.] The poem "Boris Pasternak" is also discussed in *Journals*, vol. 2.

the road. How had I walked through the House of Entertaining Science?
How had I crossed Nevsky?

I had been sleepwalking: poems had guided me, instead of the moon,
and the world had been absent.

1939

22 February 1939 *

She came – in an old coat, a faded, crushed hat, coarse stockings.

She sat on my divan and smoked, stately, beautiful as ever.

"I can't look at those eyes. Have you noticed? They seem to exist apart from the faces."†

"My neighbour doesn't love her boy.‡ She beats him. When she takes the strap to him, I go into the bathroom. I tried to talk to her once – she rebuffed me."

"Last winter I read *Ulysses*. I read it through four times before I got to grips with it. It is a very remarkable book. Although there is too much pornography in it for my liking."

"Lyova had already written scholarly works of his own, had mastered languages. He once asked his professor if such-and-such was true. The professor replied: 'If you think so, that means it's true' ... He is very hardy, because he has always been used to living in bad conditions, he's not been spoilt. He's used to sleeping on the floor, eating little."

Then she looked over my books – that is, Mitya's English ones§ – she picked out E. Browning and I set off with her to see her home. It was dry, snowless, cold. Windy. She walked with a light, quick step, but was afraid to cross the street and clung to my sleeve in the middle of Nevsky.

She stood midway for a long time, not letting me go any further, fearful of my attempts. We stood in the middle of the street, her fingers clutching my shoulder ever more tightly. She said: "I can't translate.

---

* During that time – from 10.11.38 until 22.2.39 – I saw A.A. several times, but my notes have been lost – forever or temporarily, I do not know.
† The eyes of the women in prison queues.
‡ Tanya Smirnova – her eldest son, Valya.
§ When our property – including books – was confiscated, all the English books were left behind for some reason.

Osip* once said to me so plaintively, 'Everyone tries to make me translate. Everyone says, "Translate, translate!" But I don't know how to.'
Well, and nor do I."

We stood in the middle of the street for a long time. I kept encouraging
her softly: "We can go now, we can go now."

"No, no, not yet!"

26 February 1939

I went to Anna Andreevna's and dropped the ticket off.† She was sitting
on the divan in a faded pink headscarf, her feet in worn-out shoes tucked
under her.

"You know, I reread Mme Browning. Somehow I don't like her. The
husband always dragged out one single note, yet masterfully. But she
... maybe that's exactly why she's bad, because she is so like him."

From somewhere on the top shelf, standing on the divan, she took
down a green notebook. I wanted to help – "Why, I can jump like a
goat!"

She leafed through it.

"He‡ did a lot, especially after '28."

She read me two poems: one about mighty poverty, which I had heard
before, the other, which I didn't know, about Kiev-the-Viy.[3]

"Read yours."

"I don't have anything new."

All of a sudden she pointed to her forehead – on the edge there was
some kind of small, dark brown lesion.

"That's cancer," she said. "It's a very good thing I'm going to die
soon."[4]

3 March 1939, Moscow

"What is it?" asked Anna Andreevna, jumping up from the divan and
bringing her face up to mine, wide-eyed.

This was in Khardzhiev's tiny room, somewhere in the back of beyond;
it had taken me about two hours to get there.[5] Anna Andreevna knows
and loves Moscow, but I only get irritated by its awkwardness. Leningrad,

---

* Osip Emilevich Mandelstam.
† Evidently Anna Andreevna had asked me to buy her a ticket to Moscow.
‡ Osip Mandelstam.

with its harmony, also brings harmony to one's soul, whereas Moscow
upsets one's equanimity.

It was cold at Nikolay Ivanovich's. Anna Andreevna was sitting on
the divan, her coat draped around her shoulders. We drank tea out of
mugs, and then wine from the same ones.

Nikolay Ivanovich, unshaven, yellow, is listening to the footsteps on
the other side of the wall – to the neighbour's footsteps.

Anna Andreevna talked about writers who were afraid to see her.

"Today, Zina wouldn't let him come round," she said about Boris
Leonidovich.

Conversation about Herzen. I struggled long and foolishly, forcing an
open door to prove that Herzen was a great writer and a great artist.
Anna Andreevna agreed ardently.

"Of course, he is far better than Turgenev, for example. But, I don't
like the chapters in *My Past and Thoughts* where he's so frank about
Natasha."

I tried to argue. I understood it like this: in Herzen's attitude towards
world democracy, on "family matters" lies the beautiful naïveté of the
revolutionary who senses the unity of revolution, morality and aesthetics.

"No, unity and naïveté aren't the point here," said Anna Andreevna.
"Times were like that then. In Pushkin's day, one did not reveal anything
about oneself, but *they* spelled everything out to the last word."

2 May 1939, Leningrad

In the morning, walking with Lyusha, I called on Anna Andreevna and
persuaded her to come out for a walk.

She limped slightly: a broken heel.

We walked along the Fontanka, past the circus, past the Engineers'
Castle.

"Aren't you tired of Petersburg?" she asked me after a long silence.

"Me? No."

"I am. Very. The distance, the buildings – images of frozen suffering.
And I haven't been away for so long, too long."

Walking past the circus: "Here, several years ago, a seal used to bark
during the white nights . . ."

Passing the Engineers': "You see the two windows with the different-
coloured panes? Paul was murdered in that room."

We sat down for a brief moment in the little garden. She spoke,
enraptured, about the frescoes in St Sophia's Cathedral (she had seen

photographs). And added: "St Sophia's in Novgorod is very fine too."

We set off to see her home.

"I know the Fontanka inside out," said Anna Andreevna, "I lived here, in the chapter house with Olya."

(A house with columns not far from the Simeonev bridge.[6])

"You should go for walks more often," I said on parting.

She waved her hand dismissively at me.

"Come now! How can one go for walks these days!"

18 May 1939

In the evening, a telephone call: Anna Andreevna asked me to come. But I could not – Lyushenka had the flu, I had to stay at home.

She came over herself.

She sat on my divan, magnificent, her profile like on a medal, smoking.

She had come to ask for some advice . . . In every word there was an astonishing combination of firmness, dignity and childlike helplessness.

"Look, I got this letter. People tell me: Ask Mikhail Leonidovich for advice.* But I decided you would be better. You were nurtured by Gosizdat."

(And thrown out by them too!)

The letter read: "We would be glad to publish . . . but please send us some more to facilitate selection."

"It's been like that for 20 years now. They don't know or remember anything. 'To facilitate selection!' Every time, again and again, they are surprised by my new poetry: they hoped that this time, at last, my poems would turn out to be about collective farms. Once, here in Leningrad, they asked me to bring my poems in. I did. Then they asked me to come and have a chat with them. I went. 'But why are the poems so sad? That's *done with*, after all . . .' I replied: 'Evidently the explanation for such nonsense lies in the peculiarities of my biography.'"

Together, we started going through her poetry, from memory. I tried somehow to form a cycle. She, in spite of having come for "some advice", listened to me listlessly, without any interest.

"I don't want to search, to rummage . . . Never mind them . . . I will give them 'From my Tatar grandmother' and have done with it. Besides, all that's left are some madly amorous poems."[†]

---

* Mikhail Leonidovich – Lozinsky. See note 7.

† "From my Tatar grandmother . . ." is the first line of "Tale of the Black Ring" – *FT, Anno Domini*.

She puts the publishers' letter away and, catching sight of some little volumes of Oksman's edition of Pushkin on my table, starts talking about Pushkin: "How complex *The Queen of Spades* is! Layer upon layer. I understood that for the first time when Zhuravlyov[8] recited it. He recites wonderfully. It was his recitation which revealed its complexity to me."

Both of us amiably scolded Yakhontov.

"It's simply uninteresting," said Anna Andreevna.

The conversation about Pushkin's prose led us to Tolstoy. Anna Andreevna spoke of him somewhat ironically. And then she delivered a formidable speech against *Anna Karenina*: "You must have noticed that the main idea of that great work is this: if a woman leaves her lawful husband to live with another man, this inevitably makes her a prostitute. Don't argue! That's exactly what it is! And just think: who did that rubbishy old man choose as the instrument of God? Who wreaks the vengeance promised in the epigraph, then? High society: Countess Lidiya Ivanovna and the charlatan preacher. For it is they who drive Anna to suicide.

And how vile his own attitude to Anna is! At first he's simply in love with her, admires her, with those black ringlets on the nape of her neck ... But then he starts to hate her – he even mocks her dead body ... Remember: 'shamelessly stretched out'?"

I did not argue. I am too interested in listening to speak myself. Well, yes, she is a gynophile. When she fell silent I only said: "How magnificent the pages leading up to her suicide are."

"Yes, yes, of course, there are a lot of brilliant pages. The muttering of the peasant under the wheels – marvellously *zaum*."

But on the whole, she evidently did not like Tolstoy.

"I'm very friendly with his granddaughter Sonya. She's given me an album to write in. That album has a stuffy air about it – the sanctimonious spirit of Yasnaya Polyana."

Lozinsky brought her the *Inferno*.

"The translation is remarkable," she said. "I'm enjoying it. There are forced passages, but not many. I sit there checking it against the original."

I, with my characteristic talent for making hasty remarks, without thinking, enquired whether she knew Italian.

Majestically, modestly, she said: "I have been reading Dante all my life."

In passing she complained: "It is noisy at our place. The Punins have parties, the gramophone is on till all hours ... Nikolay Nikolaevich keeps insisting that I should move."

"Exchange your room?"

"No, simply move out . . . You know, in the last two years I've started to think badly of men. Have you noticed there are hardly any *there* . . ."*

And, rejecting my attempt to explain this,† blowing smoke sideways, she quoted somebody's words: "The inferior race . . ."⁹

It was late. Lyushenka was asleep, but was coughing badly in her sleep. I ask Ida not to sleep in the kitchen but in the nursery and I go to see Anna Andreevna off. Outside, the evening was warm, the sky deep. And in those depths the bell tower of St Vladimir's Cathedral.

On the way, Anna Andreevna told me about Yaroslav's skull which had been brought here for scientific analysis ("all the teeth are intact"), and about Kiev ("spoiled by the 19th century").

Many drunks all around. The entire male contingent of the street seemed incapable of standing up. Anna Andreevna recounted how one night recently three men had pestered her, one after the other, and when she shouted at one he had retorted: "I'm not your husband, don't yell at me!"

We walked through her dark courtyard. Stumbling, she said: "Such an entertaining courtyard, don't you think?" Then we climbed the stairs in total darkness: not one single light bulb. She walked easily, more easily than I, without panting, but hobbling slightly: her heel. By her door, on parting, she said to me: "Do you know what torture by hope is? After despair, calm sets in, but hope can drive you mad."

29 May 1939

Last night, Anna Andreevna phoned and summoned me. I couldn't get away until late. I found her lying down.

"Nothing's happened. I've just got out of the bath. I'm fine."

A thick blanket with no sheet. A coarse nightshirt. Wet hair on the pillow. Her face small, dry, dark. Her mouth sunken. "This is how she'll look in her coffin," I thought.

But this impression soon dissolved. She jumped up, slipped on a black silk dressing gown with a dragon on it ("a Chinaman's coat," she explained) and brought some tea from the kitchen. There was black bread and some kind of soya sweets to go with the tea. Having finished her cup, she got back under the blanket and began to speak. She had some

---

*   There – that is, in the prison queues.
†   I said that there were considerably more men than women in prison, therefore there were more women in the queues.

new trouble and had obviously called me so as not to be alone. She did not speak about her worry, but about everything else under the sun.

"I'm rereading Saltykov. A remarkable writer. *A Contemporary Idyll* – read it again. Poor thing, they say he had to write it in Aesopian language. But Aesop's language helped him form his style."

And again about Herzen: "Yes, there's a writer ... Do you remember, by any chance, where he called Nikolay 'Dadon'? I need to know for my work.

"But there are also inflated reputations, Turgenev for example."

(I was delighted by this shared dislike.)

"He wrote so badly! So badly! Remember 'Knock, Knock . . . !' Dostoevsky was right: continual *mercis*! And the haughty manner in which he described people: superficially, disdainfully."

I said that the concept of "a Russian literary language" was wholly arbitrary, that all writers have their own: Gogol, Lermontov, Pushkin, Tolstoy, Herzen. Every one of them writes in their own language, rather than in literary Russian. I mentioned that Korney Ivanovich, after reading "While France Amidst Applause", exclaimed: "Is this supposed to be Russian? This is some other, maybe even beautiful, but other, particular language. The sound is different."

"Korney Ivanovich is mistaken," said Anna Andreevna. "It is not some special language, it is simply that in the 16th and 17th centuries in France there existed a fixed canon for beginnings and endings. Odes, for instance, had to begin with the word *aussi*. Pushkin often translated this introduction. The same goes for *while*. This was simply something obligatory for a ceremonial opening. Voltaire, in his day, was already parodying similar introductions and used them in his satirical verses. I have written a lot about that – it's all in those boxes, there. I can't even imagine any more how one understands Pushkin without this background."*

I talked about *Poltava*.

She pressed her hands to her face for a minute.

"How did he know? How did he know everything?"

Then: "I will never read it again!"†

---

* Akhmatova's observations about "this background" have now been published. See "Motley Notes", *OP*, p. 234, and also "Anna Akhmatova's Early Pushkin Studies: from materials in P. Luknitsky's Archive", annotated by V. Nepomnyashchy, S. Velikovsky (*Voprosy Literatury*, 1978, no. 1).

† I told Anna Andreevna how, having come out of prison, A. I. Lyubarskaya recited two lines from Pushkin to me:

Nikolay Nikolaevich was stamping down the corridor and jabbering away.

To distract Anna Andreevna from *Poltava*, I recounted how I had first seen her, in her azure shawl, at the Blok memorial evening.

"That was a gift from Marina," said Anna Andreevna. "And the little box."*

I asked her about the Merezhkovskys.

"They were malevolent, wicked people. And they never did anything without an ulterior motive. In 1917, Zinaida Nikolaevna suddenly started phoning me, inviting me over, but I didn't go. She needed me for something or other ..."

"And Rozanov?" I asked. "I'm so fond of him, except ..."

"Except for his anti-Semitism and his attitude to sex," Anna Andreevna finished off.

31 May 1939

Tonight Gesha was at my place.[11] Suddenly, without warning, Anna Andreevna arrived. It turned out she had had a phone call from *Moscow Almanac*, requesting poems. Meaning all her doubts had been in vain. She wanted me to deliver them.† I promised I would definitely call round before my departure. She finished her tea and left quickly, evidently Gesha made her feel uncomfortable.

1 June 1939

Today I called in on Anna Andreevna for the poems. She was lying down, her face dry, yellow, hands behind her head. I had brought her

---

My first treasure was my honour,
Torment took away this treasure,

saying that only in prison had she truly understood *Poltava*.

On A. I. Lyubarskaya see note 10.

* Marina – Marina Ivanovna Tsvetaeva.

† Akhmatova's poems were not published in *Moscow Almanac* [*Moskovskiy almanakh*]. Many years later, in December 1977, K. Simonov referred to Fadeev's ban in his letter to V. Vilenkin; Fadeev felt that some works, amongst them these poems by Akhmatova, should not be published in the first issue of this almanac. And, accordingly, they weren't. In a note to Simonov's letter, the editors also published the circular in which Fadeev gave a detailed explanation of the reasons behind his unwillingness to publish Akhmatova's and Aseev's poems, as well as Zoschenko's prose, in the almanac. (See K. Simonov, *Collected Writings* [*Sobranie sochineniy*], vol. 12. Moscow: Khudozh. lit., 1987, pp. 468–9).

rissoles, boiled eggs, cake and lilacs. Yes, lilacs too, so it would seem more like a present . . .

Soon Vladimir Georgievich arrived.*

She asked him to copy some poems: "You know where they are, don't you?"

He leafed through the exercise book a long time, searching, not finding them. She explained where and what, very patiently, trying not to get irritated, and all the same somewhere in the depths of her voice there was irritation.

Vladimir Georgievich copied slowly. I handed a rissole on a piece of bread and a cup of tea to her, in bed. She ate and drank lying down, without sitting up.

He asked her about the punctuation.

SHE: It doesn't matter in the slightest.
ME: Are you indifferent to punctuation?
SHE: In poetry – absolutely. It's a Futurist tradition.[12]
HE: Do you need an ellipsis here?
SHE (*without looking*): As you wish. (*To me.*) K.G.† said that every second line of mine ends in an ellipsis.

Vladimir Georgievich finished copying and asked her to take a look, but she waved it away: "It's all the same . . . It's not important . . ."

Taking the exercise book and glancing at the original I asked: "What's this? A hyphen or a gap?"

"No, but there, unfortunately, is a stanza . . . All my life I've dreamt of writing without stanzas, without a break. It doesn't work."‡

4 July 1939

Yesterday morning I phoned Anna Andreevna. "May I come round this evening?"

"You may, only come early, I want to see you as soon as possible."

I arrived early.

She was lying down – lying down again, hands behind her head. The window onto the garden was open. It was quiet and empty. On the floor

---

* Garshin (1887–1956): anatomical pathologist, professor at the Military Academy of Medicine, worked for many years at the Erisman hospital; nephew of the writer Vsvelod Garshin. For more details on him, see *Journals*, vol. 2.
† Kolya [Nikolay] Gumilyov.
‡ I do not remember which poem was in question.

by the window stood a picture: a portrait of Anna Andreevna in a white dress.

"Osmyorkin painted me well. He finished on the 29th. To me the face seems a great likeness."

I could not make the face out in the darkness of the corner.

After I had told her the latest, and she me, she picked up and read aloud some quite idiotic reader's letter.

"You are not keen on form, you write simply. Whereas Pasternak gets carried away by formal strivings, manipulates words . . ."

"Simply!" Anna Andreevna said crossly. "They imagine that Pushkin also wrote simply and that they understand everything in his poetry."

And I started thinking about Pasternak. He himself put it better than anyone, saying of his judges and his poetry: ". . . because we were corrupted by clichéd inanity we took it as formal pretentiousness when after long unfamiliarity we actually encountered something unprecedentedly rich in content."[13]

That's how things stand with complexity. As far as simplicity is concerned, it too is only beautiful when it has content, that is, complexity. And I don't believe that a person who doesn't understand Pasternak really understands Akhmatova. Let alone Pushkin.

6 July 1939

She came and read:

> And little signal sounds of easy rhymes . . .*

14 July 1939

This afternoon I was at Anna Andreevna's. She was rushing off somewhere, so I couldn't even understand why, when I phoned, she had allowed me to come. But then she was afraid of roads and loved having someone to accompany her.

No sooner had I arrived than we set off.

"The Punins have taken my kettle," Anna Andreevna told me, "they went out and locked their rooms. So I didn't even have any tea. Oh well, God be with them."

We went out into the little corridor and she started locking her door. It turned out to be a lengthy, complicated process. Having locked the

---

* A line from the poem "It happens thus: a kind of languor" ("Creativity") – *FT, Seventh Book*; no. 2.

door to her room, after we had already gone into the hall, she went back and, in addition, locked the kitchen.

We walked through the Entertaining entrance.

"Look at that door," Anna Andreevna said to me, and closed it slightly. An inscription appeared: MEN'S TOILET. "In the evening, when this door is closed like this, so that the inscription shows, no one calls on us."

I walked her along Nevsky to the corner of Sadovaya. We were silent, the heat stopped us from talking. Anna Andreevna crossed the road, holding on to my sleeve, she kept giving a start and looking around, although it was practically empty. Her tram came. I stood and watched as she went up the little steps, went in, grabbed hold of the strap, opened her handbag . . . In her old mackintosh, an absurd old hat, which looked like a child's cap, in her worn-down shoes – stately, with a beautiful face and tangled grey fringe.

The tram was a tram like any other. People were people like any others. And no one saw that it was her.

20 July 1939

I spent all yesterday evening at Anna Andreevna's.

She was lying down. But insisted that she was healthy.

She persuaded me to sit in the armchair, which I had been wary of sitting in until now.

"True, it has a leg missing," said Anna Andreevna, "but take no notice, it's not a problem, all you have to do is put that little chest under it."

I put the chest underneath, sat down and after the usual "What's new?", "And what about you?" as always the *Arabian Nights* began.

I admitted that I don't like Maupassant. And I was gladdened by the reply that she can't stand him either.

"His long works are particularly loathsome. Those and his short stories. I only like one story – the one where the man goes mad.[14] It's disgusting that in all his portraits he depicts himself as muscular, when in fact he'd been paralysed for a long time. The same goes for his stories."

Then we started talking about Proust, and she spent a whole hour recounting the contents of the novel *Albertine disparue* to me.

Having finished with *Albertine*, Anna Andreevna jumped up and put on her black dressing gown. (It was torn along one seam, from under the arm to the knee, but, evidently, this did not bother her). We drank strong tea with bread, there was nothing else, not even sugar, and I chastised myself for not having brought any.

On the silver teaspoons was engraved a little *a* with a stroke through it. "That's how I write it," explained Anna Andreevna.

I wanted to take a closer look at the little box, which had always fascinated me. She took it down from the shelf. It was a tiny travelling case, silver, with a handle set into the lid. Next to the case stood a small three-panelled icon, and next to the icon, a stone and a little bell. Under the bell there turned out to be a small inkpot, enchanting, made in the 1830s or so. (The bell was its lid.) There was also an empty perfume bottle.

"Smell it, isn't it a delicate scent? It's 'Ideal', the scent of my youth."

Casting a sideways glance at Anna Andreevna, I asked: "Has no one sculpted you?"

"There is a figurine by Danko, but I haven't got it.[15] One sculptor was meant to do a sculpture of me, but then he didn't want to: 'It's dull. Nature has already done it all.'"

She lay down again. She started telling all sorts of stories, jumping from subject to subject, from name to name. She asked whether I had heard of Pallada.[16]

"No."

"You haven't even heard of her? That can only be explained by your preternatural youth. She was renowned. Bracelets on her ankles, Homeric promiscuity. Once, in front of me, she said to her girlfriend: 'I had a marvellous flat on Mokhovaya. You don't remember whom I lived with then, do you?'"

I started asking her about Larisa Reysner – was it true that she used to be amazing?

"No, oh no! She was weak, confused. Once I went round to see her at Admiralteystvo, she lived there when she was married to Raskolnikov. A sailor with a gun barred my way. I asked to be announced. She ran out deeply embarrassed ... She died strangely: her mother and her brother died at the same time, also of typhoid. To me there is something odd about those deaths."

I asked: "Was Larisa as beautiful as people remember?"

Anna Andreevna replied with a thorough, methodical impassivity, as if she were making a clerical inventory: "She was very large, broad shoulders, broad hips. Like a waitress in a German tavern. Her face was slightly swollen, grey, with large eyes and dyed hair. That's it."

For some reason the conversation turned to L.E.

"She used to come round often. She was bewitchingly pretty. Her Giaconda-like lack of eyebrows suited her very well. But then she suddenly changed. She stuck eyebrows on. And she became a gendarme in a skirt. And she immediately became ugly – did you notice?"

I mentioned a good photograph of Altman's portrait of her which I had seen at a friend's house.

She did not pursue the reference to Altman but, after a silence, pronounced: "I have always dreamt that my husband would hang my portrait over the table. But none of them did – not Kolya, nor Volodya, nor Nikolay Nikolaevich. He's only hung it up now that we've separated. That is, he's placed a photograph of me and one of his daughter under the table glass."[17]

I left late. Anna Andreevna asked me to come tomorrow morning without fail. Pleading eyes.

"I will come."*

21 July 1939

I arrived in the morning, as promised.

Anna Andreevna was sitting on the divan, silent and straight. The silence was heavy, perceptible. We were waiting for some lady with whom we were to go.

The tension communicated itself to me as well. I also fell silent. Not knowing what to do, I started leafing through a copy of Byron, lying uppermost, a thick, tattered, English volume.

"Please don't look at the pictures," said Anna Andreevna to me in irritation. "They're awful. I even tore one out, see?"

"Yes, they really make a mockery of the text," I agreed.

"Even without that there isn't much sense in Byron."

The awaited lady arrived. Thinnish, oldish, her whole face covered in tiny wrinkles. The corners of her narrow mouth sagged. Without greeting me and even, it seemed, without noticing me, she informed Anna Andreevna at once about G.†

Anna Andreevna covered her face with her palms. Small, childlike palms.

It was time for us to go.

"Let me introduce you: Olga Nikolaevna – Lydia Korneevna," said Anna Andreevna suddenly on the stairs.[18]

No sooner had we stepped out of the door than we were nearly killed

---

* The next day she was due to take a parcel to the prison queue.
† About someone's arrest – I don't know whose.

by some boards which someone was hurling out of the staircase window. They flew past our heads and fell at our feet with a crash. We went back inside and stood there a long time. The crashing mountain of boards in front of the door grew.

At last, the hurling ceased. We stepped over the mountain, helping one another, and came out onto the Fontanka.

And beyond that, everything was so familiar, like a wallpaper pattern. With the one difference that every time the "kite's tail" was shorter and shorter.*

And so already it's all behind us. But we are still there. We are sitting with Anna Andreevna on a bench, more like a perch. Olga Nikolaevna met an acquaintance and moved aside. And Anna Andreevna whispered, leaning towards me: "Her son is Lyova's brother ... He is only a year younger than Lyova. He has Kolya's hands exactly."

29 July 1939

Yesterday I dropped in at Anna Andreevna's. Vladimir Georgievich and Olga Nikolaevna were there. They were drinking tea with some bread. I didn't take my coat off, just sat down for a minute. They started asking me – and I told them. If I don't speak, if I am alone, I rarely cry. But I cannot speak: my voice breaks off into tears.

Everyone pretended they hadn't noticed a thing. But Anna Andreevna, seeing me off at the door and saying goodbye, asked: "When can I come and see you? May I come tomorrow?"

(To this very day I do not know whether she was being spontaneously kind, or whether it was some nobility of mind, a highly developed aesthetic taste, that compelled her to do good deeds.)

Today she came in the evening. Zoechka was round.† We drank tea. Anna Andreevna talked lightly, freely, elegantly. I asked her where she had studied, and what kind of a student she had been.

"At the Gymnasium in Tsarskoe, then several months at the Smolny, then in Kiev ... No, I didn't like secondary school, nor the Institute. And they didn't like me particularly either.

"At the Gymnasium, in Tsarskoe, something happened to me that has stayed with me all my life. The headmistress there couldn't stand me – apparently because once on the skating rink I had had an argument with

---

* Prison queues in 1939 were incomparably shorter than in 1937–38. We did not stand in them day and night, only hours.
† Zoya Moiseevna Zadunayskaya. For more about her see note 19.

her son. When she walked into our classroom, I knew she would give me a dressing-down: I was not sitting properly, or my dress was not fastened correctly. I found it unpleasant, but I didn't think about it much, 'we were lazy and incurious'. And then came the time to part: the head-mistress left the school, she was transferred elsewhere. There was a farewell party, flowers, speeches, tears. I was there too. The party came to an end, and I was already running down the stairs. Suddenly someone called me. I went back up and saw that it was the headmistress who was calling me. I had no doubt that I was going to be reprimanded again. And suddenly she said: 'Forgive me, Gorenko, I was never fair to you.'"

Zoechka soon left. Anna Andreevna, jumping up from her chair, told me about Kolya. She was terribly excited.*

I started telling her about our Detgiz epic, about Mishkevich's provo-cations, about his tricks with my Mayakovsky.[20]

She waved her hand at me: "Don't, don't, don't torment me!"

Then she suggested she recite some of her poems to me. She recited, "And the stone word fell" and "You must celebrate our joyful anniver-sary".† She asked which I preferred.

I was in no state to answer that question: I was too happy. That I had lived to experience this. That I was hearing this. And I was too unhappy.

Not getting any sense out of me, Anna Andreevna said: "I know all about my old ones myself, as if they were someone else's, but I never know anything about my new ones, until they too become old."

Then everything happened as usual: I go to see her home, drunks outside, at the crossing she clings to my sleeve and is afraid to take a step, Entertaining entrance and pitch dark on the staircase.

"I only eat now when Olga Nikolaevna feeds me," said Anna Andreevna. "She somehow manages to make me."

---

*   Anna Andreevna told me that Lyova's friend, a student at Leningrad University, Kolya Davidenkov, who had been arrested at the same time as Lyova, had been released from prison. For more on Nikolay Sergeevich Davidenkov, see pp. 31–5 of this volume and also note 24.

†   "And the stone word fell" (from "Requiem"), the opening line of the poem "Sentence" – FT, Reed; no. 3. In Soviet editions, until 1987, "The Sentence" was published with no title and with no reference to "Requiem". "The Sentence" was first published as a poem from "Requiem" in the journal Oktyabr (1987, no. 3), and later, a more accurate version, in the journal Neva (1987, no. 6). "You must celebrate our joyful anniversary" – in its final version: "You must celebrate our last anniversary" – FT, Reed; no. 4.

The poem "The Sentence" at that time, when I first heard it from Anna Andreevna, did not end as it was to subsequently, but as follows:

> Long ago I foresaw this:
> The last day and the last home.

9 August 1939

Today when I was at Anna Andreevna's, I noticed a little picture on the wall. An enchanting pencil drawing, a portrait of her. She allowed me to take it off the wall to have a look.

Modigliani.

"You understand, he was not interested in the likeness. The pose fascinated him. He drew me about 20 times.

"He was an Italian Jew, short, with golden eyes, very poor. I understood at once that he had a great future in store. This was in Paris. Then, when I was back in Russia, I used to ask everyone who'd been abroad about him, but they hadn't even heard the name. Then monographs and articles started to appear. And now everyone keeps asking me, 'Have you really seen him?'"

About Aldington: "He's like some pupil who's top of the class."

I admitted that Freudianism annoys me, that I don't believe in Freud.

"Don't say that. I would not understand many things about Nikolay Nikolaevich to this day if not for Freud. Nikolay Nikolaevich always tried to reproduce the very same sexual set-up as in his childhood: a stepmother oppressing a child. I should have oppressed Ira. But I did not oppress her. I taught her French. Everything was wrong – she had an adoring mother, altogether, everything was wrong. But he suggested that I oppressed her. 'You didn't go anywhere with her.' But I myself didn't go anywhere ... What tender letters that girl wrote me!"

I enquired how things stood regarding her moving.

"You think they're in my way? Not in the least."

I asked about the housekeeping.

"A woman comes in to help sometimes. Every five days. She cooks me chicken. And when she's not around, I boil potatoes for myself. If Vladimir Georgievich is meant to come round after work, then I cook myself something solid, steak for instance."

Anna Andreevna took a thick exercise book, bound in black, from a pile of books lying on the armchair, and handed it to me, explaining: "This is what they returned to me. My friends had it bound. And now I write on the blank pages."

I opened it. Two stamps crossed out: one – 1928; the other – 1931 (it seemed). The poems had been typed out. Someone had made notes in red and black pencil. "I hid my face, and I implored my God" had been underlined. The word "remembrance" had been underlined. The poems "How is this age worse than those that went before?", "Everything is ravaged, bartered, betrayed", "You're an apostate: for a green island" had been crossed out.*

While I leafed through the notebook, Anna Andreevna stood behind my chair. It made me feel uncomfortable, I looked distractedly. I managed to catch a glimpse of a poem I didn't know, ending with the line:

The immortal lover of Tamara[†]

– but, here Anna Andreevna snapped the exercise book shut and pushed it back into the pile of books on the armchair.

I don't remember how the conversation turned to Nikolay Stepanovich's poetry.

"His best book is *Pillar of Fire*. He did not live to see fame. It was just around the corner. But he did not manage to know it. Blok knew it. For ten whole years he knew it.

"By the way, it has become clear from Blok's diaries that he had a very cold, unkind attitude towards people. And a lot of things are cut – about the Mendeleevs, about Lyuba."

On parting she said: "I read your husband's book. What a noble book. Usually I don't read such things, but I read this without putting it down. A delightful book . . .[21] Could I give it to Vladimir Georgievich to read?"

10 August 1939

At eleven o'clock in the morning I called in to see her, as promised. She was ready and waiting for me. I took the suitcase with the underwear, she, the bag with the shoes. I asked why she didn't sew a sack.

"I can't sew."

We headed towards the circus. In the sun-drenched square we waited for a tram. There was a horse carting wood.

"Wood which I don't have," said Anna Andreevna. "There's nowhere

---

*   All the notes were obviously of a censorial nature. "I hid my face, and implored my *God*..." is a line from the poem "In Memory of 19 July 1914" – *FT, White Flock*; "So that each day turned into/ *One of remembrance*..." is a line from the poem "We thought we were beggars" no. 22; "How is this age worse than those that went before?" no. 5. The last two poems, as well as "You are an apostate: for a green island", were not republished in the Soviet Union for about 50 years and only reappeared in 1976 in a book edited by academician V. M. Zhirmunsky: *Anna Akhmatova. Lyric and Narrative Poems* [*Anna Akhmatova. Stikhotvoreniya i poemy*]. Introduction by A. A. Surkov; text and notes compiled, edited by V. M. Zhirmunsky. Leningrad: Sovetskiy pisatel, 1976, pp. 84, 143 and 133 (Poet's Library, big series). Hereafter, this edition will be referred to as *BPL-A*.
   "Everything is ravaged, bartered, betrayed" *FT, Anno Domini*; no. 40.
†   "Here Pushkin's banishment began" *FT, Reed*.

to put it. The whole shed is crammed full of Nikolay Nikolaevich's wood."

I asked her whether she thought Nikolay Nikolaevich was making things unpleasant for her on purpose.

"No, not on purpose. He was even embarrassed when he informed me that there was no space for my wood. 'You see, Anya, it turns out our wood has filled the shed right up!'"

Our tram arrived. We were lucky: we both got a seat and put our things on our laps.

"I'm convinced one can't unlearn swimming," said Anna Andreevna. (I didn't understand why she brought swimming up, but I soon guessed.) "Once I was in Razlyv and swam far, far out. Nikolay Nikolaevich got scared, called me and then told me: 'You swim like a bird.'"

At that moment we were going down Zhukovsky Street.

"Over there, opposite, there used to be a sculpture of a little horse's head." She pointed out of the window with her chin. "That was the only monument in Leningrad which Mayakovsky celebrated. He used to pace up and down, wait and suffer here. On the day of his death I came here. Before my very eyes they were chipping away the little sculpted horse's head."[22]

The closer we came to our appointed destination the more sombre and more silent she became. When she got off the tram she immediately grabbed my sleeve.

Everything was as usual.

28 August 1939

In the last ten days I should have written down a lot, but in my usual hurry I didn't do it. I'll try to remember now.

I think it was on the 14th, during the day, I had a phone call. Not until Anna Andreevna said her name did I realize who was speaking – that's how different her voice was. "Come over." I went at once. Anna Andreevna announced her news while we were still in the hall.* "It's good that that's what I expected," she added.

We spent a moment in her room. I tried to work out where and whom to call. Anna Andreevna was the same as ever, only she kept searching through her bag for somebody's address, and it was clear that even so

---

* The news that Lyova was being sent to the north. Anna Andreevna asked me urgently to get hold of some warm clothes: she was allowed to visit and to take him a parcel of clothes.

she wouldn't find it. I managed quite quickly, by phone, to arrange for a hat, a scarf and a sweater. Everyone I called understood everything immediately, with no questions. "A hat? No, I don't have a hat, but do you need some mittens?" "Boots," Anna Andreevna said, "I do actually have, but they're temporarily at a friend's." We went to fetch the boots together (Anna Andreevna couldn't explain to me where to go). We had a long trolleybus ride. I don't remember our conversation on the way. A tall young man with a big nose opened the door to us;* she told him her news; he rushed off somewhere into the depths of the corridor and from there we heard a woman exclaim: "What are you saying!" A small woman showed us into a room, decorated rather vulgarly, then into the dining room. Anna Andreevna tried to drink some tea, but couldn't. It transpired that the boots were being mended. The young man, Kolya, promised to "knock them out of the cobbler in a flash," then told me that he would come to pick me up at eight o'clock the next morning.

I led Anna Andreevna out. On the way, I read her Miron Pavlovich's poetry. She liked it.[23]

Fate sent us our trolleybus instantly. We got out at the circus. On the bridge, Anna Andreevna told me: "August was always a dreadful month for me . . . All my life . . ."

I walked her to her house. Normally, when we part, she says "Thank you," bowing her head, but this time she said: "I'm not going to thank you. You don't say thank you for something like that."

That same evening, after calling on various people, I went to see her again – and not alone, but with Shura.† We brought absolutely everything! What luck! And the boots were already standing in their place. By the window, there was a woman I didn't know, sewing. Shura also started to sew. Anna Andreevna was quiet, absent, already deeply preoccupied with tomorrow. She didn't do a thing and hardly listened to what we tried to explain to her. She asked the same questions several times. I left soon, rushing to Lyusha, but Shura stayed. (I can't sew anyway.) Seeing me out, Anna Andreevna said by the door: "But on top of all this I have to look good tomorrow."

"Can you do that?"

"All my life I've been able to look however I've wanted to: from a beauty to a hag."

The next morning, at eight on the dot, Kolya burst in on me,

---

*   Kolya Davidenkov.
†   That is, with Aleksandra Iosifovna Lyubarskaya.

breathlessly. We decided to call on Anna Andreevna on the way, to make more precise arrangements. Kolya walked so fast that I was out of breath. Vladimir Georgievich was at Anna Andreevna's. We arranged to meet her there, in the courtyard, and we set off. It began to get hot. Kolya carried the bag. We were lucky with the tram, we got there quickly. In the courtyard, where last time Anna Andreevna and I had been the only people, a massive crowd was now queuing. However, the main question here was: what is allowed? A vicious, freckled girl with badly dyed red hair took the things. When our turn came, I asked: "Should one write the sender's name and address? Or only the recipient's?" – "We only need the address of the sender; we don't need you to tell us who it's going to," said the redhead, maliciously.

After getting the receipt, we decided to go to Nevsky for a drink of water and to buy Anna Andreevna some heart drops at the chemist's just in case. We met her at the courtyard exit. She was in a neatly ironed white dress, with a touch of colour on her lips.

"Are you leaving?" she asked anxiously.

We explained that we'd be back right away, and put the receipt in her handbag.

That accursed hot day in the dusty courtyard was endless. Torture by standing. From time to time one of us managed to get Anna Andreevna out of the queue and to make her sit down – even if it was only on a block of stone; the other one would take her place in the queue. But she left the queue unwillingly, she was afraid: suddenly something might ... She stood in silence. Kolya and I sometimes left her alone and went off to sit for a while on some logs piled up right by the railway tracks. Before my eyes, Kolya became covered in soot from head to toe. Black rivulets ran down his face; he wiped them off, like a washerwoman, with his elbow. I probably looked the same. He, clearly, was a nice person, thoughtful, brave and a bit comical.[24] He told me everything about himself, about Lyova, and our conversation began with these words of his: "There's one thing I've come to understand: you can't trust anyone and you can't tell anyone anything." Had he not "understood" properly? Or had he immediately felt he could trust me, as I him? What can you do? We are human beings, and evidently nothing can destroy our craving to trust one another ... Near the logs, I found a stump, and Kolya, panting, hauled it over to Anna Andreevna. She agreed to sit down briefly. I looked at her distinct profile amidst the indistinguishable faces with no clear features or profile. Next to her face all other faces seem indistinguishable.

Towards four o'clock, I had no choice but to rush home to Lyusha, in order to let Ida go, and I went with a heavy heart, leaving Anna Andreevna in Kolya's care, comforting myself with the thought that he, clearly, is a reliable friend.*

In the following days, she came to see me twice without phoning and found no one in. (I was in a hurry, rushing around: a thousand things to do before leaving for Moscow.)

Finally, on the eve of my departure, I managed to get away to see her – this was on the 17th, or maybe the 18th of August.

She was lying down. She had a headache and three toes on her left foot were numb. (This also happened to me – 18 months ago – and more than once.)

"Now it's not too bad," said Anna Andreevna, "but when I returned from there that day, my feet were so badly swollen that I took off my shoes and walked across the Entertaining yard in my stockinged feet."

I dared to say: "You're going to have to take care of yourself."

She made a wry face.

"Please don't talk about that now."

She got up, sat at the table between two candlesticks (the candles weren't lit, it was a bright day) and began to copy out verses.†

"Now read this," she said, when she'd finished, "and please put in the commas."

The commas were exactly where they belonged, but in two places syllables were missing.

Wanting to cut off the unused part of the page, Anna Andreevna went to look for a paper knife. She lifted the lid of a large box which stood on a little table by the window. I came closer. In the box lay a comb – the famous one in the portrait by Annenkov which she was wearing when she read poems in memory of Blok, when I first saw her. And a lot of photographs – from childhood. One of them showed children standing in rows; in the first row was a girl in shorts.

"That's me in gym class. In Gungerburg. I remember that day so well."

Next, a delightful ten-year-old girl with a shaved head. The amazing

---

* At the time Lyusha was already seven years old. The reason I couldn't leave her alone at home for a moment was that Mitya's room was at first occupied by Katyshev, an NKVD agent; on his days off he was always drunk, and after that his sister, a full-time prostitute, moved in.

† I think I was taking "The Muse" – "When at night I wait for her to come..." – to Moscow; *FT, Reed*, no. 6.

outline of her head and the oval of her face were already completely Akhmatova's.

But here she is aged 16 or 17 and nothing of Akhmatova about her. Not her at all. Something indefinably girlish.

She untied a piece of pink gauze. Inside were eggs, painted with black India ink. Three of them. And a fourth – pink, with some Oriental lettering.

"Volodya gave them to me. They have the earth, the sky and the sea drawn on them. And this one was given to me by Lyovushka for Easter."

She found the paperknife, tied the eggs up in the gauze again and shut the box.

Then she addressed an envelope.

On the evening of 18 August I left for Moscow.

I returned on the 26th. There was no time to phone her. But yesterday, on my way home from the library, I ran straight into Kolya.

"Anna Andreevna is in hospital!"

"What happened?"

"She has an inflamed jaw."

He didn't know which hospital she was in. Luckily, Vladimir Georgievich rang me in the evening. We agreed that I would visit her tomorrow. But that's not what happened: today, while I was at the library, someone phoned on her behalf and left a message saying she was already home.

Lyusha and I went to see her today. We bought lots of sweet things and also took some children's books and games with us, which she had asked me to bring for Valya and Shakalik a long time ago.* I shouted up at her window – she used to complain that she couldn't always hear the bell. Because of Lyushenka we climbed the stairs rather slowly. She was waiting for us on the top landing by her door.

"What sweet visitors are coming to see us!" she said, catching sight of Lyusha.

She was wearing her black dressing gown and for some reason her face looked younger. (I recalled Blok's lines:

> It had grown young from torment,
> Which had given back her one-time beauty.)

---

* The sons of her neighbours the Smirnovs: Valya – six or seven years old, and one-and-a-half-year-old Vova, who, for some reason, was called Shakalik. Anna Andreevna loved him very much.

When, during the war, after her evacuation to Tashkent, rumours reached Anna Andreevna that one of them – Vova – had died, she dedicated the poem "Knock with your little fist, I will open . . ." to his memory – *FT, Seventh Book*. (In fact, it was Valya, not Vova, who had died of hunger.)

In her room was Olga Nikolaevna. She was somehow cheerful, fuller –
evidently some hope had emerged.* Anna Andreevna brought the boys
in and under Lyusha's guidance they started playing with the blocks,
settling themselves on the chair by the window. Anna Andreevna was
very friendly and calm, but I saw that she could hardly cope. Sitting
very straight on the divan, she recounted: "When they brought me to
the hospital I felt as if I'd been run over by a lorry: my chin was swollen,
my back wouldn't bend, swollen feet . . .

"Vladimir Georgievich told me later that the doctor was amazed how
much I could bear. So when was I supposed to scream? Before – it didn't
hurt; during the operation – I had the forceps in my mouth, I couldn't
scream; afterwards, it was no longer worth it."

She got up, bent down towards the children. Patiently she helped
them put the cubes together to make the picture "Prince Guidon and the
Swan" (the game was "The Tales of Pushkin"). I again saw what a
strain it was for her to stay on her feet.

We said goodbye and agreed that she would bring the boys round to
visit Lyusha in a few days, to see her magic lantern.

In the doorway she said to me in her even, heart-rending voice: "I
thank you."

5 September 1939

I went to Anna Andreevna's with Lyusha again, but decided to leave
Lyusha in the garden on a little bench – let her get some air! – and go
up alone. Lyusha had *Tom Sawyer* with her. She promised to wait quietly
for me for exactly half an hour. "But don't be longer. All right, Mama?
Don't be longer."

On the staircase I caught up with Olga Nikolaevna carrying a small
basket: she was bringing Anna Andreevna lunch.

We went on together.

"See, I'm bringing her some food. She doesn't cook herself anything,
and the home help only comes in once a week."

Anna Andreevna was lying on her torn divan, covered with a padded
quilt.

"Like this, when I'm lying on my back," she said, "I feel fine. But if
I turn just a little bit, or get up, I get dizzy."

---

* Indeed, her son was soon released.

Olga Nikolaevna had already poured some broth into a cup. But forks were needed for the fish and tomatoes.

"You know, Anna Andreevna, I can't find any forks anywhere."

Anna Andreevna got up, searched around in the cabinet amongst the vases and pretty cups.

"No, they can't be here, I saw them myself in the kitchen."

She went into the kitchen, returned – not there.

"Gone! That's what it's like here with all objects. You have to tend them, if you stop for a moment they disappear in a flash. Not long ago a soap dish disappeared. Everybody had seen it, Anna Evgenevna[25] had seen it in the morning before going to work. I wanted to get it to Lyovushka, but it's disappeared. That's what happens to everything around here."

My half hour was up and I left.

9 September 1939

I have the flu. Anna Andreevna visited me yesterday. All dressed up! Rings on her fingers, a brooch on her bosom, a necklace around her neck.

She recited something on death.*

"Apart from cavities in both lungs, I probably also have Ménière's disease," said Anna Andreevna. "There was a time when specialists dreamt of observing even just one patient who had it. Now many people have it. I only have to move, turn my head – dizziness and nausea. When I walk down stairs there is an abyss before me."

I asked what she was reading now.

"Bolotov."

Then she recounted to me, in a very amusing way, how someone's kids, to whom "Osip"† had given his children's book, asked him: "Uncle Osya, can't you make this book look like *The Busy Buzzer?*"

For some reason, I don't remember why, we started to talk about human tactlessness. Anna Andreevna told me: the other day a telegram came for Anna Evgenevna from Nikolay Nikolaevich. Anna Evgenevna wasn't there, she was away.

"I rang Nikolay Nikolaevich's brother," said Anna Andreevna. "He came, read the telegram: 'Nikolay Nikolaevich, through Anna

---

*   "To Death" – "Requiem", 8; no. 7.
†   Osip Mandelstam.

Evgenevna, asks his brother for 200 roubles.' But his brother doesn't have any money. I offered him some of mine. He took it and sent it in his own name. The next day a telegram arrived addressed to me: 'Thank Sasha.'"

She laughed as she told me this.

"And there is also a man who corresponds with me, who, when we parted, said 'Give me a receipt to say that I've returned all your belongings to you.'"*

She got up. I wanted to get dressed and see her home, but she wouldn't let me. "You have a fever."

She stopped at the door.

"Have you noticed? I am in full regalia today. These are pink corals. And this is a ring from the 1820s, Olenka gave it to me. And this one is a very old ring from India, there's a man's name and inscription on it: 'God preserve him.' And this" (she pointed at her brooch) "is a signed Riquet, the head of Cleopatra."

16 September 1939

This evening I was at Anna Andreevna's.

She was lying on the divan, fully dressed, but under a blanket.

It turned out, Vladimir Georgievich had taken her to the doctor's – on account of her toes – and the doctor had ordered her to stay in bed.

"It's not gangrene, as Vladimir Georgievich feared, it's traumatic neuritis."

On a chair beside her was a little volume of Benediktov,[26] a present from Lidiya Yakovlevna Ginzburg.

"You know, it turns out he did write some good poems too, towards the end, when he was old ... Without any of those Mathildas."

And she read "Insomnia" aloud to me and also another bit of a poem about a Christmas tree: the beginning was highly banal, but then it got better.

Soup was boiling on a hot-plate.

"Olga Nikolaevna left and told me to keep an eye on it," said Anna Andreevna. She got up, added water to the soup and tried to switch the kettle on.

"It doesn't always work, only sometimes ... Go on, switch on, switch on, go on, please," she whispered to the kettle, leaning over it.

*   See footnote on p. 149.

I too was eager for the kettle to "switch on", because this time I had had the sense to bring biscuits, sugar and pastries with me.

"Now, you just sit here and immerse yourself in culture and I'll go and take care of things in the kitchen."

While she was gone I leafed through Benediktov. Behind one wall a woman was growling at a child, the child was crying. Through the other one you could hear the animated voice of Nikolay Nikolaevich's new wife.

"Olga Nikolaevna has gone out on a visit and I'm afraid we won't hear the bell. It's like that too: sometimes it works, sometimes it doesn't."

We sat down to tea.

Anna Andreevna was called to the phone. Olga Nikolaevna announced that she had gone to spend the night with friends because when she'd arrived back at Anna Andreevna's she hadn't been able to ring the bell – it didn't make any sound. When seeing me off, Anna Andreevna came out onto the landing to check the bell: it rang full blast.

"That's what living in the House of Entertaining Science is like," she said.

27 September 1939

I'm in bed. Down with something – no idea what.

Anna Andreevna phoned several times, wanted to come. I wouldn't let her: the last thing she needed was to catch it. She wasn't feeling too good herself. However, today she came anyway. Looking unwell, dark, with sunken eyes, the wrinkles around her mouth more pronounced.

Nikolay Nikolaevich is back: "He walks around irritated, bad-tempered. All because he's short of money. He always did take a lack of money badly. He's stingy. You can hear him yelling in the hallway: 'Too many people eat with us.' And they're all relatives – his and Anna Evgenevna's. Once, at table he made this remark: 'The butter's only for Ira.' And that was in front of my Lyovushka. The boy didn't know where to look."

"How on earth could you bear all that?" I asked.

"I can bear anything."

("But is that good?" I wondered.)

Rakhil Aronovna came.[27] Anna Andreevna cheered up and started talking about something else.

"I've been invited to the Bryusov anniversary. To recount my personal reminiscences."

"But I thought that you, like me, don't care for him?" I asked.

"I didn't know him personally, but I don't like his poetry, or his prose.[28] His poems are full of Heliogabalus and Dionysus – and yet there is no image, nothing. No image of the poet, no image of the lyric hero. The poems are about a variety of subjects, but they are all alike. And what a high opinion of himself: a *Kulturträger*, a European education ... In reality he was not enlightened at all; he translated the epigraph to Pushkin's 'The Page': 'This is the age of the cherubim' instead of 'Cherubino'! He had been writing articles on the theory of poetry and suddenly in a letter he blurted out: 'I intend to read Boileau's *Art poétique*' ... How did he dare write without having read it? European education! And his letters, how boring they are. I read his letters to Kolya in Paris. In them, by the way, he strongly recommends Kolya not to see Vyacheslav Ivanov: he probably wanted to keep promising young poets to himself. But Vyacheslav Ivanov was a brilliant, superbly educated man, extremely subtle and wise. Sometime later Kolya wrote to Bryusov: 'I met Vyacheslav Ivanov and only now am I beginning to understand what poetry is ...'[29] You can see from his diary what a nasty man he was. One entry reads: 'Pretending to give my brother a massage I twisted his arms.' And his brother was ill. How disgusting! And why write it down? He assumed he was a genius, and therefore personal behaviour was immaterial. But he turned out not to be a genius and he had to be judged by ordinary standards.[30]

"He really did have great administrative abilities. But that's all. For Russian culture he certainly was a harmful influence, because all those recipes for versification are harmful."

She delivered this speech with animation and energy, addressing it on the whole, out of politeness, to the shy Rakhil Aronovna who hardly said a word.

Then she said that she was selecting poems for her publishers, but half-heartedly, slowly ...

"I'm not up to it. Lyusya and I are putting marks against them. So far I've crossed out all the early ones. I can't stand them."*

Unconsciously, I drummed my fingers against the wall.

She said: "My mama, when she was very upset, used to start tapping the table. She would keep it up for hours. I had a brother who was a student. We lived in a dacha. Once our neighbours asked: 'Is that your brother typing?' – meaning pamphlets."[31]

---

* "Lyusya and I" – Lidiya Yakovlevna Ginzburg. See note 38.

I said I was reading Lyushenka *Russian Women*, and that she had cried.

"I found it myself as a child," responded Anna Andreevna. "No one ever read anything to me, they couldn't be bothered with me. Nekrasov was the only book in the house, not a single other volume."

We started talking about how wet, dark and gloomy the streets were now.

"One might say Leningrad is particularly well suited to catastrophes," said Anna Andreevna. "That cold river, over which there are always heavy clouds, those menacing sunsets, that operatic, terrifying moon ... The black water with yellow flecks of light ... Everything is terrifying. I can't imagine what catastrophes and calamities look like in Moscow: for there, you don't have any of this."

I said that Kiev is a cheerful, bright city and its antiquity is not terrifying.

"Yes, that's true. But I didn't like pre-Revolutionary Kiev. A city of vulgar women. It was full of wealthy men and sugar refiners. They lavished thousands on the latest fashions, they and their wives ... My 17-and-a-half-stone cousin, waiting at Shveytser's, the famous tailor's, for a new dress to be fitted, kissed the little icon pendant of St Nicholas around her neck and said: 'Make it a good fit.'"

Rakhil Aronovna went to see her home.

15 October 1939

During this time I went to Anna Andreevna's about three times, but I didn't write anything down. And now it's already too late to recall her words, it would be so easy to misquote something.

Still, I'll note one incident. The other night, in my presence, she and Olga Nikolaevna arranged to go in the morning to queue.* Anna Andreevna asked all the neighbours to wake her up exactly at seven – not a minute later. "Olga Nikolaevna doesn't like to wake me up; she feels sorry for me." Then, a friendly squabble over a coat – who will wear what: Anna Andreevna insisted that Olga Nikolaevna should wear her autumn coat (Olga Nikolaevna only had her summer coat here), and she herself would wear her winter coat.

"It will be hard for you to stand in your winter coat," said Olga Nikolaevna. "Better for me to put on the winter coat, and you the autumn coat."

---

* At the Prosecutor's Office.

But Anna Andreevna disagreed.

"No, *I'll* put on the winter coat. You won't be able to handle it. It's tricky. It hasn't had a single button on it for a long time now. And we won't manage to find new ones and sew them on. I know how to wear it even without buttons, whereas you don't. I'll wear the winter coat."

During the day I went to Anna Andreevna's, to take her to the out-patients', to the doctor's, for an appointment arranged by Litfond. I went to her place straight from the library, where I got her *Literaturny sovremennik* for 1937 with new material on Pushkin's duel.[32] I also brought her some butter.

"Now I have supplies for many days," Anna Andreevna told me. "I have four herrings, twelve pounds of potatoes, and on top of this you brought butter. A feast!"

We set off. We stood for about two minutes in front of the absolutely deserted Liteyny: she was afraid to step onto the asphalt.

On the way we started talking about our thyroids, which in her case is even more enlarged than in mine.

"One female doctor said to me: 'All your poems are here.'" Anna Andreevna patted her throat with the palm of her hand. "They suggested operating but warned me that, in a month, I'd weigh no less than 18 stone. Just think, me!"

For some reason we came back to the subject of Kiev and I asked if she liked Shevchenko.

"No. I had a very hard life in Kiev, and I didn't take to that country or its language ... *Mamo* [mama], *khodimo* [we walk]." She screwed up her face. "I don't like it."

Her disdain infuriated me.

"But Shevchenko is a poet of the same stature as Mickiewicz!" I said. She didn't reply.

We arrived. Took our coats off. A snow-white corridor and a queue. Anna Andreevna's appointment was for 5.45, but, as was explained to us in the queue, that "means nothing". We sat down. Five people in front of us. The queue moved slowly, half an hour per head.

Anna Andreevna started asking me about Nikolay Ivanovich: What Tsezar, back from Moscow, had said about how things were with him.[33]

"Nikolay Ivanovich's attitude towards me is strange," she suddenly said.

"How is it strange? You know very well he thinks highly of you."

"Of me – yes, but not of my poetry. For Nikolay Ivanovich is a fanatical person, and he couldn't possibly like my poetry."

"Haven't you asked?"

"Certainly not, it's not my place to ask about that!"

Finally, Anna Andreevna went into the doctor's office. I waited for her. She reappeared more quickly than the others, in about 15 minutes. We put our coats on and went outside. Only there did I notice that she was very agitated.

"He pronounced me completely healthy. I knew it. I told Vladimir Georgievich that that's what would happen. Now, when Litfond asks, he will tell them that I am a malingerer. I can assure you that that's what'll happen. He probably got angry because I showed him two medical professors' notes, with very serious diagnoses. He asked me three times: 'Do you work?' I suppose he thought I wanted a sick note. He understands his task like this: to keep in check and to expose. He prescribed salt water and pine baths for me, but he found electrotherapy and foot baths, which is what Davidenkov and Baranov recommended, 'totally unnecessary'."[34]

We walked: in her fury Anna Andreevna did not want to wait for a tram. I could have cried, I felt so sorry for her: I see her life from close quarters and understand how ill she is ... And why did fate have to make her undergo this further humiliation?

We walked in silence. I could not think of anything to console her.

I took her all the way to the door of her flat – that had already become our custom. On parting she suddenly kissed me.

18 October 1939

I'm getting ready to go to Dolosy.*

For the last few days I've been sitting over Anna Andreevna's poems. She asked me to read through those she had chosen together with Lidiya Yakovlevna.†

I've spent several days surrounded by various editions of Anna Andreevna's books, pondering punctuation, chronology, variations.

We had agreed that I would go to her place this morning. "Make it early," insisted Anna Andreevna.

I arrived at noon. I knocked and knocked on her door – no reply.

"Is Anna Andreevna home?" I asked a dishevelled girl in the kitchen. "She's not answering."

---

* A sanatorium in the mountains above Yalta, where Miron Levin was first treated for, and soon died of, tuberculosis of the throat.

† Lidiya Yakovlevna Ginzburg.

"You aren't knocking the right way," the girl replied. And she began to pound vigorously on Anna Andreevna's door, using first her fists and then, turning round, her heels.

"Anya, you've got visitors!"

"Come in."

Anna Andreevna was lying on the divan, grey, her face sickly, looking swollen, her hair grey, dishevelled. I was in despair. It turned out she hadn't slept all night and had only just fallen asleep a little while ago! And the dishevelled girl, Anna Andreevna explained to me, was not a girl at all, but herself a mother, Ira Punina.

I laid the poems, books and my notes out on the table and started to ask the questions I had prepared.

Anna Andreevna answered, listened, accepted my advice, but some-how without interest. Maybe sleep simply hadn't completely left her yet.

I complained that I didn't understand one of her poems: "Sister, I have come to take your place".*

"I don't understand it either," replied Anna Andreevna. "You've hit the nail on the head. It is the only one of my poems which I myself could never understand."

I turned the pages, asked my questions and sensed, with anguish, what a burden all this was to her.

"Please, write your comments down on a separate sheet of paper," Anna Andreevna finally requested, "otherwise I'll forget everything."

I fell silent, found a sheet of paper, started to copy my notes out: dates, sections, variations, former and current cycles.

"Have you ever seen a poet so indifferent to his own poetry?" asked Anna Andreevna. "But then, nothing will come of this anyway ... Nobody will publish anything ... And I can't be bothered with it."

I said goodbye.

"Come back soon," she said to me on parting. "I look forward to it very much."

15 November 1939

I went to see Anna Andreevna yesterday, the first time since my return.

She was lying down. Lying down again. She claimed she hadn't slept for some fifteen nights.

Her head was tossing on the pillow. Her hand was hot.

---

* "Sister, I have come to take your place" – *BPL-A*, p. 76; no. 8.

"Do you have a fever?"

"I haven't taken my temperature."

She was preparing to go to Moscow. A ticket had already been bought for her.

She had read the book which I had brought her last time, *Death in the Afternoon* by Hemingway. I told her that Mitya had opened the book by chance on the counter in a second-hand bookshop, had started to read, had become enraptured and had bought it, and he'd never even heard of the author before.

"Yes, a great writer," said Anna Andreevna. "I hate his fishing, though. Those hooks, those fish, those worms ... No thank you!"

Soon Vera Nikolaevna came, bringing food.[35] Anna Andreevna didn't touch a thing.

"I don't eat any but give it away. I can't sleep and I can't eat. I give everything away, otherwise it goes bad."

She began to have difficulty with her breathing. She asked Vera Nikolaevna to go to Punin's for some camphor.

Punin came into the room humming. He started asking Anna Andreevna questions, but didn't stop singing. He interjected questions between his singing.

"Tra-la-la-la! What's the matter, Anichka? Tra-la-la-la! ..."

"Please give me the camphor."

He brought the phial – tra-la-la-la! – put a few drops in some water – tra-la-la-la! – and she drank it.

It turned out that Vera Nikolaevna had come to get some painting by Boris Grigoriev, which Anna Andreevna had decided to sell. I accompanied her out, to help her carry it. The painting was heavy, even together the two of us could hardly drag it along. It showed some semi-decent female. We had far to lug it, down Furshtadtskaya Street, along Potyomkinskaya.

Vera Nikolaevna had already sold several of Boris Grigoriev's drawings for Anna Andreevna, at 75 roubles apiece.

4 December 1939

Yesterday morning Vladimir Georgievich dropped in for a minute and asked me to go instead of him to meet Anna Andreevna, who was returning from Moscow. The telegram read: LEAVING 10.50. He wasn't able to leave work in the morning.

"I have been to her flat, I lit the stove, tidied up a little ..."

This morning, at the appointed time, I set off for the station. But I didn't meet Anna Andreevna. There was no such train – the 10.50 from Moscow ... When I got back home I rang her number just in case. I found she was already home. She had taken the Red Arrow. And she asked me to come round at once.

She sat on the divan and recounted her epic to me.*

"Konstantin Aleksandrovich phoned Aleksandr Nikolaevich.† He had been drinking. Konstantin Aleksandrovich said: 'Come over, there's a lady waiting for you here.' The other was delighted, thinking that there really was a lady! It turned out to be me ... But he was very courteous all the same."

And she went on, step by step. Then: "Boris Leonidovich liked my poems very much. He exaggerates everything so! He said: 'Now even dying wouldn't be terrifying' ... But what a charming man! And what he liked most is what you also love: 'And the stone word fell ...'."‡

And she told me about Nikolay Ivanovich: "We always give each other things ... This time I really didn't know what to take him. But as I looked through Boris Grigoriev's album, my eye was suddenly caught by a sketch and the signature: V. Khlebnikov. Nikolay Ivanovich was happy. The gift was a success, I'm glad."§

We started to light the stove together. The flames wouldn't catch for a long time, but in the end the fire started to crackle after all.

"You know," Anna Andreevna said sadly, "Shakalik didn't remember me when I came back. He's forgotten me in a fortnight."

6 December 1939

Anna Andreevna rang me this morning: "Come at once." I went. She didn't reply to my knock at the door with her usual "Come in!" but came out into the hallway herself to meet me, and here, in an energetic whisper, told me the news she had called me over for: it concerned Korney Ivanovich and the Toad.

---

* Her efforts in Moscow on behalf of Lyova.
† Konstantin Aleksandrovich Fedin phoned Aleksandr Nikolaevich Tikhonov. On Tikhonov see note 36.
‡ Evidently Anna Andreevna read Boris Leonidovich some poems from "Requiem", as well as others on the same theme.
§ Akhmatova's inscription on the back of a drawing reads: "To N. I. Khardzhiev from Akhmatova. It will soon be ten years that we've been friends. 2 Dec. 1939." (Inscription published by E. G. Babaev in the second volume of *Papers on A.A.*, p. 205.)

"Warn your father," she said.*

Then she stopped whispering and asked me aloud to come in. Lidiya Yakovlevna was in the room. I sat by the window, and Lidiya Yakovlevna and Anna Andreevna were pacing the floor in opposite directions, continuing an argument which had obviously been going on a long time, concerning new hypotheses by someone called Emma about the killing of Lermontov: that this murder had been set up and organized by the authorities. Anna Andreevna insisted on the historical and psychological impossibility of such a suggestion.

"What sort of Venetian-hired assassins or poisoners were there in Russia in the 1830s!" she said.†

As she spoke, she walked around the room, stretching her hands towards the fire in the stove, and once she even kneeled in front of the stove and remained like that. "Actually it is very comfortable like this, I didn't think it would be," she said.

Then she jumped up and, contrary to usual, set plenty of food out on the table: cheese, cans of tinned food, and vodka in a carafe. As always, however, she searched endlessly for forks, spoons, saucers, discovering them in the most inappropriate places ... We drank vodka out of minute porcelain things that looked like saltcellars.

Anna Andreevna said she could drink a lot and never got drunk.

Then suddenly, from somewhere, Anna Andreevna got out a notebook of poems copied out by hand, which looked very neat, but the first page was torn off so roughly that some tatters had remained attached.

"I tore it off," she said. "The other day a blond, well-built, handsome young man came to see me and said he wanted to recite his poems to me. I advised him he would be better off going to the Writers' Union.

---

* A.A. called Anna Dmitrievna Radlova "the Toad" when talking to me. On 25 November 1939, K. Chukovsky had an article published in *Pravda* called "Mutilated Shakespeare" concerning Radlova's translation of *Othello*. It was this article which worried Anna Andreevna: she had strong suspicions about connections between Anna Radlova and the Big House. (I do not know whence such suspicions arose, and I haven't had the opportunity to establish to what extent they are well grounded.) However, the matter of Korney Ivanovich's article did not go beyond a polemic: on 19 January 1940, *Pravda* published an article by A. Ostuzhev in defence of Radlova's translation ("On the Rules of Grammar and the Laws of the Theatre"). The polemic continued. K. Chukovsky published a new article, "Desdemona's Asthma" (see the journal *Teatr*, 1940, no. 2). Later he included both articles in revised form in his book *The High Art* [*Vysokoe iskusstvo*]. For more on Anna Dmitrievna see note 78.

† "Emma" – Emma Grigorievna Gershteyn. The discussion between Lidiya Yakovlevna and Anna Andreevna was about an article by E. G. Gershteyn, "On the Question of Lermontov's Duel", published in 1939 in *Almanakh god XXII*, no. 16. In subsequent works on Lermontov E. G. Gershteyn didn't express her previous suggestions so categorically.

On E. G. Gershteyn see note 37.

I chased him out very quickly ... And now – I come back from Moscow and find a notebook on my table. And on the first page an inscription: 'To the great poet of Russia.' I lunged at the notebook like an animal and tore out the page."

I asked whether the poems were any good, but Anna Andreevna didn't answer. She was sure that he was a Maecenas!*

Lidiya Yakovlevna and I tried in vain to persuade her otherwise. "He's young," I said. "He may simply not be informed about the particulars of your situation ..." Anna Andreevna rejected such a possibility while Lidiya Yakovlevna supported me.

"I can't see anything blameworthy even in the inscription," I risked saying.

"But I don't want to dress up in somebody else's clothes!" answered Anna Andreevna angrily.

Lidiya Yakovlevna soon left, but Anna Andreevna kept me back: "Just stay another half hour." She again started telling me about the Toad, about her scheming against Anna Andreevna. She spoke with more agitation and more loudly than usual. The deep, long pauses, so characteristic of her speech, disappeared. Vodka does have an effect even on her, after all. She commented on Lidiya Yakovlevna along these lines: "As a person she is beyond emotion, rather cold, but I value her intellect."[38]

I asked her if she had any new poems.

"No. I have not been able to do a thing since then."

I told her about Mark Twain's *Notebook* which had appeared in *Internatsionalnaya literatura*. She hadn't read it. However, she made the following remark about *Tom Sawyer*: "An immortal book. Like *Don Quixote*."

Shakalik started to cry. Anna Andreevna hurried over to him. Apparently his parents had gone to the cinema and he was on his own.

I said goodbye.

14 December 1939

Yesterday afternoon, not knowing what to do with myself until the evening when K. was supposed to come and spell out everything I already knew, I went to the embankment.†

---

* Maecenas – a code name for informers.
† The lawyer Yakov Semyonovich Kiselyov was supposed to come and see me.[39] Korney Ivanovich and Yakov Semyonovich had already known (since about April 1939) that Mitya had died, whereas I had merely suspected it. Kiselyov brought a note from Korney Ivanovich: "... It is painful for me to write about this to you, but I have now learnt for certain that Matvey Petrovich is no longer alive. Therefore there is nothing for us to do any longer. My hands are shaking, I can't write any more."

With the help of clouds and bridges I pulled myself together a bit and went to see Anna Andreevna.

In the kitchen, I was told that she was at home.

I knocked on her door – no reply.

The explanation in the kitchen: "She's probably asleep!" They offered to wake her up, but I didn't let them and left.

It was five o'clock in the afternoon. And what an afternoon! "Day was breaking, but did not break."

In the evening, a phone call; Anna Andreevna explained something to me about herself and my unsuccessful visit. But I don't recall our conversation properly because it was already after I had received the note, when I, Tamara and Shura (they had come to me, knowing already) sat in silence on my bed, and even Tusya's attempts – not to console me of course, but gently to soothe the pain – were not successful, and even her benevolent, motherly smile could not warm me.* The only thing I remember of the entire telephone conversation with Anna Andreevna is that she asked me to drop by, and so today, after a cold wash – mechanically, in a complete stupor – I went to see her.

Everything ached: my face, feet, heart, even the skin on my head.

Her room looked even stranger than usual: newspaper stuck over the window panes, and from the ceiling, from the top light, hung a twisted piece of a shawl. She told me her good news: meaningful words. Then about the house manager: She had to have her signature in her new pension book witnessed, and she had gone to see the new house manager 16 times and not caught him once ... 16 times!

I presume I kept up the conversation very badly, as after about ten minutes she asked: "You seem to be upset about something?"

I said it – without bursting into tears.

"My God. My God," repeated Anna Andreevna, "and I didn't know ... My God!"

It was time for me to fetch Lyusha from her teacher's. I left.

15 December 1939

Today, as I was about to go to the library, the doorbell rang all of a sudden – it was Anna Andreevna.

"I was in the neighbourhood to collect my pension, so I wandered over," she explained. "Today I got hold of the house manager at last. I

---

* Tamara (Tusya) – Tamara Grigorievna Gabbe. See note 57.

held out my pension book to him and asked him to witness my signature, but he said: 'Please sign on a separate piece of paper first.' Why? What for? Does he think my signature in the book is forged? I was furious. In general I have a positive attitude towards people but in this case I was very offended. I wrote out my name on a piece of paper and said to him: 'You obviously want to sell my autograph to the Literary Museum? You are right: They'll give you 15 roubles for it.' That embarrassed him, he tore up the piece of paper. Then he said: 'You were a writer once, weren't you?'"

I sent Ida out for some cigarettes, then Ida served us tea. Anna Andreevna smoked a lot, told me about the Smirnov boys. Shakalik already says "thank you", Valya (she called him "my Valya") loves listening when he's being read to. She had been reading him Walter Scott and at the end she'd said: "He was a marvellous writer." Valya suddenly pretended to steer and hoot and said: "You mean he had a car?"

"*I* don't want Walter Scott," I said to her. "I won't steer or hoot."

She recited to me again about death, and afterwards a poem I had never heard before: "Mignonette smells of water".*

And once again, this accumulation of sorrow gives me a feeling of such happiness that it is more than I can bear. I understand Boris Leonidovich: If this exists, even dying is bearable.

1940

Today, just now, I was at Anna Andreevna's for the first time since my
return from Detskoe.* Rumours of her being honoured reached my ears
even there.†

"So, what did you hear about me?" was her first question.

She said she didn't feel well, in fact even worse than before: insomnia,
and at night either her feet go numb or her head does. In my view,
though, she looks a bit better. She sat on the divan, in a coat, with her
hair done and, in it, her famous comb.

All the rumours proved justified. Indeed, she had already been sent a
lump sum of 3,000 roubles from Moscow and her pension had been
raised to 750 roubles a month. Zoshchenko has been going around
Leningrad City Council with a petition sent from Moscow and already
signed by some people (Lebedev-Kumach, Aseev), to get her a flat.‡ She
was admitted to the Writers' Union with great ceremony.§ A secretary
and a member of the board – Lozinsky – had fetched her. The proceedings
were presided over by Slonimsky.

"I still call him Misha by force of habit. Somehow he stayed a little
boy for a long time ... Misha said that I was among those present and
suggested giving me a welcome. Everyone applauded. I stood up and
bowed. Then Mikhail Leonidovich spoke. He said some awful things.
Just imagine: You have been friends with someone for 30 years and
suddenly he stands up and says that your poems will live for as long as
the Russian language exists and then every last grain of them will be
garnered like lines of Catullus. Come now, really, how could he! There
were many people there, and all strangers. Then Brykin reported on the

---

* I had been to Detskoe, to the House of Creativity, to write *Sofia Petrovna*.
† After some phone call "from above".
‡ For more details see note 75.
§ This was on 5 January 1940.

little series of the Poet's Library. And also mentioned another edition of my work."

I brought up the subject of the flat. I so want her to have a decent place to live in! Without those footsteps and records playing from behind the wall, without continual humiliations! But she, it turned out, seems to feel quite differently: she wants to remain here, wants the Smirnovs to move to a new room and give her theirs. She wants to live here, but in two rooms.

"I truly think a communal flat you know is better than one you don't. I'm used to things here. Furthermore, when Lyova returns – he will have a room. For he will come back someday..."

This hope gladdened me.

She poured us some so-called tea which was no more than hot water, and pulled the cranberry jam over.

"I ran out of tea about three weeks ago," she explained.

Then she told me about Shakalik. He has suddenly started to speak and he can say anything. Yesterday, when the light went out, he cried out: "I'm scared, where's my mama?"

"And he already calls me 'Andreevna'. Whereas before he used to call me 'T'anna'. You understand? The direction, where to: 'To Anna.' To him, this was my name. Now he has a cold, sits in bed and tugs at the pages of Krylov's *Fables*. That's his favourite book. I'm reading it to him. He understands – and yet he's only 18 months old.

"And now I'm expecting some people from *Leningrad*. I've prepared 'To the Artist' and 'That city, loved by me since childhood' for them.* Every day they keep on coming round, from all the editorial offices. Yesterday Druzin came with his secretary and some military person. I had Shakalik in my arms at that moment. I handed him to Tanya and jokingly told her in a whisper: '....................'† She believed me. It really did seem like it ... That's just my wickedness, though. Druzin was all magnanimity and encouragement. It turns out he once suffered on account of Acmeism. Didn't you know? Neither did I. He added that the Acmeists had merit: they depicted Russian nature admirably. How kind, don't you think?"[40]

---

* A.A. gave the journal *Leningrad* not two but six poems. In issue no. 2 for 1940 the following were published: "Some gaze into affectionate eyes", "From you I hid my heart", "To the Artist", "Voronezh" and "Here Pushkin's banishment began" (*FT, Reed*). The poem "That city, loved by me since childhood..." (*FT, Reed*) was not included in that issue.
† "They've come for me." In the original entry there was a blank space: I didn't dare write down these words.

Her story was interrupted by the arrival of a young lady from the magazine *Leningrad*. The young lady oozed honey and treacle from every pore. Anna Andreevna handed her the prepared poems. And when she'd left she suddenly fell silent and put on her glasses:

O stars of heaven.

I couldn't bear to watch. Like being an accomplice in a murder.*

When I had pulled myself together we moaned a bit about the impending confiscation of all electrical appliances.

"And just when I got a new one," said Anna Andreevna, "a cigarette lighter-cum-ashtray. Vladimir Georgievich gave it to me. And this too, look, what a lovely little box. Made of lapis lazuli. It's a powder case. I like the fact that they are new, modern objects. Because, otherwise, we live surrounded by things from bygone eras."

I told her that she should go to the House of Creativity, in Detskoe, for a rest.

"No, I wouldn't get any rest there. Tsarskoe is such a source of tears for me . . ."

17 January 1940

The moon.

Because of it the city and its sorrow are still more terrifying.

But I'm grateful to the moon.

Today Anna Andreevna phoned me and asked me to go round. To tell the truth, this request was rather merciless, for it was -35°C outside. However, I pulled on my felt boots, wrapped myself in a shawl and set off. And the moon guided me safely to her through the darkness.†

I brought her half a packet of tea. She was delighted and immediately put the kettle on.

She is deeply worried that Goslitizdat sent her a contract for 4,000 lines at exactly the moment Sovetskiy pisatel had accepted a volume of her poems.

She started to look everywhere for the contract: on top of the armchair and beneath among some papers.

---

*   A.A. wrote the poem "To the New Year! To New Grief" on a piece of paper, gave it to me to read and then, as was her habit, burned it over an ashtray; no. 9.

    May I remind the reader that the war with Finland had started on 30 November 1939. The poem was published abroad 35 years later in the collection *In Memory A.A.*

    It was first published in the USSR in the magazine *Daugava*, 1987, no. 9.

†   The city was blacked out because of the war with Finland.

"Kr., the director of Goslitizdat, paid me a visit. I think she is a bitch."

I burst out laughing. I love it so much when I hear such words from her lips.

"Yes, yes, don't laugh, a bitch. I tell her: 'My poems have already been given to Sovetskiy pisatel.' And she says: 'That's no problem, as long as the material is different.' *Material*, for God's sake!"

"Judging by this remark, she's a fool," I said.

"The phone rings for days on end," continued Anna Andreevna. "They are ringing from every magazine. One person called, gave his name, but I didn't catch who he was and where from. Asking for poems. I reply: 'I have already given everything out.' Silence. And then: 'You know what? Search *there!*'"

I advised her to discuss the matter of Sovetskiy pisatel and Goslit with Yury Nikolaevich Tynyanov.

Suddenly the contract turned up. I had a look: absolutely standard.

Anna Andreevna started talking about Lev Pushkin: "You know, Modzalevsky's son established that many of Pushkin's obscene epigrams were in reality the work of Lev. And even if they are Pushkin's – I still wouldn't have published them in single-volume editions. Or the 'Gavriiliada'. Originally that poem had an anti-religious significance, but now it's just obscene. It should be included in the academic edition and nowhere else."

Then – about Smirnova's memoirs.

"It's very much a woman's book ... This lady, it turns out, was far from being the way they all imagined her ... The last chapter is something dreadful; she was already mentally ill when she wrote it. It's eroto-maniac gibberish."[41]

We went on to talk about Krandievskaya's memoirs, now published in *Zvezda*.[42] I said I liked them very much.

"No, no. I disagree. Snobbish memoirs. She was always a pampered, spoilt lady – and has remained one: 5,000 a month isn't enough for her ... Do you remember the part in her memoirs where she writes about a hungry boy whom they took in? He used to sit down at the table 20 minutes before dinner! How disgusting to write about a hungry child like that! They all laughed at him, that's why this episode stuck in her mind. You can tell at once that her children never went hungry ...*

---

* "Sergunka has put on weight, regained a bit of colour. Usually, some 20 minutes before dinner, while the table was still being laid, he'd already be in his place, spoon in hand, patiently waiting for the food." (*Zvezda*, no. 9, 1939, p. 171.)

The *Diary of S.* – now there's a truly wonderful book. A wise man and a truthful one. Everything he writes – is the truth. And it is written by a man who is already old, who has renounced everything."*

I asked whether she had known Rozanov.

"No, unfortunately not. That man was a genius. Recently Nadya, his daughter, told me that they all loved my poetry and had asked their father if he knew me. He didn't know me, and, it seems, didn't like my poetry, but on the other hand he loved Marietta Shaginyan very much: 'There is no maiden sweeter-scented than I!'[43] I like everything of his, except for his anti-Semitism and his attitude to sex."

Once again I was amazed at the coincidence of our dislikes. And I recounted one of Rozanov's stories from *Fallen Leaves* which has always angered me: how an elderly lady, a mother, advises a student, in love with her younger daughter, to marry the elder, because she is worried about her elder daughter's "maturity". The student obliges (the beast!), marries the elder one, and now the lady has a bouncing grandson to look after.[44]

Anna Andreevna waved a hand dismissively.

"None of it is true. Neither the lady, nor the daughters, nor the grandson. He, of course, invented all this himself, word for word … He was a genius of a man, and weak with it. I pitied him when he was starving in Sergievo later. I was told: he used to walk along the platform collecting cigarette butts. There was nothing I could do to help him, because I was clinically starving myself."

She was anxious about whom they would ask to write the foreword for the Sovetskiy pisatel book. She was afraid it might be Volkov, some specialist on the Acmeists.

"He was always railing against us. I will tell him to his face: One should only write about what one loves."[45]

"Cup of sorrow."†

23 January 1940

Vladimir Georgievich called me yesterday saying that Anna Andreevna had completely gone to pieces; she wouldn't eat, wouldn't drink, that in a few days the publishers would be sending someone for her manuscript but the manuscript wasn't ready. I arranged to have the rest typed up

---

* The *Diary of Suvorin*, I think, but I can't be certain.
† A title thought up by Anna Andreevna for one of her cycles of poems. Which one, I do not recall.

immediately. That evening I went to see her. This time the moon didn't fulfil its duty and I hurt my head badly in the Entertaining entrance: there wasn't a single light bulb.

Anna Andreevna looked in bad shape, yellow, greyish. She smiled for a second when I handed her a small packet of sugar: "Now there's sugar – but the tea's run out."

"I don't sleep at all. And all night long I write. Everything is dying off – I can't walk, can't sleep, can't eat, but this for some reason remains."

And she recited: about a willow tree, about poetry, about a portrait, about emeralds.* She recited calmly, in her even, deep voice, breathing easily.

I was totally lost for words. Anna Andreevna had probably never had such a muddle-headed listener. The poems – a miracle.

"I've been trying to steal up to this for a long time," said Anna Andreevna, "but somehow I couldn't quite get to it."

I tried to talk Anna Andreevna into giving me these poems for retyping too, so that they could be included in her book.

She agreed to three.†

Someone knocked at the door.

"That's Aleksandr Nikolaevich," said Anna Andreevna. "Let's put the shade on the lamp. I don't look my best today."

A tall young man entered. Anna Andreevna sat him down next to her on the divan. They discussed some things concerning the Hermitage.[46] I broke into their conversation and asked Anna Andreevna to set me up for copying in the meantime. She searched for her notebook for a long time, on the armchair and under it, then she looked for paper. She pointed out the pages in her notebook containing new poems and asked me, while I was at it, to copy out a few of her old, previous ones "which once could not exist": "Little Song", "I both wept and I was penitent", "Not for your love do I ask", "White is the sky with frightening whiteness".‡

---

* I think this list of poems can be deciphered as follows: "The Willow"; "I have no need of a host of odes"; "When a man is dying"; "The Cellar of Memory" – that is: *FT, Reed*; *FT, Seventh Book* [*Sedmaya kniga*]; *FT, Reed* and *BPL–A*, p. 196 (no. 10; no. 11; no. 12; no. 24). As to how A.A. and I later reconstructed "The Cellar of Memory" together, see volume 2 of my *Journals*.

　　When I first heard the poem "I have no need for a host of odes", A.A. recited the last line as: To your joy and my *torment*.

† She did not agree to offer "The Cellar of Memory" to the publishers.

‡ "Little Song" ("From Morning I Would Hold My Peace") – *FT, Anno Domini*; "I both wept and I was penitent" – *BPL–A*, p. 53; "Not for your love do I ask" – *FT, Rosary*; "White is the sky with frightening whiteness" ("The White Night") – *BPL–A*, p. 281.

"But please put the punctuation in yourself, I don't know how to ... Dates? Please don't ask about dates. People always talk to me about dates as if I were a dangerously ill person who can't be told frankly about her illness."

I finished copying and said goodbye. She announced that she wanted to get out of her den and tomorrow, when the typist had copied everything for me, she would come to my place for the poems.

Today, after I'd got everything from the typist and proofread it, I phoned Anna Andreevna at two and at three o'clock – she was asleep. At five o'clock Lyusha and I took the poems round to her place ourselves and handed them over to Vladimir Georgievich in the kitchen: he said that Anna Andreevna was unwell and had only just fallen asleep.

"What's wrong with her?"

"She's utterly incapable of fighting her neurasthenia. She has turned night into day, and of course this is bad for her. On top of that, she doesn't eat a thing. And besides, nothing is organized. Maybe I'll manage to talk the Smirnovs into giving her lunch."

(It's all true, but one might ask: Why, if a person does the most necessary and most difficult task in the world – and afterwards naturally feels battered and worn out – should this state be described as "incapable of fighting her neurasthenia"?)

31 January 1940

This morning Anna Andreevna phoned me: "Come over!" Her hair was combed, she was dressed, wearing a necklace (dark blue, almost black).

The stove had been lit.

I asked: had she got up early or not slept at all?

"I didn't sleep at all."

A long conversation about Pushkin: about the Requiem in *Mozart and Salieri*.*

Then about Pushkin's themes: first, Europe and second, Petersburg.†

---

*   Pushkin had nothing to do with it, this is a code. In reality A.A. showed me her "Requiem" that day, written down for a moment, to check whether I had memorized everything. At that time the cycle comprised the following poems: "They led you away at daybreak", "Quietly flows the quiet Don", "Young mocking-bird, full of fun and mischief"; "Seventeen months I've cried out", "Lightly the weeks fly by", "The Sentence", "To Death", "A choir of angels glorified that hour", "I learnt how faces fall apart". Whether "No, it's not I, someone else is suffering" was already included, I do not recall; I am also not completely sure about "Quietly flows the quiet Don".

†   Apart from "Requiem", she recited two poems to me: "Not like a European capital" and, apparently, "It was only then that the dead", no. 13. (The latter was not included in

She explained to me, as an expert on Pushkin, whom he had had in mind when he wrote about Europe.*

Then silence set in. The stove crackled peacefully and cosily.†

I didn't have the strength to go straight home. After a while I found myself on the Field of Mars.

4 February 1940

Today was a big day for me. I read my historical research on Mikhaylov to Anna Andreevna.‡

In the early evening Vladimir Georgievich had brought her to me. Had brought her and had left.

I read for a long time and, all the time while reading, I felt ashamed of my bad prose. To read it to her! What made me do it? But there was nothing I could do now, so I read on.

"Requiem" at that time; A.A. added it to the cycle only in 1962. I remembered the lines: "It was only then that the dead/Used to smile – to be at peace were glad" – differently: "to be *unfeeling* were glad").

* She explained that her poem "Not like a European capital" is dedicated to Osip Mandelstam. In 1974 it was published in Paris in the collection *In Memory A.A.* not exactly as I remembered it at the time. Here is the previous version:

> Not like a European capital
> With a first prize for its beauty –
> In the stifling midnight of the Enisey,
> Changing transport towards Chita,
> To Ishim, to waterless Kirghiz,
> To celebrated Akhbasar,
> With a transfer to the camp Svobodny,
> With the corpse-like stench of foul bunks,
> Thus that city seemed to me,
> In the pale blue of that midnight,
> The city praised by the first of our poets,
> And by us sinners – and by you.

In the Paris collection this poem is entitled "A Little Geography". I do not know when this title came about; in any case, considerably later than the poem; I came across the same title unexpectedly in P. Luknitsky's book *Journey through Pamir* [*Puteshestvie po Pamiru*] (Moscow, 1955). It is the title of one of the sub-chapters.

A.A. and the writer Pavel Nikolaevich Luknitsky (1900–73) had known each other since 1924; for more details about him and their joint work see vols. 2 and 3 of my *Journals*. A book has now been published: P. N. Luknitsky, *Meetings*.

The poem "A Little Geography" was first published in Russia in 1987 by M. Kralin, in the journal *Znamya*, no. 12. He chose the Paris version.

† Once I had memorized all the poems A.A. burned them in the stove.

‡ In code. I read *Sofia Petrovna*.

I first conceived the idea of a story about M. Mikhaylov in 1937. The stimulus for this was provided by Herzen's piece entitled "They Killed Him", about the poet's death in penal servitude. I started to collect material on him. But I never did write about Mikhaylov, I wrote *Sofia Petrovna* instead – a novella dealing "directly" with 1937. That is what I was referring to. On *Sofia Petrovna* see note 47.

For the first half, I got the impression that she was bored.

I took a break, and we drank some tea.

She listened to the second half intently, with undivided attention and, it seemed to me, great emotion. At one point she even wiped away a tear, I think. I wasn't sure of it, however, as I read not raising my eyes.

All this lasted an eternity. What a long story!

When I finished she said: "This is very good. Every word is true."

At half past two I took her home.

This time, our journey was a difficult one, as though through the circles of hell.

At first Anna Andreevna could not go down our staircase. For some reason she had got it into her head that the steps began right outside the apartment door, and I could not persuade her to cross the landing for anything. At last, I led her down the stairs.

As we were about to cross Nevsky, totally empty at this time, and just as we'd stepped onto the street, Anna Andreevna asked me, as always: "Can we go now?" – "We can," I said, and we took two more steps towards the middle. "And now?!" she suddenly screamed in such a high-pitched, terrifying, inhuman voice that I almost fell over and couldn't answer her at once.

Finally, down along the Fontanka, we reached her gates. They appeared to be locked. I pushed at them in vain with my shoulder. We peered through the fence into the darkness of the courtyard, looking for the yard-keeper. No one there. And suddenly it turned out that the wicket of the gate was not locked.

We passed safely through the Entertaining entrance, but at her staircase – new torments. On the landings she wouldn't believe that they actually were landings, she didn't want to walk as if on an even surface but on stairs, and became frightened.

At long last, the door to her flat. She put the key in the keyhole and then it proved that the door was not locked. This also scared her. We went in together. She walked along the corridor, turning the lights on as she went – in the bathroom, in the kitchen. I got her to the door of her room.

"Thank you for listening to it all so patiently," I said to her as we parted.

"Shame on you! I wept, and you say 'patiently'."

I left.

8 February 1940

Once again I received a present from the notebook with the little lock.

Yesterday, opening her notebook, Anna Andreevna read "Cleopatra" to me.* She read it, finding it hard to make out the pencil writing.

"Is it good?" – "Yes! Very!" – "I can't tell yet. I can't tell straight away, I will only understand after some time ... Would you like some wine?"

We drank wine from crystal glasses with funny little handles and ate cakes off plates from the Directoire period and, through all of this, I repeated to myself all the time the lines I had just heard. Even the conversation with Anna Andreevna herself was a distraction to me, I wished to be left alone with the poems. "They say that one should not eat off these plates, that they should be kept safe, but I don't like having to keep things safe ... Aren't they delightful? Drawings in the style of David."

She offered to read me some poems – not hers, someone else's. Usually I like hearing other people's poems from her; they sound different, pronounced with her intonation. This time, though, I didn't want anyone else's poetry – I wanted "Cleopatra" – but, of course, I didn't argue. She recited Fyodor Kuzmich from memory (splendid),† Tsvetaeva (no, I didn't like it, too much is spelled out – but, perhaps, I'm simply not used to it); Kuzmin is good, but too intricate for my liking.

I said that poets are very like their poetry. Take, for example, Boris Leonidovich. When you hear how he speaks, you understand the complete naturalness, the spontaneity of his poems. They are the natural continuation of his thoughts and speech.

"In Boris Leonidovich's case there really is a great resemblance," agreed Anna Andreevna. "But I? Am I also like mine?"

"You? Very."

"It's not good, if this is so. It's most disgusting, if this is so. But take Blok, he didn't resemble his poetry at all, neither did Fyodor Kuzmich. I knew Fyodor Kuzmich well and was friendly with him. He was a remarkable person, but difficult."

I said that I remembered him only as an old man.

"He always looked like an old man, from 40 onwards," explained Anna Andreevna.

---

* *FT, Reed,* no. 14.
† Fyodor Kuzmich: the poet Fyodor Sologub.

I started asking about Vyacheslav Ivanov, about the Tower.

"That was the only real salon I ever got to see," said Anna Andreevna. "Vyacheslav's influence was enormous although publishers didn't seek to acquire his poetry at all. Vyacheslav knew how to influence people, and his faithful pupil in that respect was Max ... Once, in Moscow, a young girl visited me. Of the 'archive miss' variety – have you ever heard that expression? I brought it into circulation ... She was telling me about Max with delight, breathlessly: 'He was in Moscow ... we all met up ... and he said ...' – 'He said to one' – I interrupted her: 'You are the Muse of this place', to the other: 'You are Sappho ...' – 'How do you know?' cried the girl, taken aback by my astuteness ... 'I just made it up,' I replied. The thing is that Max, like Vyacheslav, loved seducing people. That was his second occupation. Whenever a young girl came to Koktebel he used to walk her along the seashore in the evening. 'Do you hear the sound of the waves? They are singing for *you*.' And later the girl would tell everyone that Max had made her understand herself. She would worship him all her life, because neither before, nor after him, had anyone ever spoken to her like that, for the perfectly good reason that she was stupid, talentless, plain and so on.

"Vyacheslav, of course, was more subtle. But he, too, had a need for seduced devotees of his own. He also knew how to entice. He tried his charms on me as well. You would go to see him, he would lead you into his study: 'Recite!' Well, what could I recite then? Twenty-one years old, plaits down to my heels and fantasies of unhappy love ... I would recite something like 'The slender shepherd boy'.* Vyacheslav was ecstatic: since the time of Catullus and so on. Then he would take you into his sitting room: 'Recite!' You would recite exactly the same thing. And Vyacheslav would demolish you.

"I stopped going there very soon, because I saw through him. I was already very spoilt by then, and seduction had little effect on me."

Seeing that Anna Andreevna was in a story-telling mood, I asked her about Zinaida Nikolaevna. Was she beautiful?

"I don't know. I saw her at a rather late stage, when she was already quite affected. I had been invited, with the three of them, to the Morning of Russia party. I messed it up there: I read the first stanza of "Apostate",† but I forgot the second. In the dressing room, of course, it all came back

* "Over the Water" – *BPL–A*, p. 49.
† "You are an apostate for a green island" – *BPL–A*, p. 133.

to me at once. I left without reciting anything else.* In those days I had many troubles. Things were bad for me ... Zinaida Nikolaevna was wearing a red wig, her face looked enamelled, she was wearing a dress from Paris ... They kept trying to get me to visit, but I avoided it because they were nasty – in the simplest, most elementary sense of the word."

I asked about Larisa.†

"Once I was at the Prival – the only time – and was already leaving. I was walking towards the door through the empty room – there sat Larisa. I said 'goodbye' to her and shook her hand. I don't remember who helped me into my coat, I think it was Sergey Ernestych – I was putting my coat on, suddenly Larisa appears, two tears in place on her cheeks: 'Thank you! You are so magnanimous! I'll never forget that you held your hand out to me first!' – What was that about? A young, beautiful girl, why this self-deprecation? How could I know then that she had had an affair with Nikolay Stepanovich? And had I known – why shouldn't I have held my hand out to her?

"Another time, much later, she came to me to confess. At that time I was poverty-stricken, hungry, sleeping on bare boards – a real Job ... Then I once went to see her on business. She lived by the Admiralty: three windows onto the Bronze Horseman, three onto the Neva. She took me home in her carriage. On the way she said: 'I would give everything, everything to be Anna Akhmatova.' Stupid words, aren't they? Which everything? Three windows onto the Neva?

"And just think, when we all die," finished Anna Andreevna, "I and Lily Yurevna and Anna Dmitrievna – historians will find something common to all of us, and all of us – Larisa and Zinaida Nikolaevna – will be called 'women of their time ...'. They are sure to find a common style."

I said goodbye.

"You know," said Anna Andreevna to me, already at her door, "that evening when you saw me home and came into the flat with me, Nikolay Nikolaevich imagined that I was having a highly romantic adventure."

---

* Akhmatova is talking about her appearance with the Merezhkovskys at the Tenishev College hall at the start of 1918. This event, in which other famous writers also participated, was organized for the benefit of the Political Red Cross. On this see *Petersburg Memories* ... [*Peterburgskiy dnevnik* ...] by Zinaida Gippius (see the Pamyat collection, issue 4. Paris: YMCA-Press, p. 365), or *Black Notebooks* [*Chyornye zapisnye knizhki*] by Zinaida Gippius (in the collection *Links* [*Zvenya*], vol. 2. Moscow and St Petersburg: Feniks-Atheneum, 1992, p. 61).
† Larisa: Larisa Mikhaylovna Reysner.
‡ Radlov.

"Did you put him right?"
"I said that it was you."
"Did he believe you?"
"Oh, it's all the same to me."

15 February 1940

Last night, when I was already dressed to go to Shura's, Anna Andreevna rang and asked me to come over. "I can only come for one hour," I said in dismay. "Well then, come even for just an hour."

I arrived. She was sitting in a fur coat by the burning stove. She walked over, limping – still that same broken heel! – to the divan and sat me down beside her.

At my request she recited "Cleopatra" for the second time. I couldn't tell last time whether it was *shalost* [mischief] or *zhalost* [pity]: it was *zhalost*. Well, of course, *zhalost*!* (She can't pronounce *sh* and *zh* clearly – some of her teeth are broken.)

Then came complaints about Kseniya Grigorievna.[†]

"She talks to me as if I'm mentally ill or suicidal. The constant refrain: 'Pull yourself together.' When I was not well: 'Why are you lying all alone?' With whom was I supposed to be lying? With the Commander-in-Chief of the Fleet? She insists I get myself a maid. But where am I going to put her? 'She can sleep in your room.' That's how she sees my insomnia! She doesn't realize that my way of life is like this and not different because it is so closely bound up with my state of mind. Vladimir Georgievich is right in saying: 'She doesn't understand that you have a hundred times more willpower than she.'

"You see, today my room has been washed and cleaned. I went out to the Rybakovs', while Tanya, at Vladimir Georgievich's request, washed, cleaned and even put down a doormat. And a tablecloth on the table: Kolya Gumilyov brought it back from C. sometime.[‡]

Vladimir Georgievich came to fetch me from the Rybakovs' and on the way back let slip about the room. I got very scared and said: 'Then I'm not going there.'"[§]

---

*   "And then to place with a careless hand on her dusky breast/ A black asp as a parting gesture of pity . . ."; **no. 14.**
†   Davidenkova, the mother of Lyova's friend Kolya . . . Kseniya Grigorievna was very fond of Akhmatova, but didn't understand a thing about either her work or her character and constantly infuriated Anna Andreevna with her tactless attempts to take care of her.
‡   Cairo? I don't remember.
§   For more about the Rybakovs see note 73.

While taking me down the corridor Anna Andreevna muttered a poem. Hearing it, I was afraid to say a word, even "goodbye". But she interrupted herself: "So it's all right if I treat Kseniya Grigorievna badly?"

"Go to it!" I said. "Down with her! May the devil take her!"

3 March 1940

During this period I saw Anna Andreevna four times. What is not written down right away can be considered lost. I recall just a few things.

For about two weeks it was very cold at Anna Andreevna's, she ran out of wood, she lived in her overcoat. But, evidently, she had started sleeping better.

She was terribly worried about Shakalik – he had pneumonia. "He's so touching," said Anna Andreevna.

She was rereading Vyazemsky's *An Old Notebook*.

Last night she stayed at my place for a long time. Vladimir Georgievich, who had gone to fetch her from the Rybakovs', where she had had lunch, rang me and brought her round.

She settled right back into the divan, and we drank tea.

"You know," she said, worried, "already two people have said to me that 'a joke' does not work. What's your opinion?"

"Nonsense," I said. "This 'Cleopatra' is not pseudoclassical but real. They should read Maykov then..."

"Yes, yes. That's it, Maykov. That's what I'm going to tell them! Everybody has forgotten Shakespeare. But my "Cleopatra" is very close to the Shakespearean text. I'll read it to Lozinsky, he'll tell me the truth. He knows his Shakespeare extremely well.

"I read 'Cleopatra' to Boris Mikhaylovich* – he didn't object to 'a joke'. But he did say something that made me walk home in a daze: 'The last classical poet.' I get very scared when people talk like that...

"Bukhshtab sent me a copy of Dobrolyubov. I read the whole volume from cover to cover. What bad poetry! The words seem glued together in a line. And what a *Diary*! You can't see anything or anybody. Somehow in the beginning you sense his way of life, there is a glimmer of something. But later on – boredom and women. And nothing else ... I never read Belinsky, not a single line – did he write as badly, too?"

I told her what I honestly thought, in spite of knowing that to argue with her about literature is unwise and unnecessary: "In my view, too,

* Eykhenbaum.

Dobrolyubov's *Diary* is vile and hollow," I said, "and his poems are somehow not poems. Whereas from the articles one can see that had Dobrolyubov not died early he would have become a genuine critic. Belinsky, for his part, is a remarkable writer, sometimes on a par with Herzen. The intensity of his spiritual life is astounding. I like many of his articles and particularly his letters."

Anna Andreevna heard me out without anger but without much trust. I don't think my speech will have persuaded her to take up reading Belinsky.

"Are Bukhshtab's comments good, conscientious?" I asked.

"Yes, very. Too conscientious, even . . . Just think – why give different versions of such bad poems?"[48]

She told me about her library which she had sold in 1933.

"Books were stacked all over the floor of the large room. All of them rare, and all had inscriptions. Now, of course, Nikolay Nikolaevich says: 'It never happened.' He has a knack for not remembering what he doesn't want to remember . . . Now I have no books.

"I never liked seeing my poems in print. If there was a copy of *Russkaya mysl* or *Apollon* containing my poems on the table, I would grab it and hide it. I considered it indecent, as if I had left a stocking or a brassière on the table . . . And I simply couldn't stand having my poems recited in front of me. If Nikolay Nikolaevich or Lyovushka ever quoted a line of mine in my presence I would throw something heavy at them."

Then she read me the newly found lines from Pushkin's *Requiem*. "The Circle of the Moon".*

I walked her home after midnight. For a long time we couldn't cross Nevsky. She could hardly bring herself to set foot on the road. "Can we go now?" – "We can." – "And now?" – She suddenly cried out in the middle of the road, in a high-pitched voice, as if drowning and calling for help. Again!

As we walked along the embankment I asked her about the river.†

---

* A line from Akhmatova's "Requiem" ("Dedication").

What do they sense in the haze of the moon?

I take this opportunity to point out that in contrast to the text published first abroad and then in 1987 in Russia (see the journal *Neva*, no. 6), I remembered the epithets in the first five lines of "Dedication" differently: "The *powerful* river cannot flow" instead of "the great" and "*great* anguish" instead of "deathly". I cannot be sure whether these were changes made later by Akhmatova, or my memory lapse; no. 15.

† I asked what the line "Quietly flows the quiet Don" means? Why the Don? ("Requiem", 2); no. 16.

"Well, Nikolay Nikolaevich worked it out," she answered by way of an explanation.

"He understands poetry amazingly well. His ear for poetry is as good as his eye for painting."

6 March 1940

Yesterday, out of the blue, the doorbell rang, and there was Anna Andreevna on the threshold. She had been to the savings bank nearby, so had come to ask after Lyusha's health and to recite some new poems.

We sat in Lyushenka's room, because Lyusha was lying in my room – it was warmer in there. Anna Andreevna kept her coat on, just took off her hat. She had some ugly scarf wrapped around her neck – actually, I'm not even sure it was a scarf.

She recited a poem addressed to Mayakovsky, stumbling a bit, uncertain. The line: "That which you tried to destroy – was destroyed" is a marvel of energy. I asked her to recite it once more and, when she hesitated a bit, I prompted her with the first two lines.

"What? Already?" exclaimed Anna Andreevna. "I get the feeling that you know my poems by heart five minutes before I've written them. Maybe not ten, but five certainly.

"Do you agree that it's not at all like my poem to Pasternak? Not a bit? I'm glad if that is the case."*

Then I told her about Shura's and my article;[49] from there we somehow moved on to folklore, and from folklore to Homer. I confessed that epic poems usually bore me. I understand that the poems are remarkable, I can explain *why* they are marvellous, but I feel no urge to read them. Going to bed, I don't get *The Iliad* out from under my pillow. " 'I've read the list of ships halfway through' – that's not for me."

"I don't think", said Anna Andreevna, "that anyone reads *The Iliad* just like that, in bed, these days ... Do you know *Gilgamesh*? No? It's magnificent. It's even more powerful than *The Iliad*. Nikolay Stepanovich translated it from a crib, but V.† translated it for me straight from the original and that's how I can judge."‡

* "Mayakovsky in 1913" – *FT, Reed*; no. 17.
† I think V. is V. K. Shileyko.
‡ For more about the two translations of *Gilgamesh* by N. Gumilyov and V. Shileyko, see the article by Vyach. Vs. Ivanov, "Gumilyov's translation of *Gilgamesh*", in the collection *19, Novo-Basmannaya* [*Novo-Basmannaya, 19*] (Moscow, 1990).

Then she told me about the *Rezets–Zvezda* conflict and about the authorization which Kr.* had given her.

I absolutely had to go to the chemist's – Lyusha was asleep, but as soon as she woke up I would have to make her gargle. Ida had gone to the market. I asked Anna Andreevna whether she would keep an eye on Lyusha, and what I should give her to read in the meantime. She agreed at once to look after her, but as for a book she replied: "Give me some Mayakovsky, but it has to be an annotated edition. I have to check whether it's true that *Vladimir Mayakovsky* was performed in the Luna Park."

When I returned, Ida was already home. Lyushenka woke up in good spirits, despite having a temperature of 38.5°C. I gave her something to gargle with and then Ida applied a compress to her throat. And I saw Anna Andreevna home.

I told her she looked well today, a rosy complexion, eyes wide open – all of which I attributed to Tanya's care.

"No, I'm simply putting on weight ... It's age, the time has come ... Did you notice how well I crossed the road today?"

Indeed, she had crossed Nevsky without stumbling and had hardly even held on to me.

On the way: "I met Mayakovsky in 1912 ... I had to meet someone on business in Luna Park, so I went there. And that's where Vladimir Vladimirovich was introduced to me. Young, toothless. He begged me very insistently to come to his première but I couldn't, I don't remember why now."

I asked her at what age she had started writing.

"Eleven ... God, what shamefully bad poems I wrote! I read them again not long ago, I wanted something as a keepsake. No, nothing can be kept. Everything is a disgrace. Nothing was my own, everything was other people's, standard stuff – the sort of thing third- or fourth-rate authors used to write then. I am sure that Mayakovsky also had a lot of this – early, bad work – but when Burlyuk revealed to him who he really was – he destroyed everything. And rightly so."

When we had already turned into her courtyard, this time from the Liteyny, I said that I'd been reading *Ruslan and Lyudmila* to Lyusha and that, this time, I did not like the poem.

"Yes, of course, it's very brilliant and very cold. He was young then

---

* The "conflict" was probably a dispute over her poems. About the authorization which Kr. had given her, see p. 54.

and used everything he'd managed to learn from his mentors – Ariosto, Voltaire. And these mentors were rather cold people ...* But what brilliant verses, what daring! I read it to Valya recently and marvelled at each epithet."

"Do you have a very clear picture of Pushkin as a person?" I asked.

"Yes, absolutely ... 'A blackamoor who threw himself at Russian women,' as S. used to say.† You didn't know that? No, he couldn't stand Pushkin. Hated him. Perhaps he envied him: a rival! S. was such an odd character that he could have envied even Pushkin. Olenka, who knew S. much better than I did, says that that's how it was ... And if you want to visualize Pushkin as a person, read his notes in the margins of Batyushkov's poems. In his articles Pushkin used to restrain himself – as everybody in art always exercises self-restraint, it doesn't do to present oneself *au naturel* – there, however, in the margins of the book, he wrote freely, for himself. By that time, Batyushkov was already dead or already insane, in any case he no longer counted as a living poet. Criticizing 'Dying Tasso', Pushkin wrote: 'Surely this isn't Tasso dying? This is Vasily Lvovich dying.' Charming, isn't it?"

We entered her little courtyard through the Entertaining entrance.

"What a pity your little garden is fenced in," I said.

"Yes, it really is. Nikolay Nikolaevich was given a pass for it, but I wasn't."

"Why is that?"

"For the same old reason. He is someone, a professor, but what am I? Carrion."

"All the same, these are your trees, your house and garden," I thought but did not manage to say. Tanya was coming towards us. She told Anna Andreevna that Vladimir Georgievich was waiting for her upstairs. Anna Andreevna quickly said goodbye to me and went up the stairs. I walked along beside Tanya. I told her that to my mind Anna Andreevna looked much better and all thanks to her, Tanya's, efforts. "Yes, well, I does what I can for her," replied Tanya, flattered. I asked her what she was going to feed Anna Andreevna now. "Oh, I'll give her some cabbage soup and then I'll make meself pancakes and let her have some of mine. We don't keep no account – when we gets hers or she gets ours."

---

* On the connections between the works of Pushkin and the traditions of West European classical poetry, and on Anna Akhmatova's observations, see footnote on p. 19.

† Seemingly, Fyodor Sologub. This is clear from the following text: O. A. Glebova-Sudeykina, whom A.A. mentions later was friends with Sologub. About F. Sologub's animosity towards Pushkin see also E. Danko's memoirs, published in the almanac *Faces*.

9 March 1940

Anna Andreevna came to visit me this evening. I sat her down in Lyusha's room – at the time Lyusha was lying in my bed, being examined by a doctor. When the doctor left, Ida carried Lyushenka back to her own bed. Anna Andreevna sat affectionately next to her whilst I made my bed and tidied the room.

Leaning right back into the divan in my room, Anna Andreevna lit a cigarette and began to talk.

"I am so tired ... I've been writing every night ... 'The wedge'.*

"Nikolay Nikolaevich has now discovered a new reason for taking umbrage at me: why didn't I write when we lived together, when I write so much now? I couldn't write for six years.† The whole atmosphere weighed so heavily on me, more heavily even than my grief. Now at last I have understood: for Nikolay Nikolaevich, Anna Evgenevna was always the model wife: she works, earns 400 roubles a month and is an excellent housekeeper. He constantly tried to force me onto that Procrustean bed too, but I am neither a housekeeper nor an income earner ... Had I lived longer with Vladimir Kazimirovich, I would have forgotten how to write poetry too."

"And what were you supposed to be there?" I asked.

"There, nothing, but the man was simply impossible to live with."

I asked whether Nikolay Nikolaevich liked her poetry.

"It's impossible to tell whether he does or not. You see, he is ruled by the subconscious."

I told her that although I didn't understand "the wedge" it was clear that the author is speaking about something familiar to her, which really did take place: this happens in Pasternak's poetry very often. The direct meaning is unclear, but it's clear that the poem is about a real event.

"Yes, with him it is like that, you're right. And often. Sometimes, however, it is different. Here, for example" – she jumped up from the divan and took a book of Pasternak's poetry off the shelf – "here for instance, in 'Ballad'. Try hard as you might, you won't understand a thing. To make matters worse, there is even the hint of a subject here ...[50]

---

* She recited the poem "All this you alone will guess" (dedicated to Boris Pilnyak), which contains the line "That sunny, lily-of-the-valley wedge ...". She did not say to whom this poem was dedicated then, and somehow I did not understand it properly, especially the word *wedge*; no. 18.

† See footnote on p. 148.

"He gave me this book with the inscription: 'To Anna Andreevna, prolonged in sound. After a quarrel.' This is what the quarrel was: When he arrived in Leningrad, Boris Leonidovich gave one of our mutual acquaintances 500 roubles for me. I was sick at the time and didn't see him. When I had recovered I went to Moscow, sold my archive to Bonch.* I brought the money to Boris Leonidovich. He wouldn't take it, made a fuss, wouldn't accept it. 'I never expected this from you. I brought it to you with the purest sentiments.' – 'I sold my archives with the purest sentiments, too.' He was so angry that he even grabbed me by the knees, without realizing what he was doing."

I asked: "The human soul is oddly made, don't you find: poems, even the greatest, don't make the author happy? Take Pushkin: he knew that it was he who had written *The Bronze Horseman,* and yet he wasn't happy."

"He wasn't. But you can say with confidence that what he wanted more than anything else in the world was to write more and more ..."

Vladimir Georgievich came for her. She changed at once. Either he was in our way or I was in theirs. They soon left.

11 March 1940

Today Anna Andreevna phoned – couldn't I come round? I went.

The same black dressing gown, but from underneath, the large white collar of a new nightdress protruded. It made her look like Byron or Mary Stuart.

"Here, have a look," and she handed me a report. "Zh. brought it round in person yesterday."†

I read it. First there was wooden praise, then a rejection of the poems, one after another, totally arbitrarily. One justification, for example, was: "It's insipid".

She put the reader's report to one side. And recited a new poem. Something wondrous but rather elusive.‡ I asked her to recite it again: I hadn't fully understood it. She refused: "It's not finished."

---

* That is, to the State Literary Museum, which was founded in 1933 by one of the oldest activists in the RSDRP-BKP (b)-KPSS, Vladimir Dmitrievich Bonch-Bruevich (1873–1955). For more about him see the biographical dictionary *Russian Writers* [*Russkie pisateli*], vol. 1 (Moscow, 1989).

    [RSDRP-BKP (b)-KPSS – the Russian Social Democratic Party–All Union Communist Party (of Bolsheviks)–CPSU.]

† I can't remember who that was. Evidently Anna Andreevna had been shown somebody's "in-house" report on her collection *FSB.*

‡ She recited "Thus dark souls take flight"; no. 19. The first half.

"You aren't obliged to understand *this* ... That's how I sit all night long in my armchair. I go to bed when everybody else is already getting up and going out for sugar."

Conversation about a flat.

"I won't move to a new housing development. Neither in Strelna, nor in Lesnoy. Here, all my friends are close by, I can reach them all on foot. There, I'd be cut off. And Vladimir Georgievich wouldn't be able to visit me more than once a week."

I don't remember how, but the conversation brought us to her leaving Nikolay Stepanovich.

"Three years of hunger. I left the Gumilyovs' without taking anything with me. Vladimir Kazimirovich was ill. He could do without anything but tea and tobacco. We rarely cooked – there was nothing to cook or to cook in. We had to ask the neighbours for each little saucepan: I didn't have a fork, a spoon or a saucepan."

I told her that during the hungry years I had felt most humiliated by my footwear, or rather, the lack of it. When I was about twelve, in winter, to be able to go outside, I had to put Korney Ivanovich's huge galoshes on over my slippers. And that's how I went around, in galoshes that kept flapping and falling off."

"For *me*, the most humiliating thing was matches. There weren't any, and in the morning I had to run into the street to get a light off somebody."

It turns out she likes Goncharov's *Oblomov*, but not his *Precipice*.

"In *Oblomov* there is the flow of life, continuous, deep and dense, which Turgenev never has. With Turgenev it's always surface, lightness. But *Precipice* is a failure: the novel was written too much as a blunt response to the times. Obviously, this is inappropriate for art."

Without knocking, Tanya entered the room, bringing a thin and sullen Shakalik, wrapped in a blanket.

"Want to go to Anya?"

"Don't want to!" – and he turned away.

"Anna Andreevna, hold him a minute," said Tanya. "I haven't had any grub since this morning."

20 March 1940

I hadn't been to Anna Andreevna's for quite a while. She had phoned several times but somehow I just couldn't get away. Today, at last, I went, but it wasn't a great success: she had people round.

Anna Andreevna herself opened the door. A touch of lipstick, a shawl over the dressing gown.

"Osmyorkin[51] and Verochka are here."*

Anna Andreevna was silent and absent-minded, most of the time she sat in an armchair, arms spread out. Soon I. arrived. Anna Andreevna kept going to the kitchen, searching for spoons, cups – there and also in her own cupboard. At last everybody settled down to drink tea. The conversation revolved around the Hermitage and the Russian Museum, the hanging of paintings, the life span of paints and so on. From behind a cupboard, Anna Andreevna pulled out a canvas and everybody (except me) began guessing: was it Sudeykin or Grigoriev? Osmyorkin gave a whole lecture on each artist's style.

Anna Andreevna settled back in the armchair again, spread out her arms, and fell completely silent. The general conversation carried on without her. I., who was sitting on the divan, slipped off twice (obviously the divan was also broken); each time it made me jump almost to the ceiling; I. hurt himself – but none of this made the slightest impression on Anna Andreevna. Finally, I. and Osmyorkin asked her to recite something. First she stubbornly refused: "For the last three nights I've been reading aloud, I've got a sore throat from it." Nevertheless, she did recite "Cleopatra" (with an alteration in the stanza about children), "I have no need for a host of odes" (with an alteration in the last line). She recited in a tired voice, sometimes short of breath. And she also recited, until the end, the one which I hadn't understood last time: "The Hundredth". What weariness it contained – not even pre-death, but posthumous weariness. And then release:

> Nothing at all do I need on earth ...
> Soon I shall be treading the blissful shore ...

And that dream, which gnaws at me too, and not only at me of course: if only that which happened had not happened – to awake in the morning:

> ... And Troy has not fallen. Eabany still lives ...†

At half past one everybody got up. In the courtyard I. and Osmyorkin decided to go to Vera Nikolaevna's for a drink and insisted on my coming, too. I refused, with the excuse that I had to be up early. Osmyorkin offered to walk me home. I refused that as well, so as not to break up

---

* Verochka: Vera Nikolaevna Anikieva.
† A reference to the poem "Thus dark souls take flight" – see *BPL–A*, p. 196; no. 19.

their company, but mainly because I wasn't afraid and felt good walking by myself.

> ... And Troy has not fallen. Eabany still lives,
> And has been drowned in a fragrant mist ...

> ... Nothing at all do I need on earth –

> Nor the thunder of Homer, nor the wonder of Dante.
> Soon I shall be treading the blissful shore ...

21 *March 1940*

I set off to the library with my notebooks but instead went to Anna Andreevna's.

She was drinking tea in her room which had been tidied up, freshly swept.

I suggested a walk in the sunshine. "I knew you would come," she said and agreed. "Let's just wait until the stove burns out." She settled in the armchair in front of the stove, I sat down on the little trunk next to her. Her face, momentarily lit by the fleeting glimmer of the fire in the stove, seemed to me today dry and dark, like a face on a coin or in an icon.

I asked who had thought up her pseudonym.

"Nobody, of course. In those days no one was interested in me. I was a sheep without a shepherd. And only a crazy 17-year-old girl would choose a Tatar surname for a Russian poetess. That's the surname of the last Tatar princes of the Horde. Taking a pseudonym occurred to me because, having found out about my poems, my father had told me: 'Don't bring shame upon my name.' – 'I can do without your name then!' I said."

She handed me the proofs from *Leningrad*. I read them and suggested some changes in the punctuation which would emphasize the rhythmic structure. She accepted them all.

"What talent God bestows!" said Anna Andreevna, looking over my shoulder as I was making the corrections. "I would never be able to learn that."

It was very amusing.

Tanya came in: "Anna Andreevna, it's time for your dress fitting!"

Anna Andreevna hesitated a bit, but I explained to her that I had to go out on business for about 15 minutes.

When I returned, Anna Andreevna was already in her room and

waiting for me, wearing her coat. By the time we got outside the sun had already begun to wane, however. We headed for the garden near the Engineers' Castle.

"I see you like this garden," I said.

"Yes, it is my permanent residence ... The dress is rather macabre, by the way. Do you know who's making it? A lady plumber. The plumber's wife."

We sat on a bench flooded in sunlight. Two birches stood facing us, their white trunks so brightly lit that our eyes hurt.

"Yesterday you spoke disapprovingly about Esenin," Anna Andreevna said. "Osmyorkin loves him, though. He was upset. No, I can't understand that. I have just reread him. He's very bad, very monotonous, and it reminded me of an apartment during the NEP: the icons are still up but the place is already overcrowded, and there's someone drinking and pouring his feelings out in front of strangers. Yes, you are right: all the time – drunken, definitive truths, interminable effusions, although really there is nothing to effuse about. Always the same theme; Browning also had only one theme, he, however, mastered it with virtuosity, but what virtuosity is there here? Then again, when I read other poems, I think I'm being unfair to Esenin. They, poor things, don't even have one theme."

We walked along the Fontanka towards the Summer Garden. Soldiers were at drill in the courtyard of the Engineers' Castle. Music carried over from the Field of Mars. From Panteleymonovskaya Street we could see banners being waved. Anna Andreevna tried to make out what was going on there, but the Panteleymonovskaya was thick with crowds and cars. Nothing could be distinguished. The sun blazed blindingly off the polished sides and windows of the cars. We turned back home.

For a long time we couldn't cross the Fontanka: she was fearful.

"How I envy those who are not afraid!"

She told me about her brother who had poisoned himself when his child died of malaria.

"He left us a letter – a marvellous one. Not a word about death. It ended like this: 'I kiss Mama's hands, which I remember as so beautiful and delicate and which are now so wrinkled.'" His wife had taken poison together with him, but when they broke down the door and came into the room she was still breathing. She was saved. She turned out to be pregnant and gave birth to a totally healthy child.

9 April 1940

Anna Andreevna came round in the evening of the 29th, that is on the eve of my departure for Moscow. Dressed up, her hair done, wearing a necklace – she was obviously going somewhere or coming from somewhere. Shura was there. Anna Andreevna recited "Who at this fearful hour can weep" to us.[*]

Yesterday I returned from Moscow, and hardly had I unpacked my suitcase – the telephone. "You're back? Come over! Come as soon as possible!"

I went during the day.

Joyfully, happily I walked through town.

Anna Andreevna herself opened the door.

"Well, how successful has it been?" I asked after we'd sat down.

"Only unsuccessful so far. I gave a reading in the Vyborg House of Culture. The tickets must practically have been forced on people. The moment I went on I thought: 'God! How much they'd all rather be at the cinema or at a dance!'"

She handed me *Leningrad* no. 2.

"Have you seen this yet?"

"No."

I began leafing through it. An ocean liner, sailing in a pond. She took the journal out of my hands: "Better, let me read you something new."

She recited something about mourners.[†]

She told me how the poems were arranged in both books.

Then about her visit to Tynyanov.

"And I even complained to you – remember? – that he had been a bit limp on the phone. I feel guilty about that. The truth is, he is ill. Very ill. A mane of youthful chestnut hair, and underneath, a tiny, shrivelled old man's face. He came into the hallway to see me off and suddenly collapsed on the floor, and just imagine, I picked him up myself. All on my own! Oh, how light he was – like a little rag."

Then she told me that she had been to the publishers to get her savings

---

[*] She recited a poem dedicated to Boris Pilnyak: "All this you alone will guess". When I first heard it, it seemed slightly incomprehensible: "the wedge" – *FT, Reed*; no. 18.

[†] Evidently part of the poem "The Way of All the Earth": "A flock of mourners/ Behind me I lead" – *FT, Reed*; no. 20. I take this opportunity to correct the misprint and censor's changes in *FT*. On p. 284 instead of "From aquamarine/ Blazes forth the sunset" it should say: "O Salve Regina! –/ Blazes forth the sunset"; on p. 287 "For a new loss/ I make my way home" should read "Through the crucified city/ I make my way home"; and on p. 288 it should say: "There, like a lark,/ Hovers ancient pain".

book seen to and they had talked her into going up to the editorial office.

"Did they treat you with appropriate deference?"

"Yes! Divine! They gave me a lot of books as well. I read them. Awful. After that, you don't want to read poetry, let alone write any. They're all the same.

"Tsezar Samoylovich came to see me.* Listen, he's very ill. Look how he inscribed his book to me – see: 'To Anna Andreeva'. I'm often given different names. One of my admirers who stutters recently said at someone's house: 'Sh-sh-sh-she w-w-was p-p-published.' 'Who's she?' 'Astafeva.'"

She questioned me thoroughly about Nikolay Ivanovich.

"Was he glad to hear that I was coming?"

"Very!"

A short silence. Then: "You know," Anna Andreevna said, "Nikolay Nikolaevich is furious about 'From you I hid my heart'. He walks around black as a cloud."

"Didn't he know before?"

"Of course he knew, but for some reason he's just now decided to take offence. It doesn't bother me, though."†

Vladimir Georgievich came, they discussed her ticket to Moscow and her recital on the 11th.‡ I said goodbye.

"I will see you before I leave, won't I?" said Anna Andreevna, seeing me off. "I'll come over."

3 May 1940

On the 1st, at Anna Andreevna's request, Vladimir Georgievich phoned me: Anna Andreevna had returned and was asking me to come over. But I didn't have anyone to leave Lyusha with: Ida was celebrating. I tried to enlist one of my friends – no luck.

On the 2nd, yesterday, towards evening, she came herself. Dressed up and almost rosy.

"How well you look," I said.

"Oh, come now! I just washed my face with hot water and put some powder on. Actually, I feel very bad. Moscow tired me out. There was central heating where I stayed, and my thyroid can't take that."

---

* Volpe.
† May I remind the reader that this poem appeared in print in March 1940 (in the journal *Leningrad*, no. 2); no. 21.
‡ Which one, where, I do not remember.

"Did you do much visiting in Moscow?"

"No. All I did was take a taxi and go to Nikolay Ivanovich's. What a brain he has! What do you think – it's important for me to know – is he able to talk with admiration about poems he doesn't like?"

"No. Of course not. In general he can't be bothered to lie. Certainly not about poetry!"

"Do you know what he said to me? 'I have always loved you, but I used to be indifferent to your poetry. But now I understand that your poetry is even better than you are. You make me love the hateful.' That's what he said, but in reality it isn't like that. I've just read the proofs and see clearly what a mediocre, trivial, insignificant book it is."

I didn't contradict, I wanted to understand. And she explained it to me.* I didn't console her. How can one console her. I merely reminded her: things will change.

She waved her hand wearily.

Then she told me her new idea: (a) "We thought we were beggars"; (b) "Fear, which picks out objects in the dark"; (c) "But it's arrant nonsense that I live in sadness"; (d) "Wild honey smells of freedom", and others.† And added: "The late Alighieri would have created the tenth circle of hell."

She recited two new poems. About a tower. And impressions of poems.‡

"And how was 'The Way of All the Earth' received in Moscow?" I asked.

"Tishenka§ was in raptures over 'Back in time', but Boris Leonidovich didn't like it. He didn't say so but I guessed."

Then: "If only you knew what a welcome Vovochka gave me! 'Our Anya is back!' And as I was leaving, already in my coat, and Tanya was coming out into the hallway with him, he reached for the door: 'You should open the door for Anya.' He is so touching. I have made up my mind to rent a dacha for him. I'll ask Litfond to give me one, and I'll

---

* She was troubled and depressed that her most cherished poems – from "Requiem", "A Wreath for the Dead" and many others – could not be included in the book.

† The above-mentioned poems never appeared as a separate cycle. But they were published in various years in various publications: (a) *White Flock* [*Belaya staya*], no. 22; (b) *BPL–A*, p. 168, no. 23; (c) the journal *Moskva*, 1966, no. 6, no. 24; (d) *BPL–A*, p. 191, no. 25.

‡ "Impressions of poems" is apparently "About poetry" – *FT, Seventh Book*; no. 26. "About a tower" is probably "My youthful hands", containing the lines: "Who knows how completely empty the sky is/ On the spot of the fallen tower,/ Who knows how quiet the house is,/ Where the son has not come home?" – *BPL–A*, p. 195; no. 27.

§ Aleksandr Nikolaevich Tikhonov.

take him and Tanya with me. Valya will be sent to a summer camp. But Shakalik really needs fresh air."

I asked how her recital at the Capella had gone down.

"Everything was very strange. In my eyes it was a most ordinary reading. I didn't notice anything special. But Verochka and all the others maintain that there was an ovation."

6 May 1940

Yesterday I got very tired and on my return from the library I lay down. The phone rang. It was Vladimir Georgievich: "Anna Andreevna is unwell and *begs* you to come."

I rested for a bit and went. I went, even though I realized that nothing had happened, that she simply couldn't sleep, was depressed and wanted someone to sit beside her.

Indeed she "simply couldn't sleep" – but I did the right thing in going.

Again the dressing gown, the divan, the crumpled blanket, the dishevelled, unkempt hair. It's hard to believe that just two days earlier she had looked so youthful, so well dressed, so triumphant. Now this sallow, pinched, old face. She complains of a pain in her foot.

The proofs will be ready on the 7th. From Goslitizdat? From Sovetskiy pisatel? I don't remember, I've got confused. At any rate – the proofs will be ready. Anna Andreevna wants to give me the task of reading them and, most important, of making sure that everything – including the punctuation – is consistent with the proofs which Lozinsky has just read.

I promised.

"Bear in mind that there are eleven printer's sheets to be done," said Anna Andreevna.

"I'm not afraid," I replied.

"In the Goslit edition there are 150 fewer lines than in the Sovetskiy pisatel edition. In the Sovestkiy pisatel edition, apart from what was agreed, only one poem, "The Last Toast", has been removed so far.* I ordered 40 copies at the reduced price for myself; I will give my friends the Sovestkiy pisatel book, but I won't give anyone the Goslitizdat."

She fell silent. She performed the ritual.

"Nor the agitated linden shadows."†

---

*   No. 28.
†   A.A. wrote down, gave me to read and burned over the ashtray: "Already madness with its wing", a poem about a visit to her son in prison; no. 29.

And I immediately understood everything: her sallowness, her dishevelled hair, her sleeplessness.

"Did you do that last night?"

"No, yesterday. Between continuous phone calls from the publishers."

She put on her glasses and began to leaf through her notebook. I saw that the notebook was filled to the very last page. She snapped it shut, without having read anything to me.

"You'll have to get a new one," I said.

"I've got two new ones! Just look at them."

She pulled two albums out of her chest of drawers; one was antique, wonderful, with thick paper.

"Nikolay Ivanovich gave it to me. From Pushkin's time, see?"

She sat on the divan, feet tucked beneath her, and took a cigarette. She was very agitated – why? – probably because of the imminent publication of her book, although she was hiding it. She showed me her portrait by Tyrsa, which was going to be included in the Sovetskiy pisatel volume. I didn't like the portrait – too superficial. She liked it, though. (From the end of the '20s.)

Lighting a cigarette, she said: "And all this for nothing: the portrait, the proofs ... There won't be enough paper, or something else will be in short supply. We'll see. You know, I've at last understood why I can't stand my early poems. Now I see them all perfectly for what they are. I hadn't seen them for a long time, but when I was looking at the proofs with Lozinsky I realized exactly what they're like: unkind in their attitude to the protagonist, unwise, naïve and shameless. I assure you, that's precisely what they're like. And I just can't understand why people like them so much."

I said that I could perhaps agree on only one point: unkindness towards the protagonist.

"No, no, it's exactly as I say ... Art is a dangerous thing. You don't realize this when you're young. What a terrible fate, with traps, snares. I now understand parents who try to shield their children from poetry, from the theatre ... Just think, what terrible fates ... You don't see it when you're young, and even if you see it, you 'don't give a damn' ..."

It was first published with many censorial distortions and under the heading "To a friend" in the collection: *Anna Akhmatova. Selected Works* [*Anna Akhmatova. Izbrannoe*] (Tashkent: Sovetskiy pisatel, 1943). Then in 1974, with censorial distortions and with misprints in the collection: *Anna Akhmatova. Selected Works* [*Anna Akhmatova. Izbrannoe*] (Moscow: Khudozhestvennaya literatura). For the most authentic text see: *Neva*, 1987, no. 6 ("Requiem").

She was agitated and focused. She obviously wanted to talk.

"You do know Lotta,[52] don't you? The sharpest of women. Razor-sharp. She's charming. A few days ago I told her: 'I would like to recite to you, Lotta, I've written a poem...' And she said to me: 'Who? You?' Charming, isn't it? It's very funny: 'Who? You?'"

We started talking about Dostoevsky.

"I've recently reread Dostoevsky's *The Idiot*, *A Raw Youth* and *The Insulted and Injured*. Yes, you are right, *The Idiot* is the best. An astounding novel. And you know what I've noticed? Have you ever thought about the little old men in Dostoevsky? Those perfumed, courteous, naïve old men, who flutter around, clicking their heels, trying to be French, always falling in love? I've understood that they are all people from Pushkin's days, who've overstayed their time in this world, and he depicts them as they appeared to his generation. That's how he and his contemporaries saw people of Pushkin's day – that's what Prince Vyazemsky, for instance, was like for them."

I began to question her about Moscow, about Boris Leonidovich.

"He is slowly dying at home ... He's not writing his own poetry anymore, because he's translating other people's – nothing destroys your own poetry more than translating other people's. Take Lozinsky, he started translating and stopped writing ... But in Boris Leonidovich's case the main problem is something else: it's his home life. I feel infinitely sorry for him ... Zina loses herself in card-playing for days on end; Lyonechka is neglected. He himself says: Lyonechka goes around in rags, and when you try to explain to her – she starts screeching. From the very start everybody around could see that she was a coarse and vulgar woman, but he didn't see it, he was blindly in love. Since there was absolutely nothing to be enraptured by, he admired the fact that she washed the floors herself ... And now he sees everything, understands everything clearly and says terrible things about her ... Had he said them to me in private, of course I wouldn't have repeated them to anyone, but he spoke about Zina in front of Nina Antonovna whom he hardly knows. Nina and I couldn't bring ourselves to look at each other, that's how embarrassed we felt.[53] 'She's a storm on a parquet floor, who has been to the beauty salon and acquired a veneer of bad taste.' Accurate, isn't it? Then: 'If she was at least extreme in some respect, you know, like a hovel, which you can point out to foreigners and say, "Look at this terrible hovel of ours!"' – like the one I had (she pointed her finger at the wall, behind which lived Nikolay Nikolaevich) – 'but she is merely common as muck.' He understands everything, but he won't leave, of course. Because of Lyonechka. And, besides, he belongs to the breed of conscientious men who cannot get divorced twice. But is it possible to work in such conditions? Side by side with vulgarity? Poverty has never hampered anybody. Neither has grief. Rembrandt painted all his best works in the last two years of his life, after having lost everybody around him: his wife, son, mother . . . No, grief doesn't interfere with work. But a Zina like that can ruin everything . . ."

"But if she is like that," I said, "I don't understand why she needs Boris Leonidovich. It's not only that he needs a different wife, she too needs a different husband. He can't be any good for her either."

"You see, their romance began at the height of his prosperity. He was proclaimed the best poet, there was plenty of money, they could go off to Tbilisi in a sleeping car. Oh, if only one could find her some well-off book-keeper. But, I fear, it won't happen."

I said that I liked Pasternak's translation of *Hamlet* very much.

"Yes, yes, I also grew to like it. I'm so happy for Boris Leonidovich: everybody praises it, everybody likes it, and Boris Leonidovich is pleased. The translation really is superb: a powerful wave of verse. And, strange though it may seem, not a trace of Pasternak. Marshak told me that in his view Hamlet, in Pasternak's translation, is too much of a schoolboy, simplified, but I don't agree. My only regret is that it has now become fashionable to praise Pasternak's translation to the detriment of Lozinsky's. Yet his is very good, although totally different. Lozinsky's translation is better for reading as a book, whereas Pasternak's translation is more suited to the theatre. As a matter of fact, there is no need to favour one over the other; one should simply rejoice in such a feast of Russian culture."

I began talking about Boris Leonidovich's taste in poetry, which I find incomprehensible; I had seen his letter to our Kolya* in which he praises Vsevolod Rozhdestvensky's poetry effusively.

"Oh, he always does that. On my last visit to Moscow it was also like that. He brought Spassky to Fedin's, as the former wanted to hear my poems. And right there, in front of him, he repeated endlessly: 'Sergey Dmitrievich has created something so grand, that for the past three days I have been living on his last poems.' And it's all nonsense. Rozhdestvensky's poetry is so poor, there isn't a word of his own and, of course, Boris Leonidovich has no use for it. He often praises things for the

---

* "Our Kolya" is my older brother, Nikolay Korneevich Chukovsky. For more about him see my *Journals*, vol. 2.

most naïve, trifling motives. I can assure you. He imagines he's doing
somebody a good turn. And sometimes he himself doesn't understand
what he's saying. For instance, he didn't like 'The Way of All the Earth'.
Yet he heaped Homeric, boundless praise upon it."

"How on earth do you know that he didn't like it?"

"I guessed. First of all he said it was like Mandelstam. But he can't
stand Mandelstam, and he had forgotten that he'd told me so earlier.
Then he said: 'It is so beautiful that it can't exist on its own. I am sure
that somewhere something like it must exist.' Later I guessed: 'something
like it' meant real poems, his own, which he hasn't written yet, whereas
I have already written; but what is mine is not the real thing, it happened
by chance, whereas the real thing – 'something like it' – is his, it is what
ought to be and will be . . . That's what his subconscious thought is; he
himself doesn't understand it yet, but I've guessed it."

The kettle came to the boil. As always Anna Andreevna started to
wander around the room, in search of the essential requisites for drinking
tea: "Where on earth has the sugar disappeared to? Tanya managed to
get hold of some sugar for me and was very proud of herself, and now
it's gone."

The sugar was found. She sat down, poured tea into the cups and
once more returned to what she had been saying.

"But the main reason for all this wild praise of Boris Leonidovich's
is an occupational disease affecting all writers. Like a callous on a plough-
man's hands. A writer, a poet is incapable of having a calm attitude to
his work and its fate. Take Boris Leonidovich – at the moment he's
frightfully upset because Korney Ivanovich and Samuil Yakovlevich
didn't like his translation. But what's so upsetting about that? Some like
one thing, others another. And, what's worse, he stops liking people
who don't care for something of his. The main reason he is fond of me
is that I dedicated some poems to him, and that I like his poetry."

"But does he like your poetry?"

"I doubt it. Some time ago he used to read my poems – very long
ago – and he has forgotten them. He may remember the odd line. But
basically he has no need for poetry. Haven't you noticed that poets don't
like the poetry of their contemporaries? A poet carries within him his
own enormous world – why does he need someone else's poetry? When
they're young, about 23 or 24, poets like the work of poets in their own
group. Later though, they don't like anybody else's – only their own.
They have no use for other poetry, it feels superfluous or even hostile."

After a pause she said: "I have many failings, vices even, but human

ones; I don't have any occupational diseases. It doesn't bother me at all
if a person doesn't like my poetry. Look what Mandelstam wrote about
me! 'A stylite on a pillar of parquet'! What could be more offensive."[54]

"But he did love you, didn't he?"

"Yes, probably. And I loved him very much. How I love them both,
Osip and Boris Leonidovich."

"Who could not be fond of Boris Leonidovich!" I said.

"Such people do exist, though. Aseev for instance . . . But I can assure
you that not being fond of Osip was very hard, too, although he was
completely different from Boris Leonidovich . . . It's difficult to talk about
him, to explain him. When Boris Leonidovich dies it will also be difficult
to explain what was so charming about him. Osip and I were friends
from youth, but our friendship became close in '37. Yes, in '37. He didn't
like my poetry,[55] but he couldn't have been more trustful of me had I
been his sister. He told me, behind Nadya's back, about all his loves:*
his whole life he used to fall in and out of love easily . . . And once he
told me: 'I'm ready for death now.'"

I got up, saying goodbye. She stood up.

"I can assure you I have no occupational diseases. And you know
why? I am not a literary person."

She walked me right up to the door. It was two in the morning. At
the door she said: "Only please don't think that I was saying something
bad about Boris Leonidovich to you."

10 May 1940

Three days ago, Anna Andreevna rang me in the morning and asked me
to come over. Goslit were sending the proofs over to her at once. I went.
We sat around for a long time, drinking tea, watching the clock, waiting.
Anna Andreevna complained that Goslit's selection is much worse than
that of Sovetskiy pisatel: it is 150 lines shorter, has no epigraphs and all
in all is "Akhmatova pour les pauvres".†

A book in colour. Its table of contents.‡

---

* "Nadya": Nadezhda Yakovlevna, wife of Osip Mandelstam. For more about her see E. G.
   Gershteyn. *New Material on Mandelstam* [*Novoe o Mandelshtame*] (Paris, 1986); my *Journals*,
   vols. 2 and 3; *Anna Akhmatova. Mandelstam. (Pages from a Diary)* [*Anna Akhmatova. Mandelstam. (Listki iz dnevnika)*]; and also: Nikita Struve, "Eight Hours with Anna Akhmatova"
   in *Works*, vol. 2, pp. 176 and 327, 1968.
† *Pour les pauvres* (Fr.): for the poor.
‡ I am unable to decipher this line. Evidently, it concerned some planned but unrealized
   book.

The proofs were delivered at last. They really did look pitiful, shoddy. Anna Andreevna insisted that the new poems should be checked against the Sovetskiy pisatel proofs, that is, against the set Mikhail Leonidovich had checked. I rang our dear Tanya[56] at the publishers, but she said that the proofs had already gone to the printers and nothing could be done about it. Anna Andreevna got angry and made me phone back several times: "Tell her that the dotty old lady doesn't understand a thing and keeps insisting." But I *did* understand and felt very embarrassed at doing this to Tanechka who, even without my phone calls, would have been prepared to do anything for Anna Andreevna. Within the hour Tanya herself phoned and suggested the following – Anna Andreevna, using the author's prerogative, should keep the Goslit proofs for four days, as she was legally entitled to do, by which time the proofs would be back from the printers. But Anna Andreevna said: "I don't have the strength to squabble with them, Goslit is pressuring me."

Taking the proofs, I set off for Tusya's.* She would do everything perfectly, no worse than Lozinsky. We worked avidly, hardly stopping, from four o'clock in the afternoon until 1 a.m. When we had finished I phoned Anna Andreevna. She asked me to bring the proofs over, not in the morning, but at once.

I did.

Last night she came round to my place with a briefcase. It was the first time I had seen her carrying a briefcase! She was listless, irritable – obviously the fuss over the book had exhausted her, and then there had also been news from Moscow about B.'s fruitless effort.†

She unfolded her list of corrections – some were amendments, some new punctuation and some misprints. One misprint which infuriated her was "needle" [*igloi*] instead of "arrow" [*streloi*] in the lines:

> And on the tower clock the large hand
> Does not seem to me a deadly needle.

"How absurd! You have arrows of death, not needles. How carelessly people read poetry. They all read it, they all like it, they all write letters – and they don't notice that it's utter nonsense.‡

Then she showed me the new punctuation at the end of the poem

---

*   Tusya: Tamara Grigorievna Gabbe. See note 57.
†   Some failure concerning efforts on Lyova's behalf.
‡   The misprint "needle" instead of "arrow" in the poem "Weak is my voice, but my will does not weaken" appeared in the collection *White Flock* (1917); and to my amazement, in spite of Anna Andreevna's correction, that very same misprint was repeated in the collection *FSB*, on p. 122. In all subsequent editions, including *FT*, it says "arrow" (p. 93).

"Like a white stone in the depths of a well": the line "That my wonderful sorrows should live for ever" should be separated from the following line "You have become a memory of mine" by a punctuation mark; it doesn't relate to it.*

Then I began putting questions to her from a list of queries Tusya and I had prepared. I suggested some changes in the punctuation. She responded and agreed willingly. Only once, when I suggested inserting an ellipsis, did she reply: "Don't ... I don't like it." Sometimes she couldn't answer the question – this or that punctuation mark? Then I would ask her to read out two or three lines, putting in the punctuation marks myself according to her intonation.

She dictated to me a stanza from the poem "Boris Pasternak" which had been included in the Sovetskiy pisatel book but had for some reason been omitted from the Goslit edition. And she restored several epithets.†

Tanechka had sent her the set of proofs which Yury Nikolaevich had brought back from Detskoe for her – the very one, with Anna Andreevna's and Mikhail Leonidovich's corrections. I took a look: it really did have a totally different appearance. Yu. N. and Tanya had fought hard to obtain an old-fashioned typeface.

I checked all the new poems in the Goslit proofs line by line against the Sovetskiy pisatel text. Anna Andreevna wasn't a help to me, and even distracted me by talking, but she looked at the proofreader's marks with reverence and took an amused delight in my ability to put them in.

I finished.

"Do you really think all the poems are bad?" I asked, remembering our recent conversation.

"All, or almost all of them ... I assure you: the poems are bad, the book's bad. But this – 'The heavy amber day drags on for ever' – this I do like."‡

I said that the poem "Tall woman, where is your little gypsy boy" always nearly moved me to tears.§

"That's history," Anna Andreevna replied cryptically. And, without any explanation, she dictated some minor corrections to the poem "We shall not drink from the same glass" to me.§§

---

* However, in both collections – in *FSB* and in *FT* – the punctuation does not correspond to my notes.

† Which stanza – I do not remember; one of three: IV, V or VI; I think the epithets were "deadly" [*smertelnyy*] and "graveyard" [*kladbishchenskiy*].

‡ *FT, Rosary*; no. 30.

§ *BPL–A*, p. 109; no. 31.

§§ *FT, Rosary*; no. 32.

"Mikhail Leonidovich was offended to see that I had changed it, made it different from the way it had been in our youth. And so, I'm restoring it to how it was," she explained.

"What? That means, it was to him!" I thought, but didn't say.

Ida served us lunch. Anna Andreevna tried to be friendly and gracious but was cold and distracted. She did, though, speak very nicely of our Daniil Ivanovich; she had met him a few days ago and had liked him.

"He told me he believes that a genius must possess three qualities: perspicacity, authority and intelligibility. Khlebnikov possessed perspicacity but did not possess intelligibility and authority. I recited 'The Way of All the Earth' to him. He said: 'Yes, you do seem to have authority, but not much intelligibility.'"[58]

She was in a hurry to get home: Vladimir Georgievich was supposed to bring some doctor back with him by six o'clock.

She left. And Goslit sent someone to my place for the proofs. I wrote out instructions for the technical editors and the proofreaders; I also enclosed a photograph which Anna Andreevna had brought (1936, "a good photograph, here I wasn't trying to make myself look younger anymore").*

That evening, when she got home from the publishing house, Tanya phoned me. It turns out that there is a big intrigue surrounding Anna Andreevna's books – and she was right not to want to sign contracts with two publishers at once. Goslit had tricked her with the assurance that they had some special authorization. They did not and could not have any: on the contrary, the publication of two identical books at the same time in two different places is categorically prohibited. And now both publishers are rushing to get the book out first, in order to jeopardize the other.

And caught up in all this is a person who so earnestly does not want, so passionately does not want to be put in a false, unworthy position . . .

I'm not going to tell her. It would make her ill. Anyway, nothing can be done about it now.

And what if "Akhmatova pour les pauvres" comes out first? And the Sovetsky pisatel edition doesn't come out at all?†

---

* This concerns a photograph of Akhmatova taken by L. Gornung on the Starki estate at the Shervinskys' in 1936. I take this opportunity to point out my mistake in the previous publication of my *Journals*. The photograph by L. Gornung opens the volume, but I gave the wrong year.

    For more on the Shervinskys see *Journals*, vol. 2; on the photographs taken by L. Gornung see *Memoirs A.A.*, pp. 194, 196, 198, 203, and 208.

† Fortunately the reverse happened: *FSB*, the Sovestkiy pisatel collection compiled by Yu.

11 May 1940

Last night, while Shura and Tusya were at my place, Vladimir Georgie-vich phoned and said that Anna Andreevna was seeking my permission to come over and show me the proofs from *Zvezda*. It wasn't particularly convenient for me (we were working) but, of course, I said: "I'll be expecting her."

She arrived very late, after eleven, dressed up, all in black silk, amiable, gracious and even cheerful. After being introduced to Tusya (she'd seen Shura before), she immediately informed us, rather gaily, that she'd lost a brooch, an Egyptian one; she'd looked for it for two hours and hadn't managed to find it. "The brooch had been lying on the chest of drawers . . . The trouble is, the Punins have a new domestic help."

"Today two unpleasant things happened to me," she cheerfully explained, "first, I lost the brooch; second, I acquired this book."

And she handed Tamara the book which she'd got as a gift from Shklovsky today. Tusya read out the inscription . . . It ended like this: ". . . it is very hard for me."[59]

Anna Andreevna spoke of the book with extreme disapproval. Then she gave me the proofs of her poems in *Zvezda*. I read them. Numerous misprints. Anna Andreevna was utterly inconsistent in allowing me to insert the new quatrain into "Boris Pasternak", but not allowing me to replace the epithets.[*] Then, to ensure their accuracy, the proofs were read by Shura and Tamara in turn.

It was decided to drop "The Last Toast" in order not to stir up a hornets' nest.

Shura left. We sat down to drink tea. We started talking about Pyotr Ivanych's activities.

"It's like the bubonic plague," said Anna Andreevna. "You're still pitying your next-room neighbour, and next thing you yourself are on the way to M."[†]

I asked Anna Andreevna to recite some poems – asked and immedi-ately regretted it: she didn't feel like it, but she felt uncomfortable refusing me and Tusya after all the trouble we had taken over the proofs.

"Tell me, Lydia Korneevna, what should I recite?" she asked in an overly submissive tone of voice.

N. Tynyanov and M. L. Lozinsky was published; the Goslit edition was never published. I do not remember when it was killed off or under what circumstances.

[*] In the fifth quatrain "of February" (instead of "of Moscow"), "transparent" instead of "death"). See *Zvezda*, 1940, no. 3–4; no. 1.

[†] To Magadan.

She read about memory (with new opening lines), then she started on some poem from 1924, but stumbled and gave up, then "The Way of All the Earth".*

Tusya commented on "The Way". She said that it was a very contemporary work, a work that responded to the rumble of the times.

"I keep trying to work out a general rule," said Anna Andreevna, "about who likes it, and who doesn't. But the generalization just doesn't work. I thought connoisseurs of literature would like it, simpler people wouldn't. It proved to be totally different. Boris Leonidovich for example didn't like it at all. Kharms accused it of insufficient intelligibility. But Aleksandr Nikolaevich† liked it so much that he walked around the table to kiss my hand and spoke all sorts of lofty words ... So, what else shall I recite? I can never remember."

"Don't recite anything," I said.

"Is that all right? Then I won't."

But as soon as Tamara started to describe her work on a historical reader and mentioned several headings, Anna Andreevna, probably by association, herself came out with the suggestion: "I'll recite 'Cleopatra' for you."

She did. Then she related an amusing story about a conversation she had had in Moscow with a young poetess.

"In Moscow I was feeling rather ill, I was getting tired, I was suffering because of the central heating and was waiting for a phone call. And then I started being asked very persistently to receive a young woman who writes poetry, dreams of meeting me, etc. I was asked by the people I was staying with and could not refuse them. A time was arranged. She appeared, apologizing profusely because for some reason she couldn't bring me her book as a gift, and recited her poems. Imagining that she was interested in my opinion, I commented in detail on one of her poems and told her, by the way, that in his poem 'The Commander' Pushkin managed to fit the Hermitage, Barclay, time and himself into a relatively small space, whereas her poem was long but not substantial enough. She replied: 'Pushkin didn't always manage that either.' Then I recited my poems to her. I recited several poems; after one she said: 'Now *that* is good.' When she left it was explained to me that she was a very big fish. Meaning that my playing the maître with her had been pointless."

---

*   "About memory" is "The Cellar of Memory"; the poem from 1924 is "Russian Trianon". For the surviving fragments of this poem (and rough drafts of it) see *In Memory A.A.*, p. 12, and also *BPL–A*, p. 326.

†   Tikhonov (Serebrov).

"Evidently," said Tusya, "she had imagined something quite different: a meeting of two representatives of poetry from different generations. In her dreams, on parting you present her with your portrait, inscribed 'To a victorious pupil from a vanquished teacher . . .'"

By the time Anna Andreevna and Tusya decided to leave it was two in the morning. All three of us went out together. Outside, it was warm, half light and quiet. From time to time we came across drunkards. One of them shouted at us: "Come on, gggirls."

"Once I was walking home from your flat," recalled Anna Andreevna, "it was some holiday, and the only man who didn't accost me was one who was at that moment accosting another woman. They don't really care: anything between 15 and 65 will do."

We approached Nevsky. It was deserted. Anna Andreevna crossed it together with us freely and easily.

"When will we ever stop loving this city!" I said.

"I already have," responded Tusya.

"I've also seen another face of it," said Anna Andreevna, guessing at once what Tamara had in mind.*

"Have you noticed: at the end of Liteyny, whenever you look, there is always a storm cloud? It may be different colours, but it is always there."

Continuing the conversation about drunks, Anna Andreevna told us how once, when the heel of her shoe had twisted in the street and she had stamped her foot to put it back in place, one passer-by had said: "Go on, you, just stamp at me, stamp at me, just you dare!"

"What a pity horses have almost disappeared from the city," Tusya said. "I used to love hearing that harmonious clatter through the windows, or the soft sound on the wooden pavements."

Anna Andreevna started to tell us about riding, or rather, that is, about the way N.S.† used to ride.

"After K.G.‡ had enlisted in the army, I visited him near Novgorod and he told me that he was learning to ride all over again. I was surprised – he had been an excellent horseman, used to ride beautifully and could ride for a long time, for many miles. It turned out not to be the kind of riding required in the field. The arm absolutely had to be held like so, the leg like so, otherwise either you or your horse would get tired, etc.

---

*   That is, she meant the torture chamber.
†   Nikolay Stepanovich Gumilyov.
‡   Kolya: Nikolay Stepanovich Gumilyov.

And whipping was an essential part of the exercise. The riding-instructors would even whip the grand duke about the legs, he told me.

We reached her gates from the Liteyny side. Tusya said goodbye to us there. Anna Andreevna graciously promised to send her her book as a present. As always, I accompanied Anna Andreevna through the court-yard and up the staircase right to her door. And, as always, walking home from her house, for some reason I wasn't frightened at all. Besides, the nights are no longer black, but grey.

14 May 1940

Anna Andreevna has suffered some bad luck – the usual thing. Nothing has come of her kind white magic.

Today she asked me to come over, sat me on the divan, settled herself next to me and told me in detail of her latest misfortune.* She is somehow solemn, quiet, her hair neatly done, with a fringe, and even with her famous comb in her hair. But it is sticking out a little lopsidedly.

"It was Vovka who put it in for me like that," she said, following my gaze and taking the comb out of her hair.

The boys came in, Vovka and Valya, she kissed each on both cheeks and told them to go to their room.

"Shakalik is so affectionate. Today he said: 'Nya, my pet, my darling.'"

I sat beside her, finding no words, no consolation. I am not Shakalik and I can't say to her: "Nya, my pet, my darling." But perhaps she felt a little better just having somebody sitting next to her and listening – short words, long silences . . .

15 May 1940

This evening I was at Anna Andreevna's. Lotta was there. Anna Andreevna was sad, sallow, she was sitting in her armchair, arms spread out, and Lotta chattered nonstop, evidently trying to cheer her up. She chatted too freely, but sometimes it really was witty. Anna Andreevna replied briefly, sometimes she didn't answer at all, but she did laugh at the witticisms.

Lotta drew my attention to a new piece in the room, a trunk. It was large, iron-mounted. "Sixteenth-century," Anna Andreevna explained to

---

* Her latest misfortune in her efforts on behalf of Lyova.

us. "I keep books in it. My room looks very unintellectual: no books in sight. They are in the chest of drawers, and here in the trunk."

"And underneath the armchair," said Lotta.

She decided that the trunk would be a very good place for keeping silk dresses and long candles in.

"Oh, how I would love to have a wedding!" concluded Lotta. "In church, and everything as it's supposed to be."

"I had a wedding," said Anna Andreevna, "at which all the rules were observed. But I can assure you it's much more interesting watching other people getting married than getting married yourself."

Lotta started telling all sorts of jokes about illiterate teachers. Really, it was funny and frightening. Anna Andreevna recounted how a few years ago Anna Evgenevna and Irina had gone to the Caucasus and hadn't returned for the beginning of the school year.

"A stern note came from the school. Nikolay Nikolaevich asked me to go up there and talk to them. I went. I see: STAFF ROOM. I enter – there's some woman there. I hand her the note. The blood rushed to her cheeks, she even grew prettier. 'Do you realize that she may be expelled?' She expected me to plead. Instead, I suddenly started to yell: 'Go on, then! Expel her! What do I care! I couldn't give a damn! I'm just a neighbour in the flat." (Anna Andreevna uttered these words, so unusual from her lips, a few times – 'Go on! I couldn't give a damn!' – obviously enjoying their coarseness.) All of a sudden she seemed to wilt and fell abruptly silent.

It turned out Anna Andreevna and Lotta were waiting for Roz.,* who had phoned from the Sovetsky pisatel and promised to bring the advance copy at seven o'clock. It was already nine, however. Lotta started trying to persuade Anna Andreevna not to wait for him but come for a walk with us.

"No, I'll wait for him," said Anna Andreevna.

"You can't stand being separated from your book for one more minute? Admit it!" yelled Lotta.

"No, it's not that. I promised him I'd be in."

"What boorishness to be so late. He said at seven o'clock and now it's nine."

"He imagines," said Anna Andreevna, "that if he has an object like that in his hands, he can come whenever he likes. And, if it's very late, for the night!"

*   ?

"Well, if it's for the night," declared Lotta, "then we're leaving. Come on, Lydia Korneevna!"

And we left.

20 May 1940

Today, having got Anna Andreevna the issue of *Russkaya mysl* containing an article by Nedobrovo – which she'd long been asking for – I tried to phone her. I try: once, twice, three times – it's engaged. And no sooner had I hung up, annoyed, than it rang: it was Anna Andreevna asking me to come over.

She looked sallow, ill, lying on the divan under a heavy blanket, in her dressing gown, her hair dishevelled.

"My heart is playing up. I'm tired today. I went to VTEK. They put me in category two, whereas I used to be in three. I'm gradually approaching an ideal state of disability. I was found to have degeneration of the mitral valve."

But today she wasn't as sad as the last few times. Apparently the reason for this was that blue telegram, which she let me read.*

I noticed a book on the armchair – the advance copy – and, of course, I grabbed it eagerly and started to examine it.

"Please put the book in the drawer," ordered Anna Andreevna, almost rudely. "Deeper, deeper. And shut the drawer. I don't like seeing it."

"What you have is the occupational disease in reverse," I said.

"I recited 'The Way of All the Earth' to another very perceptive person," Anna Andreevna said. "He was overwhelmed."

"So was I."

"Maybe it's because it has a new intonation. Quite new, as there's never been before. For only the new overwhelms ... But two listeners admitted that they hadn't understood it: Sandrik[†] and Kseniya Grigorievna.

And, probably remembering how interestingly Tusya had discussed this work, she suddenly added: "Come round some time with Tamara Grigorievna, all right?"

"Here, take a look, Vladimir Georgievich brought me a whole pile of poetry from the Writers' Bookshop." She bent over like an acrobat, reached for a pile of little books on the chair and placed them on my

* ?
† A. N. Boldyrev.

knee. "At the bookshop they always say to him: Some poems have come out, Anna Andreevna may be interested. Find A.E. Read it."

I read a short poem about love; it was languid and eclectic.

"Just think, how cold, how indifferent," Anna Andreevna kept saying. "And what he's writing about in this way! The most important thing in poetry is to have one's own, new intonation . . . But here all the intonations are somebody else's. As if he himself had never loved."

I asked her how she feels about Ostroumova – I was planning to take Lyusha to her exhibition.

"Yes . . . I like her . . . but, I suppose, not particularly. When I was little I too was taken to the Hermitage and the Russian Museum, which had only recently opened. We lived in Tsarskoe; Mama used to take me from there. What I couldn't stand were the *Peredvizhniki* exhibitions. Everything was lilac. I used to go up the stairs thinking: How much better these old paintings hanging on the staircase are."

Anna Andreevna asked me to give her the topaz from the chest of drawers and placed it on her breast, over her heart.

"It's cold," she remarked. "It feels good."

The conversation turned to Mayakovsky and the Briks; I told her about our Detizdat single-volume edition and my trip to the Briks' in Moscow with Miron Levin. I found it hard being with them: the whole style of the house was antipathetic to me. Besides, I had the feeling that Liliya Yurevna had no interest whatsoever in Mayakovsky's poetry. I liked neither the hazelhens for dinner, nor the jokes at table . . . Around the table, besides Miron and myself, who had come on business, were Primakov, Osip Maksimovich and "our Zhenichka". Above all, I disliked Osip Maksimovich – his protuberant lower lip, prominent ears, but most of all, his tone, hovering between the literary master and the fop. The only one I liked at this family table was Primakov – taciturn and somewhat distant from them.[60]

"I find it hard to see Mayakovsky fitting in there, amongst them," I said.

"Well, you shouldn't," replied Anna Andreevna. "Literature was put aside, all that remained was the Briks' salon, where writers used to meet Cheka agents . . . And you, and not only you, are wrong in separating Mayakovsky from the Briks in your imagination. It was his home, his love, his friendship; he liked everything there. That was the level of his education, of his sense of camaraderie and of all his interests. He never left them, you see, he never broke with them, he loved them to the end."

I said that I had no right to discuss Mayakovsky's relationship with the Briks because I didn't know much about it, but that I was surprised by the shoddiness of their work, by their total indifference as to whether the single volume for which they were responsible would be good or bad.

"That's a different matter. But in his attitude to writers and literature he himself was on their level, that is, on a very low one. Once Nikolay Leonidovich* asked him about Khlebnikov. He replied: 'Why publish Khlebnikov now?' That was how he spoke of his friend, his mentor ... What is the difference between him and the Briks then? They are indifferent to the publication of his poems, he to the publication of Khlebnikov's poems. There is a difference, and a great one, but of a different nature: his great talent. As for the rest, there is none at all. He, like they, could sometimes be shady, hypocritical and insincere ... But this didn't stop him from becoming one of Russia's greatest 20th-century poets."

Vladimir Georgievich knocked and entered. She very affectionately sat him down at her feet on the divan. He complained of utter exhaustion: post-mortems, exams. He had come to find out the results of the medical examination. Anna Andreevna, bending over acrobatically again, reached for the medical certificate on the armchair. He read it, declared: "It's all nonsense, semiliterate rubbish," and got up. Before leaving he leant over her, looked closely into her eyes and asked, in the infantile tone in which he often spoke to her in my presence: "Have you been good today?"

"Yes," replied Anna Andreevna and handed the blue telegram to him.

(Indeed, in spite of being ill today, she has been much more cheerful than lately.)

I wanted to leave with V.G., since we were going the same way, but Anna Andreevna put her hand on my knee: "Stay with me a little longer," and I stayed.

Anna Andreevna got up for a moment, found the jam and sugar, put the kettle on and lay down again. We started talking about someone who's been collecting material.†

"He came to see me and told me about everything he had collected. That's how I learnt how badly people think of me. One lady promised him to remember by next time whose son Lyova really is – Blok's or Lozinsky's. But I was never intimate with either Blok or Lozinsky. And Lyova looks so much like Kolya that it frightens people. There are hardly any traces of me in him ... The things they've said about me!"

---

* Stepanov. For more about him see note 61.
† ?

"And has he collected anything of substance?" I asked. "Or nothing but gossip?"

"Trifles! And anyway, he himself turned into one of the great writers in the land of Russia."

Then she told me about an outrageous deed by *Leninskie iskry*. Without asking, the newspaper had published the poem about Mayakovsky which Anna Andreevna had given to *Literaturnaya*, not *Iskry*, and furthermore it had published it with errors: "in '12" instead of "in '13"; "until now" instead of "until then".

"And the title! It couldn't be more banal: 'A Poetess to a Poet'. How disgusting! I feel ashamed even to go out now."

I told her about Blaginina's poem, in which, just as in Akhmatova's famous lines, flags are hung out on the trees in autumn.* "By the way," I added, "I like Blaginina's poem."†

"So what?" said Anna Andreevna, "I can't see anything wrong in that. Pushkin also always did that. Always. He took anything he liked from anybody. And made it his own for ever."‡

She started to ask me about Lyusha, I told her about Lyusha's favourite books – Dickens, Pushkin – from there we moved to Charskaya. I recounted Tamara's story to her about how Tamara and Zoya, on behalf of Litfond, had taken Charskaya some money and how Lidiya Alekseevna had told them, with modest pride, very graphically, about the schoolgirls who visit her and put questions of destiny to her. "They come to me with what's closest to their hearts," Lidiya Alekseevna had said, clasping both hands to her heart, slightly breathless.

"They come to me, too, all brimming over with questions about destiny and the things that are closest to their hearts," said Anna Andreevna. "But they don't show up a second time, the way I receive them."

For a while there was silence. Whenever she is silent for a long time,

---

*   An early autumn has covered
                                The elm trees with yellow flags . . .

lines from Akhmatova's poem "It's fun to be with you when you're drunk" – *FT, Evening* [*Vecher*].

† A mistake in my entry: no such lines exist in Elena Blaginina's poems.

‡ "A genius," said A.A. to Pavel Nikolaevich Luknitsky, "is a catcher. He accumulates, pounces on words, similes, images, etc., from all around. Both the most simple and those which no one has noticed before, but which are the best."

    And she continued: "Pushkin's creativity is a furnace which melts down the entire material Pushkin used. After 'melt down' something quite new emerges, which is pure Pushkin. (See V. Luknitskaya's publication in the journal *Ogonyok*, no. 6, 1987, p. 10 – excerpts from P. N. Luknitsky's diary.)

I have already learnt, she is preparing herself. And so it was: the black ritual. The lock and the door.*

"What harshness, what force," I said.

"Do you think so? That's what I wanted."

We fell silent again. I remembered this morning's coincidence with the telephone: I was calling her – and she me. Simultaneously. I told her about it.

"That always happens to me," she explained. "It happens with everyone."

21 May 1940

Today I remembered one story of Anna Andreevna's, which I hadn't written down immediately – in reply to a question of mine. I remembered it exactly.

I had once asked her how could it be that sometimes you don't understand poems, yet you love them. Why had it been like that with Zhenya Lunts[62] and me – I was eleven and she was ten, when we fell in love with Blok's "The Unknown Woman" and, after our lessons, hiding between two solid doors – that is, in a cupboard, actually – we would read enraptured, in unison or in turn:

---

* She wrote down, gave me to memorize and burnt the poem:

> And this, despite the fact that death
> Is staring into my eyes,
> Again according to your words
> I am voting *for*:

> A door to become a door;
> A lock a lock once more,
> For the gloomy beast in my breast
> To become a heart . . . But
> We are all fated to learn
> What it means not to sleep for three years,
> What it means come morning to find out
> About those who perished in the night.

Reciting this poem to me A.A. read out the epigraph, saying: "'In the forest trees cast their vote.' N. Zabolotsky." However hard I subsequently tried to locate this line of Zabolotsky's I could not find it . . . It turns out (Vyacheslav Vsevolodovich Ivanov drew my attention to this) that for her poem A.A. wittingly or unwittingly adapted the lines of Zabolotsky's poem "Nocturnal Garden" from the original version:

> And the souls of lime trees raised up their hands,
> All are casting their votes against the crimes."
> *Literaturny Sovremennik*, 1937, no. 3.

In the Soviet Union this poem of Akhmatova's was first published by R. D. Timenchik in the journal *Daugava* (1987, no. 9, p. 125).

> And ostrich feathers, lightly drooping,
> Are swaying slowly in my brain,
> And fathomless blue eyes are radiant
> On the shores of that far domain.

We had not yet drunk wine, had never seen drunkards with rabbit eyes, had never seen a restaurant – and we did not understand what lay behind those verses, but we loved them ecstatically.

"For you they were a new harmony, that's what they were," Anna Andreevna said. "That's what Innokenty Annensky was like for me. Once I arrived at K.G.'s.* He was finishing off some urgent proofs. 'Look at this book in the meantime,' he told me and handed me a book by Annensky which had just come out. And immediately I stopped seeing or hearing, I couldn't tear myself away, I repeated those poems day and night ... They opened up a new harmony for me."[†]

24 May 1940

Last night, late, at about eleven o'clock when I arrived at Shura's, she greeted me with the words: "Not finding you home, Anna Andreevna rang here."

My heart stopped, out of fear. And it probably showed.

"Oh no, nothing's happened!" said Shura. "On the contrary, it's something good! Anna Andreevna asked me to tell you that she's got the author's copies and you can go round even now to collect your copy."

I should have rung straight away in response to such a kind and swift invitation, but Shura's mother slept by the phone, and I felt uncomfortable about disturbing her.

I rang her this morning and, while Zoechka took Lyusha and Tanya[63] to the Café Nord – to celebrate their achievements at school – I went to Anna Andreevna's.

There were roses in her room on a little table, but I hadn't even thought to bring flowers on such a day!

Anna Andreevna was lying down; on a chair next to the divan were little stacks of white books. So we did live to see this joyous day. I

---

*   Kolya Gumilyov's.
[†]   Only recently did I notice that, speaking to me about the "new harmony", A.A. was using an expression of Pushkin's. Thus, in his letter to P. A. Vyazemsky of 5 July 1824 Pushkin wrote: "Lamartine is good in 'Napoleon', in the 'Dying Poet', he is good in general because of some new harmony." *A. S. Pushkin. Complete Collected Works* [*A. S. Pushkin. Polnoe Sobranie Sochineniy*], in 10 vols, vol. 10 (Moscow and Leningrad: Publishing House of the Academy of Sciences USSR, 1949).

wanted to grab the little book at once and have a close look at it but I didn't dare.

Anna Andreevna looks bad, her face is mournful, sallow, her hair is pinned up any old how.

It transpires she is to have an operation tomorrow – she has a tumour on her breast, not alarming, non-malignant. She'll be back home the same evening. I asked under which anaesthetic.

"I don't know. And I have no interest in knowing. I don't care. Even if it's without any anaesthetic. I have never been afraid of physical pain. An acquaintance of mine once mentioned in front of me, in passing, that he was afraid of having his tooth out without an anaesthetic – and that instant I lost interest in him. I am unable to respect such people.

"I will be operated on tomorrow afternoon at three, but I forgot about it so completely that I even told a lady to come and get a copy of the book at three o'clock tomorrow.

"It turns out that Obllit banned the book," continued Anna Andreevna. "That's why, for a few days, the publishers kept replying so vaguely to my question about when the author's copies would arrive. It turns out that the book was banned on the 16th and on the 22nd it was allowed. Yesterday the Writers' Bookshop received it, 300 copies were distributed to the writers on their list, but they hadn't put a single one on the counter . . ."

I said that would mean that only those who were friendly with her, who – one way or another – already knew those poems anyway, would receive them.

"You mean to say, *unfriendly* with me," Anna Andreevna corrected me. "Members of the Writers' Union never knew and never wanted to know my poetry, they didn't like my poetry and now only take the book in the bookshop for the reason that mere mortals cannot get it, but they – if you please! – can. That reinforces their feeling of superiority, of privilege. They can't stand my poetry, however. You see, they always, all these 20 years, thought there was no reason to retrieve this old junk from the mothballs . . . But what I would like is for my book to reach a wide audience, real readers, young people . . ."

Then she asked me whether I'd read Nedobrovo's piece in *Russkaya mysl* and what I thought of it.

I said: "The article is profound and intelligent, he speaks particularly interestingly on protagonists in poetry. But . . ."

"A stunning article," Anna Andreevna interrupted me. "Prophetic . . . I read it at night and was sorry that there was nobody with whom to share my admiration. How could he foresee the severity and steadfastness to come? How did he know? It's a miracle. For at that time the conventional opinion was that all these little poems were so-so, sentimentality, lachrymosity, whimsy. Drawing-room affectation. I think Ivanov-Razumnik's article was even entitled: 'Capricious People'.[64] But Nedobrovo understood my path, my future, he divined and predicted it, because he knew me well."*

We started talking about the book again: it would certainly sell out in a day.

"Poetry is much loved in our country," I said.

"Yes, amazingly. Nowhere else in Europe is it like that. In Paris I told one poet how many times poetry books are reprinted here – he could hardly believe it. Public readings are not customary there. If a famous artist does drawings or vignettes for a new volume of poems – then it has a chance of selling out. Because of the drawings – just think! In Russia, people have always loved poetry, but the French are primarily interested in painting."

I rose. Anna Andreevna took two copies of her book and inscribed one for me and one for Tamara. I drew her attention to the odd way the word break had been done on the book's spine: "Poe-try".

Vladimir Georgievich came in with a bouquet of lilies-of-the-valley. Anna Andreevna took it from his hand, found a glass and, putting the flowers in the water, told us: "In the morning I lay here on the divan, surrounded by flowers, flowers ... Just like a corpse."

29 May 1940

I didn't write things down at the time. Now I only remember snatches.

I came to see Anna Andreevna on the evening of the 25th, the day

---

*   Evidently A.A. was thinking of this passage from Nedobrovo's article: "These torments, complaints and such extreme humility – isn't that a weakness of spirit, isn't that simple sentimentality? Of course not: Akhmatova's voice pattern itself, firm and rather self-confident, her very calmness in accepting pain and weakness, finally, the very abundance of poetically transformed torments – all this testifies not to tearfulness in the face of life's trifles, but reveals a lyrical soul, firm rather than too soft, cruel rather than tearful, and clearly dominant rather than submissive." (N. V. Nedobrovo, "Anna Akhmatova" in *Russkaya mysl*, 1915, Book 7, p. 639.

For more about Nedobrovo see Yulia Sazonova-Slonimskaya's study "Nikolay Vladimirovich Nedobrovo. An Experiment in Portraiture" (*Russkaya mysl*, 1923, no. XI–XII, and also the book: *Anna Akhmatova. Poem without a Hero: Book 5* [*Anna Akhmatova. Poema bez geroya: kniga 5*]. Introductory article by R. D. Timenchik. Compiled and annotated by R. D. Timenchik and V. Ya. Morderer (Moscow: Publishing House MPI, 1989, p. 232). In addition to this I also refer the reader to *BPL–A*, p. 461, and venture to express my conviction that V. M. Zhirmunsky unjustly omitted to mention, among the poems addressed to Nedobrovo, the poem of 1928 "When horror of the moonlight quivers"(*FT, Reed*).

of her operation. She was lying down, covered up and bandaged, her face calm and, I would say, serene. The operation had gone well and lasted 20 minutes. She returned home on foot, as Vladimir Georgievich hadn't managed to get a car; walking had made the bandage slip, so at home the dressing was changed by a nurse, an acquaintance, who would come and change it tomorrow as well.

That time, I think, we didn't talk about anything interesting, only one thing stayed in my mind: in passing, she informed me that the husband of one of her friends had come back after a two-year separation.

"It always sounds strange to me," I said. "He came back, she came back ... I think love is quite as unresurrectable as a corpse."

"Yes, of course..." said Anna Andreevna, pausing. "One returns not to the person, not to the former love, but to the walls, to the room."

Yesterday, Tamara and I went to see her. Tusya and I met in a little park, after buying flowers and cakes, and sat for a while on a bench while Tusya examined the book which I had passed on to her.

Anna Andreevna was not lying down, she was wandering about the room. She said she had had a heart attack. "My father died from his first," she said. She looked haggard. She was amiable throughout, especially towards Tusya; only occasionally did she become distracted and silent.

Tusya enquired whether there were any misprints in the book. Anna Andreevna, not answering, suddenly declared: "One line has been vexing me all my life: 'Gde milomu muzhu detey rodila [Where she bore her dear husband children].' Do you hear: Mu–mu?! Can it be that neither of you, both such lovers of poetry, has noticed this mooing?"*

Tusya burst out laughing, and then replied, very seriously: "First, you don't hear mu-mu at all. The syllables are long, drawn out: Mílomu Múzhu: the two mus don't collide, there is a mi at the beginning of one word and a mu at the beginning of the other. The mu–mu juxtaposition is purely visual but not aural, which means it is of no consequence to the poem. And, second, these two mus are completely natural, embedded in the language itself, they exist there – why avoid them? What could you substitute? Tolstomu muzhu [fat husband]? Dobromu [good]? Glupomu [stupid]? Anything will have mu in it – such are the rules of declension in our language."

Anna Andreevna settled in her favourite tattered, shaky armchair and,

* "Lot's Wife"– *FT, Anno Domini.*

spreading out her arms as was her wont, recited Pushkin's "Monument".*

Tusya said: "There is an expression which goes: as necessary as bread, as air. From now on, I am going to say: as necessary as the word ... Forgive me, Anna Andreevna, but even you who created this, even you don't know how necessary it is. Because you haven't been *there*, to our great, common fortune ... But I remember being *there*, and remember faces and nights ... If they, *there*, could only imagine that *this* exists ... But they will never know now. So many lips have fallen silent, so many eyes have closed forever..."

We were quiet for a while. "Thank you," said Anna Andreevna. Then she started talking about something else, in a calm voice: "The 23rd was a special day for me. A courier from the publishers brought me copies of the book; friends came, brought flowers. I was lying down, I felt unwell: it was my heart. Tanya entered my room, looked at me, looked at the flowers, sniffed scornfully: 'Restless old age!' – and went out.

"That same day, Nikolay Nikolaevich also had his say. He dropped in for a minute, looked at the flowers, looked at the books: 'I see, Anichka, you are going through your second youth!' And he stormed out very angrily. That is how my neighbours – on one side and on the other – congratulated me."

Tusya and I rose. It was after one in the morning. Seeing us to the door, Anna Andreevna said to Tusya: "So, I don't have to be ashamed of the *mu–mu*? And there's no need to rewrite the line?"

1 June 1940

Anna Andreevna rang yesterday morning asking me to be sure to come round. But our place was full of nails, ropes, bundles, boxes, utter havoc; friends had suddenly managed to get hold of a small truck for me for nothing, and I had to make the most of such good fortune. Ida is going with the large things in the truck and I'll have to feed the girls, collect their bits and pieces and take the train three hours later. Ida and I are rushing around. The girls are excited, packing their dolls' suitcases, and

---

* In a whisper; making us sit beside her; and not Pushkin's, but her own epilogue to "Requiem", where there are these lines:

  If they think some day in this country
  To raise a monument to me ...

No. 33.

are dying to get to the station, even though it's a while yet before our train.

I told Anna Andreevna that I would definitely go and see her, but not at once and not for long.

After sending off the truck, I took the suitcase with the lighter things, Lyusha and Tanya took their dolls' cases, I locked our rooms, and we set off for the station, but on our way called in on Anna Andreevna. The girls promised to wait for me downstairs on some planks, guarding our stuff, while I went up to Anna Andreevna's.

It turned out she wanted to show me an article, written by some young man for *Literaturny kritik*, an article which Katya* had brought to show her. I read it. The article was uncontrolled and inaccurate. The author, someone called O., says that Akhmatova resurrects the pseudo-classical tradition of Racine in her poetry, that the heroine of Akhmatova's poetry is the heroine of Racine's theatre.

"But I hadn't read any Racine when I started writing poetry, and I didn't know his theatre," said Anna Andreevna.

"Whether or not you've read Racine is beside the point!" I yelled. (My yelling was clearly provoked by the stupidity of the article and also by the fact that the girls were waiting for me and I was in hurry.) "There isn't anything pseudoclassical in your poems and there's nothing of Racine. They have grown out of the Russian classics, transforming them, and there's nothing rhetorical about them, they are completely devoid of grandiloquence, they are the epitome of naturalness and quietness, they are written in living Russian and, furthermore, in contemporary language. Where does he get the idea of Racine from? And, you know what?" – it suddenly dawned on me – "he invented all this on account of four lines by Mandelstam:

> Half falling from her shoulders
> Her pseudoclassical shawl turns to stone.

and

> Thus – like indignant Phèdre –
> Stood once upon a time Rachel.

There you have the entire reason for his learned guesses about your poetry!"

"Osip didn't have my poetry in mind at all when he wrote that," said Anna Andreevna. "At that time, we used to meet almost every day in

---

* Katya: Ekaterina Romanovna Malkina. For more about her see note 66.

the Guild, and he was simply writing about a woman whom he liked."

I asked her how she was feeling.

"Very bad. I don't think I've ever felt worse. Five heart attacks in five days. Vladimir Georgievich got scared and even advised me to go into hospital. Maybe that's why I recovered immediately: yesterday and today I haven't had any attacks."

We returned to the article.

"It's upset me," said Anna Andreevna. "It reminded me of a party attended by the majestic Balmont. Oh, he was always majestic, not for a moment did he forget that he was no mere mortal, but a poet. (Incidentally, however odd it seems, he truly is a poet. There was a volume called *The Siren* published once. It represented poets minor, major and average, but the best proved to be Balmont. His poem about the moon is delightful.[65]) So this lavish party began with dinner; then some guests left, others remained, and people started to dance. I didn't dance. Balmont was sitting next to me. He glanced into the drawing room where couples were waltzing, and intoned to me: 'I am so delicate – why are they showing me this.' I, too, want to say about this article: 'I am so delicate, why are they showing me this.' The article by Pertsov, who wrote about me once, 'This woman forgot to die on time,' offended me much less."*

"I don't understand how you can be offended by such rubbish," I said, but there was no time to argue. Looking out of the window, I saw Lyusha and Tanya. They were sitting dolefully on the planks, their eyes glued to the door from which I was supposed to appear. Tanya had a very mournful expression on her face, exactly like the boy in Picasso's painting *An Old Man and a Boy*. The dolls' cases were lying on the girls' knees, but my suitcase, half-open, had fallen to the ground.

It was time to go. I rushed back to them.

3 June 1940

I came into town to get food and do many other things. It was late by the time I had finished, and I rang Anna Andreevna in the evening from Tusya's place. She asked me to come. She was still deeply downcast by

---

* V. Pertsov, "Across Literary Watersheds". (In the journal *Zhizn iskusstva*, 27 October 1925.) Deriding Akhmatova and her poems, Pertsov wrote, among other things: "... contemporary language has no common roots with that spoken by Akhmatova, modern, living people remain and will continue to remain cold and heartless towards the laments of a woman who was born too late or *did not manage to die on time* ..." (*My italics.* – L.Ch.)

O.'s article, she was wondering whether she should meet him in person or let Katya convey her views to him.

"Advise me – in person or through Katya? . . . Of course, I won't contest his opinions, but I'll point out factual mistakes."

Remembering her numerous heart attacks, I advised her not to talk to O. in person, but through Katya. Because that pseudoclassical sage might, in passing, come out with some other nonsense which she would keep refuting, inwardly, for days afterwards.

(Incidentally, a thought crossed my mind: is it not from this gift for polemicizing with such concentration, for refuting, for exposing, that her love poems, so scorchingly dramatic, are born? But this is only by the way. I had to advise her on the article.)

I insisted on her seeing Katya.

"You are right, it would be better through Katya, but, strangely enough, Katya likes the article. She is so engrossed in the turmoil of her work that she doesn't understand anything anymore. I noticed long ago that if women have a profession, a job, they let themselves become blinkered by it."[66]

She complained that Kaminskaya, who was planning to arrange an Evening devoted to the poetry of Blok and Akhmatova, kept phoning her, asking if she had anything against it.[67]

"Certainly – everything. Tell me, what should I say to her, so as not to offend her?"

"Blok and Akhmatova make a very incongruous combination," I said. "And as a rule, one should never, during the course of one evening, perform the poetry of two great poets at the same time – one should not immerse the listeners in two different worlds. Besides, Blok is dead, whereas you are alive and can read your poems yourself. And anyway, why have somebody other than you *perform* them? I can't bear it when actors read poetry."

Nikolay Nikolaevich knocked and entered. Anna Andreevna met him amiably, but didn't ask him to sit down. He reported the latest news from the front and left.

Anna Andreevna told me that she'd been to Pushkin House for the funeral service for Yakubovich.

"It was good, everyone spoke very warmly about him. Especially Tomashevsky. Yakubovich would have been so happy to hear these words, all his life he adored Tomashevsky like a schoolboy.[68] And now – he didn't hear them . . . When the coffin was carried downstairs, the clock started chiming on the landing – there is an antique clock there with a lovely melodic chime. But he no longer heard it. On the steps under the feet of all those carrying the coffin, and those following, flowers were strewn at random – chrysanthemums. I walked around them, I could not step on them – they are alive. He no longer saw them."*

I got up to say goodbye. But Anna Andreevna held me back.

"Are you going home? Is it night already? During the white nights, you never know when to go to bed..." (Unfortunately, I always know only too well when it's time for me to go to bed – even without a watch, during the white nights, always.)

Anna Andreevna picked up her notebook, put on her glasses and I heard: "The Air of Tsarskoe Selo", "The fifth act of the drama" and "In that house it was terrifying to live" – oh how terrifying, even more terrifying than "Fear, which picks out objects in the dark".†

"I've never read this to anyone... (It even frightens me...) What do you think, can it be published? If it can be, it should come third: 'Now I do not know where the dear artist is', 'The Temple of Jerusalem', and this one about the house..."‡

I resolved to ask her: now, after so many years of work, when she writes something new, does she have a sense of being armed, of having experience, of a path already trodden? Or is it a step into the unknown, a risk, every time?

"Naked, on naked soil. Every time."

After a pause, she added: "A lyric poet follows a terrible path. A poet has such difficult material: the word. Do you remember Baratynsky already writing about this? The word is much more difficult material than, for instance, paint. Think about it, really: for the poet works with the very same words that people use to invite each other to tea..."

---

* Is it not these chrysanthemums that later inspired the lines in "Poem without a Hero":

> And for me that particular theme,
> Was like a chrysanthemum on the ground,
> Crushed, as the coffin is borne by.
>
> "Tails" [Reshka]

† The first three poems were written at the start of the '20s and are dedicated to the memory of Gumilyov: "All the souls of those I loved are on distant stars", "The fifth act of the drama" (*FT, Seventh Book*; no. 34 and no. 35) and "In that house it was terrifying to live"; no. 36. A.A. intended to include "In that house..." in "Epic Motifs", and still later in "Northern Elegies" (placing it third). But the work on the elegy remained unfinished, and therefore A.A. did not want to publish it. (The elegy was published as an incomplete draft in *In Memory A.A.*)

"Fear, which picks out objects in the dark" *BPL–A*, p. 168; no. 23.

‡ "Now I do not know where the dear artist is..." and "The Temple of Jerusalem..." are lines from "Epic Motifs", from sections 2 and 3 (*FT, Anno Domini*).

Then she added further: "In my youth I was very sociable, I loved having guests, I loved being a guest myself. Kolya Gumilyov explained my sociability this way: 'When left alone, Anya writes poetry nonstop. She needs people in order to rest from her poems, otherwise she would write without even taking a break or resting.'"

Then, without any transition, she added: "His second marriage didn't work either. He imagined that Anna Nikolaevna was made of wax, but she turned out to be a tank ... Have you seen her?"

I said I had seen her: very pretty, with a meek, gentle little face and a pink ribbon around her forehead.

"Yes, yes, all true: a gentle little face, a pink ribbon, but she herself is actually a tank. Nikolay Stepanovich lived with her for some three months and sent her to his relatives. She didn't like it, she demanded he bring her back. He brought her back but he himself left at once for the Crimea. She is a very disagreeable, quarrelsome woman, and he was counting on having obedience and submission at last.*

Walking home and remembering O.'s stupid article, wholly out of place, wholly irrelevant – I thought about the one I would write one day. It will be an article about courage, femininity, about will, the constant awareness of oneself and one's fate within Russian culture, within the history of mankind and Russia: Pushkin, Dante, Shakespeare, Petersburg, Russia, the war ... She is unable either to love or to quarrel in her poems without showing the reader, with absolute precision, the exact moment on the map of history ...

8 June 1940

Yesterday morning, I called Anna Andreevna and invited her to come with me for a few days to join the girls at the dacha. I would squeeze in with Lyusha and Tanya and would give her my room. She replied: "I can't today. Come round quickly."

I arrived about two. She looked very bad, tired eyes, her face drawn and blurred, as if the features had lost the clarity of their outlines.

"What's the matter with you? Have you been ill these last few days?"

"No."

And she told me her latest Dostoevskian episode, truly both horrifying

---

* Anna Nikolaevna Engelgardt (c. 1897–c. 1942): Gumilyov's second wife.

and tiresome. What an imbroglio – those children she looks after, and this Royal Court of Wonderland.*

She was getting ready to go to the Rybakovs' for lunch, but would not let me leave, and we talked for a long time. I admitted that I was very hungry, and Anna Andreevna, to my surprise, very deftly warmed up a rissole and potatoes for me on the electric hot plate.

"So, you really are perfectly able to rustle up a meal," I said.

"I can do everything. And if I don't do it, it's just out of spite," replied Anna Andreevna.

I said that today I'd been at Tusya's since early morning, and, instead of doing our work, we had discussed Anna Andreevna's poetry, and Tusya had expressed her own theory on that score.

"Please tell me, she's a clever woman, and I'm interested," asked Anna Andreevna.

Immediately, I regretted having let it slip. Tusya has a remarkable gift for words, which I lack. She herself would have developed her idea much more forcefully and profoundly, whereas I could only get the outline across.

When you first apprehend it, Akhmatova's poetry does not strike you by the novelty of its form as does, say, the poetry of Mayakovsky. You can hear Baratynsky and Tyutchev and Pushkin – sometimes, more rarely, Blok – in the movement of the poem, in its rhythms, in the fullness of the line, in the precision of the rhymes. At first it seems like a narrow path, going alongside the wide road of Russian classical poetry. Mayakovsky is deafeningly novel, but at the same time he is unfruitful, barren: he brought Russian poetry to the edge of an abyss, one step further – and it would have disintegrated. One should not follow him or one comes to the abyss, to the total disintegration of poetry. Akhmatova's little path turns out to be a wide road in fact; her traditional style is purely external; she is daring and innovative and, while maintaining the appearance of classical verse, within this she brings about earthquakes and upheavals. And, in contrast to Mayakovsky's poetry, one can follow Akhmatova's – without repeating and without imitating it, but continuing, carrying on the tradition of great Russian poetry.

---

* A.A. suspected that Tanya Smirnova, her neighbour, Valya's and Vova's mother, had been assigned to keep watch on her, to spy on her, and she even detected some signs of this surveillance. "It always turns out," she told me, "that I end up paying my own informers."

A.A. called the watch kept on her and her manuscripts, which she felt constantly, the activity of the Royal Court of Wonderland.

Anna Andreevna listened attentively and, it seemed, sympathetically, but did not respond to me.

I asked if she had written anything in the last few days.

"Very little. I'm finishing 'Dusk falls and in the dark blue sky'. I'm working on the end."

She told me that some lover of books, catching sight of a pile of copies of her volume on a chair at her place, had suggested: "Give me five of them, I'll bring you 500 roubles tomorrow."

"That means that speculation has already started. How disgusting ... And just think: it turns out that the writers are already signing a list at the Writers' Bookshop for the next one, the Goslit edition. What do they want it for? How outrageous. Again, nobody, except them, will get the book."

She sat on the divan, legs tucked under, and smoked one cigarette after another. I asked her something about her previous readings, she told me about one – and moved from that to Sologub. She told me that more than 20 years ago, once, at Sologub's – or organized by Sologub? – there had been a party for the benefit of exiled Bolsheviks where tickets were being sold for 100 roubles.

"I took part too. I wore a white dress with big flounces, with a wide, high collar and had awful tuberculosis ... For several years Sologub was extremely celebrated, the most celebrated of poets. Nastya loved lavishness but had no taste whatsoever, so the luxury of the house was heavy, vulgar.* They needed a lot of money, so Sologub published lousy little stories in insignificant little magazines, and they lived lavishly. Nastya was plain but had a lively, intelligent, attractive face. I was friends with her through Olya, rather not with her, but with her sister. And I was also friendly with Fyodor Kuzmich."

"Was he difficult to get on with?"

"Yes ... Actually no, not very. And how terrible he looked when I saw him in 1922 at Blokh's. Old, trousers unpressed, gone to seed ... He came to offer one of his books for publication. Blokh wasn't there, he was told: 'You'll have to wait, wait a bit ...' and he sat down to wait.[69]

"I know what destroyed Nastya. Nobody really knows why, but I know how and why it all happened. She became mentally ill as a result of unhappy love. She was about 42 at the time; she fell in love with a

---

* Nastya – Anastasya Nikolaevna Chebotaryevskaya (1876–1921): writer, translator, wife of the poet Fyodor Sologub.

cold and indifferent man. At first he was surprised at receiving frequent invitations to the Sologubs'. Later, when he found out about Anastasya Nikolaevna's feelings for him, he stopped going there. She would take me to her room and talk and talk about him endlessly, for hours. Sometimes she would put on a white dress and go and declare her love to him ... In general she did frightful things which no woman should ever do. The last time I saw her was a few days before she died: I was going to meet Volodya at the Marble Palace and she walked with me. The whole way, she talked about her love – she was no longer able to talk about anything else. When she threw herself into the Neva, she was on the way to her sister's. It was established precisely that she had set off from home in order to go and see her sister, but two doors from her sister's house she threw herself into the Neva ... Fyodor Kuzmich later moved in with Nastya's sister and lived there, not knowing that Nastya had drowned beneath his window.

"Somewhere, I still have the newspaper in which he put a notice searching for her. I got it by chance. A stranger sent me flowers – it does happen to me sometimes – and the bouquet was wrapped in the newspaper carrying this notice."

Sensing that Anna Andreevna was in the mood for reminiscing today, I asked whether Nikolay Stepanovich liked her poetry.

"At first he couldn't stand it. He'd agree to listen and pay close attention because it was me but he was very critical; he suggested I occupy myself with something else. He was right: I really did write appalling poems then. You know, like those published in little magazines as fillers ... And then it was like this: in April we married. (We had been engaged for a long time before that.) And in September he left for Africa and spent a few months there. During that time, I wrote a lot and had my first taste of fame: all around everybody praised me – Kuzmin, Sologub and at Vyacheslav's. (They didn't like Kolya at Vyacheslav's and they tried to tear me away from him; they used to say: 'There you are, there you are, he doesn't understand your poetry.') He came back. I didn't tell him anything. Then he asked: 'Have you written any poetry?' – 'I have.' And I read it to him. These were poems from the book *Evening*. He gasped. From that time onwards, he always loved my poetry very much."*

And once again she returned to the subject of Anna Nikolaevna.

---

* On N. Gumilyov's attitude to Anna Akhmatova's poems see her own prose in *Literaturnoe obozrenie*, 1989, no. 5, pp. 11–12.

"When I was young I had a difficult character, I strongly defended my inner independence and was very spoilt. But later even my mother-in-law held me up as an example to Anna Nikolaevna. It was a hasty marriage. Kolya was deeply hurt when I left him and he married somewhat hastily, on purpose, out of spite. He thought that he was marrying a simple girl, made of wax, that he would be able to shape a person out of her. But she is made of reinforced concrete. Not only is it not possible to shape her, you couldn't even make a mark, a scratch on her."

I asked whether Kaminskaya had been to see her, and whether she'd succeeded in talking her out of holding the Evening.

"She did. No, I didn't succeed. But the Evening won't take place before the autumn. Perhaps I will have died by then, or she will have died – you know, like in the joke. Imagine, she asked me: Is it true that 'The Grey-Eyed King' is about Blok and that Lyova is Blok's son? How do you like that? But 'The Grey-Eyed King' was written four months before the moment that Aleksandr Aleksandrovich bowed and said: 'Blok' . . . Imagine, the impertinence! After all, I don't ask her about anything or anybody."*

Suddenly Anna Andreevna noticed my new, wide-brimmed, white hat, lying on the chair. And she tried it on in front of the mirror. It was time for her to get changed to go to lunch at the Rybakovs', and I offered to wait for her downstairs in the courtyard.

"No, no, don't go anywhere, I always open the wardrobe door and get dressed behind it and then I'm not visible."

At her request, I read her some poems (by Shefner and Lifshits from the latest issue of *Literaturny sovremennik*) while she was changing. She didn't like them.

She came out from behind the wardrobe door in a new silk dress and started rubbing some cream into her cheeks in front of the mirror, then she put on a white necklace and bright lipstick. Now she looked completely different from an hour ago, elegant, majestic, even the absence of a few front teeth somehow became unnoticeable.

She put my hat on again and went to get someone's opinion of it; Anna Evgenevna's, I think.

"I've made up my mind, I'm going to buy one like it. This is the only hat I've ever liked: no hat looks good on me . . . Would you know where I could buy some gloves?"

I didn't know.

---

* "The Grey-Eyed King" – *FT, Evening*.

We left. In the courtyard I noticed that she was wearing a new coat and new, elegant shoes. I was pleased: money in action.

We got on a trolleybus. Anna Andreevna made her way towards the front while I stayed behind to pay. And suddenly, for the whole bus to hear, not even turning her head towards me, she asked in an uninhibited, resonant voice: "And how much does that hat cost?"

12 June 1940

Yesterday I called Anna Andreevna to make more specific arrangements for today: she had promised to come. She said: "Come to me now, and then we'll go to your flat together . . ." It was already late, but, as ever, I obeyed.

She herself opened the door. She greeted me with the words: "I tricked you: I'm not coming to you today. I'm tired. You stay with me for a while."

She told me the bad news. First of all, according to Nadya R., F. had been summoned to see the director in connection with the book. This displeased me greatly.*

"Boris Mikhaylovich says," continued Anna Andreevna very seriously, "that the book is a major one, an important one."

(As if we wouldn't have known that without Boris Mikhaylovich!)

"Letters have already started pouring in. Today I received two: one a typical gushing woman's letter, the other – very nice – from Kruchyo-nykh. Read it."

I read it. To me the letter seemed not a bit nice, but very stupid and not interesting in any way.

Kruchyonykh writes that the poems "burnt through" him, and as proof he encloses "endings" which he had thought up himself for some of the poems – for "When a Man Is Dying" for example; his "endings" were extremely empty and flat. Could it be a joke? If it is a joke, it's not funny. His own poem dedicated to Anna Andreevna is also included: now she is no longer a "Lady of the Evening" but something else.

Seeing that this letter did not amuse or please me, Anna Andreevna put it away in her handbag. And she recited to me the end of a poem "Dusk falls and in the dark blue sky"†

---

* Who F. is, and why "F.'s being summoned" was a bad omen for Akhmatova's book, I do not recall.

Nadya R. – Nadezhda Yanuarevna Rykova (b. 1901): literary critic, translator, specialist in French and English literature; at the time she was working as an editor at Goslitizdat.
† The lines after "Which were tumbling in the black ice-hole . . ."; no. 37.

"Now it is no longer a fragment, but a finished work, wouldn't you agree?" she asked. And we started to discuss whether it would be possible to include it in the Goslit edition, which had been delayed for so long. It depends on the proofs – if there is room on the same page. But above all – on the editor's wishes.

We started talking about *Anna Karenina* at the Moscow Art Theatre. Criticizing this play, I said that what appeals most to the public is the chance of seeing "the opulent life of high society."

"Historically, it's quite untrue," said Anna Andreevna. "The supposed opulence of high society never even existed. High society people dressed very modestly: black gloves, a black collar buttoned to the throat . . . They never dressed according to fashion: a gap of at least five years was obligatory for them. If everybody wore enormous hats, then high society ladies would wear small, modest ones. I saw many of them at Tsarskoe: a luxurious landau with a coat of arms, the coachman in furs – and on the seat a lady, all in black, in mittens, with a sour expression on her face . . . Now that was an aristocratic lady . . . But the ones who dressed luxuriously, according to the latest fashion, and walked around in gold shoes were the wives of famous lawyers, or else actresses or courtesans. Upper-class people behaved very calmly, freely, simply in society . . . But it is not the theatre which is at fault here: it is impossible to convey modesty and a kind of old-fashioned style on stage . . ."

Then she started talking about not liking *Anna Karenina* at all.

"Haven't I told you why? I don't like repeating myself."

I lied, saying no – and I don't regret it. This time Anna Andreevna explained her dislike in more detail, more fully and differently.

"The entire novel is based on a false physiological and psychological premise. While Anna lives with a middle-aged husband whom she does not love and whom she finds repulsive, she doesn't flirt with anyone, behaves modestly and morally. Whereas when she lives with a young, handsome one whom she loves – she flirts with every man around, holds her hands in a certain way, walks around almost naked . . . Tolstoy wanted to prove that a woman who leaves her lawful husband inevitably becomes a prostitute. And his attitude towards her is vile . . . Even after her death he describes her 'shamelessly naked' body – he has created some kind of morgue by the railway. And she loves Seryozha, but not the girl, because Seryozha is legitimate but the girl is not . . . I assure you . . . That is the point of view of the people around him: his aunt's and Sofya Andreevna's. And can you please tell me, why did she imagine that Vronsky had stopped loving her? Eventually he dies for her . . ."

"Eventually," I said. "Yes, eventually he does."

This time, I couldn't contain myself and started to argue with her. Vronsky really doesn't love her as before. I reminded Anna Andreevna of their meeting on the carriage platform: "Why are you going?" Anna asks Vronsky, who has suddenly appeared beside her. "To be where you are," replies Vronsky. And later, when she has already left her husband and son, and they are together, he is bored with her, seeks ways to amuse himself, and once stays out late at his club. Anna asks: "Why did you stay?" – "I wanted to stay so I stayed," replies Vronsky.

"You must agree," I said, "that between the first and the second exchange something has altered in Vronsky's feelings, and fundamentally so. Love is always dependence ('I am going in order to be where you are'), but when it starts being a question of asserting your independence ('I wanted to stay so I stayed') – that's the end of love. And as for his dying eventually, that's because his conscience troubles him: it's no joke having driven the woman you loved under a train."

Anna Andreevna did not agree with me on anything.

"Rubbish," she said. "She did not have any grounds for thinking that he had stopped loving her. Or for doubting him. Love always manifests itself a hundred times a day. And this excessive suspicion of hers is not without purpose for Tolstoy: Anna thinks that Vronsky cannot love her because she herself knows in her heart that she is a prostitute ... And please don't try to defend that rubbishy old man!"*

Our conversation turned to Freud. I said that I didn't like and didn't believe him; the only thing that appealed to me in his teachings was the

---

* In those years when A.A. and I spoke about *Anna Karenina* her point of view seemed interesting to me, but incorrect, invented ... About two years later, by chance, I picked up one of the old Tolstoy volumes of *Literary Heritage* [*Literaturnoe nasledstvo*]: a chapter was published there which Tolstoy subsequently removed from the final text. During one of Vronsky's absences, Anna, bored and angry, asks a Guards officer, who she knows is in love with her, to escort her to a flower show; in the semi-darkness of the carriage she behaves so provocatively that when they reach their destination he opens the door for her – that gesture contains more contempt than courtesy.

Having read this chapter, I understood that in spite of Tolstoy's having deleted this page, A.A. had profoundly understood his intention.

I will return to this attitude of Akhmatova's to Tolstoy more than once in volume 2 of my *Journals* ("a demigod" is how she used to refer to him sometimes ...). The jokey nickname "rubbishy old man" came about like this: soon after Tolstoy's death, B. V. Tomashevsky visited Yasnaya Polyana and tried to question the local peasants about him. In reply to all the questions about Lev Nikolaevich they persistently talked about Sofya Andreevna. When B. V. Tomashevsky still tried to steer the conversation on to Tolstoy, one of the peasants replied: "What is there to remember about him! He was a rubbishy old man!"

idea that early childhood plays a huge part in every person's life. The longer you live, the more clearly you see that.

"Yes, maybe so," Anna Andreevna agreed without enthusiasm. "But as far as the rest goes ... all you see in these sexual arguments and myths is the reflection of the stagnant, stale, provincial milieu in which he lived ... I read a book by that banal Zweig about Leonardo da Vinci. In it he quotes Freud: 'Leonardo, of course, had an Oedipus complex and if he loved birds, that's because babies are brought by storks ...' Just imagine, what nonsense: why does he assume that the custom of lying to children about storks existed even in those days?"

We agreed that she would come round tomorrow at four, and I left.

13 June 1940

At four today it started pouring, and Anna Andreevna came late and not for long. She was tired, sad and complained of a chill. She looked through various editions of Pasternak on my shelf; she railed against *Second Birth* ("an attempt to be understood"), spoke rapturously of my favourites, *The Childhood of Lyuvers* and *Safe Conduct*.

"Every word of these is believable."

She left early.

18 June 1940

Yesterday I dropped in at Anna Andreevna's for a minute, to find out what news she had. Anna Andreevna told me in full detail about her march ... She is hopeful and happy about it – but at the same time slightly humiliated.

"And on her knees shed tears before Augustus," she said in the middle of her account.*

Then she held out an issue of the magazine *Leningrad* containing an article about Esenin in which her poetry was highly spoken of. "When Verochka told me about it, I didn't believe her."†

Vladimir Georgievich arrived. I got up but Anna Andreevna held me back.

---

*   This refers to some episode in the history of efforts on behalf of Lyova, and is therefore coded. I cannot remember now exactly what we were talking about.
    "And on her knees shed tears before Augustus ..." is a line from the poem "Cleopatra".
†   *Verochka*: Vera Nikolaevna Anikieva. Akhmatova's "highly spoken of" poetry refers to lines in L. Rakhmilevich's review of a book by Esenin, where Akhmatova is named as one of the "remarkable poets" (see *Leningrad*, no. 5, 1940).

"You don't look well at all," she said to me. "What's happening to you? You came back from the dacha thin, pale . . ."

And she started asking Vladimir Georgievich how to get Baranov to see me as soon as possible.*

I didn't argue. It goes without saying that her plan made no sense whatsoever. But if it put her mind at rest – so be it.

Turning to Vladimir Georgievich, who was sitting next to her on the divan, she gave him a detailed account of Vera Nikolaevna's illness.

Then she said: "Would you believe it, Osmyorkin amazed me yesterday. He was here. I suggested to him that we go together to visit Vera. And suddenly I see that he doesn't want to. Not for anything. He's afraid. I was amazed. In the first place, Verochka was lying down in a most proper state, her hair curled, she was dressed, had no fever, and there was no threat to him of oxygen bags and cold sweat. Secondly – how shameful! He can drink cognac with her, but seeing her ill – oh no! I can't stand that."

I said that you often come across people who reason this way: If I can't help, why should I torment myself by watching?

"Yes, yes, it happens," said Anna Andreevna. "How wretched! And besides, it's not true: if one person wants to help another, ardently and unselfishly wants to, then he always can. But I knew a lady who claimed that she was incapable of visiting her sick friend: she couldn't bear the sight of hospitals, white gowns, sick people. And there are those who don't want to see the dead: it is too hard for them."

"Well, if it were their *own* dead, their beloved dead, they would certainly want to see them," I said. (And their graves – I thought to myself.)

"And I've noticed," continued Anna Andreevna, "that the people who have such fears are always the ones who have the most terrible fates: it is they who are destined to see many dead people."

20 June 1940

I called Anna Andreevna in the middle of the day and said that I was ill, in bed. She immediately offered to visit me (unlike Osmyorkin!).

And she did come. She brought me some lilies-of-the-valley. She was wearing black silk, a white necklace. Her face was calm today, and, as on any tranquil face, the cheeks, mouth and forehead are less prominent

---

* At that time I was suffering terribly from goitre.

– but the eyes are brighter. Today they were large and grey. Settled on my divan, she greatly resembled her Paris portrait.

We brought up the fact that the Goslit book is not delayed without reason. No, of course not.

Then Anna Andreevna told me of the sudden arrival of Sh. and the vile things she had hurled at her.

"'You were such a stunning woman! How could you let your hair get so grey?'; 'Now that you have written something Soviet, you get advances from everywhere'" (by 'Soviet', she meant the poem about Mayakovsky, explained Anna Andreevna). "'You would not listen to me, and now ...'

"Well, I immediately put a stop to the stream of vile things which she still had in store by asking her to pass on 1000 roubles. I did not even try to disabuse her as far as the advances were concerned."*

I asked whether there were any new poems.

"No ... Would you like me to recite a short, very old one to you? It has never been published."

And she recited:

> On both sides
> The pillow has grown hot ...

– so amazingly accurate that anyone with insomnia will memorize it instantly. And what elegance, what perfection. And what – I might say – virginal purity.†

"This poem was supposed to be the last one in the volume *Evening*. First I wanted *Evening* to be called *Goosefoot*, and the first poem would have been 'At the rising of the sun/ I do sing of love,/ In the garden on my knee/ Goosefoot I do weed.'‡ But I was talked out of it."

"But why didn't you at least include it in the current volume *From Six Books*?"

"You will laugh, teacher sir. I didn't include it because when I started to copy it, I didn't know how to put the punctuation in."

(She has the same complex about punctuation marks as about crossing

---

* I think "Sh." is Shura, that is, Aleksandra Stepanovna (married name Sverchkova, c. 1875–c. 1952), half-sister of Nikolay Stepanovich Gumilyov, his father's daughter from his first marriage. "You would not listen to me ..." is a reproach to Lyova. I believe A.A. wanted to send some money to her mother-in-law, Anna Ivanovna Gumilyova, of whom she was very fond.
† *FT, Evening;* no. 38.
‡ *FT, Evening;* no. 39.

the road. She *knows* perfectly well how to put them in, but for some reason she doesn't trust herself and is afraid to.)

I told her one can see from her poems that she is very fond of goosefoot.

"Yes, very, very, nettles too and also burdock. Since childhood. When I was small, we lived in Tsarskoe, in a little side street, and burdock and goosefoot used to grow in a ditch there. I was small and they were large, with broad leaves, scented, warmed by the sun – I've loved them ever since then."

I plucked up courage – we were drinking tea, she was smoking – and I dared ask whether some of her poems had been letters.

"No . . . People have been saying that for a long time: they seem like letters or a diary. No. Once, it's true, I did turn a letter I received into a poem. When I die, that letter will be found."

She was in a hurry to go: she still had Davidenkovs to visit.

24 June 1940

I phoned today to find out what had happened on the 23rd. She said: "Please, come over, only hurry, because unfortunately, I have to leave. Vera is very ill, we're going to see her."

Two people were at her place: Vladimir Georgievich and a man I didn't know, who was young but looked rather old. Anna Andreevna had her hat on: evidently I had held her up.

"Tanya has haemocolitis. She has just been taken to hospital by ambulance. Vovochka saw his mama being taken away."

Then: "Sofya Ivanovna from the publishers rang me today and asked when I would be able to receive their director. I said not today, today is my birthday after all."

Ah, that's why there were roses on her table!

Anna Andreevna asked me what I thought about the director's forthcoming visit. "I think they want to cut two or three poems out," I said.

Anna Andreevna shook her head.

I asked her about yesterday's visit. It turned out the conversation had never taken place; she had not been supposed to go on the 23rd, but on the 25th, to sign up for the 28th.

I offered to go instead of her tomorrow, the 25th: for it was impossible for her to go, she had to stay home with Vovochka, as Tanya wasn't there.

She agreed. The four of us left. Outside, Anna Andreevna took my arm and led me ahead. I noticed that, leaning on my arm, she was walking somehow heavily, awkwardly, as if in pain. Anna Andreevna expressed her gloomy forecast about the book to me, and not only about the book, brushing aside my objections. We parted on the corner of Panteley-monovskaya and Liteyny. I repeated my promise.

25 June 1940

The morning's errand took me no more than three hours. After completing it, I went straight to Anna Andreevna's. She was already anxious and waiting for me. She questioned me about everything and was satisfied.

She sat in the armchair in an old faded dressing gown. I suggested going to buy the hat at last. (She was able to go out because Vovochka's aunt had taken him.) But she didn't want to – the heat. She complained that since Tanya had been in hospital, she hadn't eaten anything and "at last I'm hungry". I offered to go and buy something, we could have breakfast and go for lunch at the House of Writers in a couple of hours.

"If you get butter, ham, bread, then why have lunch? *That* will be our going out."

I took my bag and left. I noticed with surprise that I even found queuing for Anna Andreevna pleasant. Afterwards, I was caught in a thunderstorm – magnificent, blustery, refreshing...

"Are you soaked?" cried Anna Andreevna opening the door for me.

But I was dry. Except for my shoulders.

We had breakfast.

Standing by the mirror she suddenly asked: "Do you like *Spektorsky?*"

"On the whole – no. But certain passages ... bits ... to the utmost degree."

I recited:

> Space is asleep, fallen in love with space,
> The city adream, up to its ears in water,
> And a sea of requests, forgotten yet passionate,
> Half asleep is splashing, no one knows where.
>
> There's a murmur, which plucks at the heart,
> Of courtyards, suburbs, of a wet roadway,
> Of side gates, of raindrops ... a wondrous rumble without shape,
> Like swooning, having a chat with oneself.

"It is an unsuccessful work," said Anna Andreevna. "I don't mean the passage you recited. I mean the work as a whole. I always disliked it.

Above: Anna Gorenko, 1904

Right: Anna Akhmatova, 1911

Below: Nikolay Stepanovich Gumilyov, Anna Andreevna Akhmatova and their son, Lyova, 1916

Above: The house at Five Corners
– Zagorodny Prospekt, 11 –
where L. K. Chukovskaya and
M. P. Bronshteyn lived in flat
no. 4

Right: Akhmatova and Punin, 1927

Below: Fontanny House, the former Sheremetev Palace in Leningrad, in an
annexe of which Akhmatova lived for about 30 years from 1921. The building
was also the home of the House of Entertaining Science

Above: Matvey Petrovich Bronshteyn, mid-1930s

Below: Anna Akhmatova, Starki, Summer 1936

Above: Lydia Chukovskaya, Kiev, 1938

Below: Lev Gumilyov, 1930s

Top left: Vladimir Georgievich Garshin

Above left: Shpalernaya 25, the House of Preliminary Detention

Left: The "Big House" – NKVD Headquarters, Leningrad

Above: "White Night" (1940). Portrait of Anna Akhmatova by A. A. Osmyorkin

Below: The Kresty Prison, Leningrad, where Lev Gumilyov was held in the late 1930s

Top left: Lydia Chukovskaya with Lyusha, Moscow, 1943

Top right: Lyusha, Leningrad, 6 May 1937

Above: Lyusha and Tanya Volova (*left*) in the Summer Garden, Leningrad, 27 June 1938

Right: Anna Akhmatova and Vova Smirnov (Shakalik), Leningrad, 1940

Left: Korney Ivanovich Chukovsky, late 1930s

Centre left: Akhmatova's dedicatory inscription to Chukovskaya on the back of a photograph: "To Dear Lydia Korneevna Chukovskaya on the day we read Annensky. 30 June 1940"

Centre right: Yury Nikolaevich Tynyanov

Below left: Tamara Grigorievna Gabbe, Leningrad, late 1920s

Below right: Aleksandra Iosifovna Lyubarskaya, two months before her arrest, Moscow, July 1937

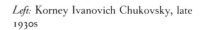

Left: Leningrad under siege. Nevsky Prospekt, 1941

Below: One of the first drafts of "Poem without a Hero", autographed in pencil. The dedicatory inscription on the title page reads: "I give this notebook to my dear friend L. K. Ch. with love and gratitude, A."

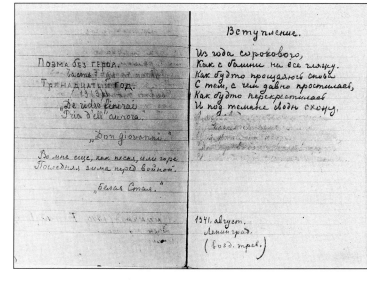

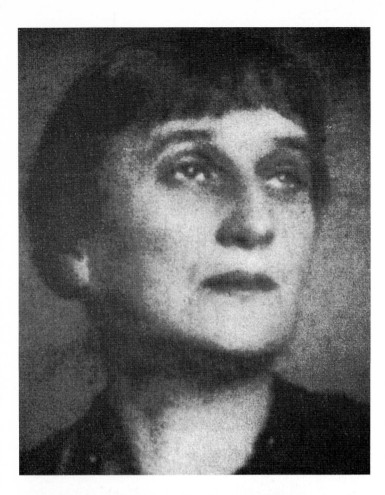

Left: Anna Akhmatova, Tashkent, 1942

Below: Photograph of Anna Akhmatova, Tashkent, 1942, inscribed on the back: "To my Captain, L. K. Ch. from Akhm."

But I only worked out why today. The point is that Pasternak's poems were written before the sixth day, when God created man. Have you noticed there are no people in his poems. There is everything you want: thunderstorms, woods, chaos, but no people. True, sometimes he makes an appearance himself, Boris Leonidovich, and he comes across well ... He really could have shouted out of the window to the children: 'My dears, what millennium are we living in at this moment?' But other people don't come into his poetry, and he doesn't even try to create them. Whereas in *Spektorsky* he tried. And immediately, disaster. The name and surname 'Mariya Ilina' sounds foolish in his poetry, preposterous ..."

We talked for a very long time, and when I noticed that I had taken up her whole day, I got up to say goodbye, but she said so plaintively: "Oh, why are you leaving? Stay a while longer!" – that I stayed.

I asked Anna Andreevna about her family. She is such an exceptional person, both inwardly and outwardly, that I very much wanted to understand whether she has something about her that comes from her ancestors, her family, something shared. Could it be possible that she resembles anyone else?

She told me about her sisters – Iya and Inna.

"Both died of tuberculosis. Iya, when she was 27 years old. I would have died too, of course, but I was saved by my thyroid disorder – which destroys tuberculosis. We had terrible TB in the family, though my father and mother were absolutely healthy. (My father died of angina pectoris, my mother of pneumonia at a very old age.) Iya was very special, severe, stern ...

"She was the way readers always imagined me to be, but I never was," continued Anna Andreevna, after a pause.

I asked whether Iya Andreevna had liked her poetry.

"No, she considered it frivolous. She didn't like it. The same thing, over and over again, all about love ..."

Anna Andreevna stood by the window and dried the cups with a coarse towel.

"We didn't have any books in the house, not a single book. Only Nekrasov, a thick, bound volume. My mother used to let me read it on feast days and holidays. This book was a present to Mama from her first husband, who shot himself ... The secondary school I went to in Tsarskoe was like a real reformatory ... Later in Kiev, school was a bit better ...

"I have loved poetry ever since I was a child and I managed to get hold of it somehow. At the age of 13, I already knew Baudelaire, Voltaire and all the *poètes maudits* in French. I started to write poetry early, but what is surprising is that before I had even written a line, all those around me were convinced that I would become a poetess ... My father even teased me by calling me a decadent poetess ..."

An old woman came in, without knocking, covered in shawls and wrinkles – Tanya's mother. Anna Andreevna explained Tanya's illness to her in detail and very clearly and wrote the hospital address on a piece of paper in big letters. No sooner had the old woman left than there was a loud knock and a young man in a dirty white gown entered – a hospital attendant, I suppose. He sat himself down and started to put questions to Anna Andreevna about Tanya's illness, very rudely and insistently. It may well be that he didn't mean to be rude, but he simply could not be otherwise. A real interrogation. Anna Andreevna answered patiently, calmly, humbly, without any trace of offence.

At last, he left.

Anna Andreevna asked me about my childhood. And I suddenly told her many things which I had never told anyone. She understands, guesses and grasps things with astounding subtlety and accuracy.* She was so

---

* I ask the reader to compare this observation of mine to several lines from N. V. Bannikov's article "An Exalted Gift" (i.e. from his afterword to the book: *Anna Akhmatova. Selected Works [Anna Akhmatova. Izbrannoe]*. Moscow: Khudozhestvennaya Literatura, 1974, p. 552).

"'She understands,' wrote one of her interlocutors, 'guesses and grasps things with astounding subtlety and accuracy,'" quotes Bannikov from my *Journals*. He grasps and quotes with complete accuracy, only there is no reference to the source, and I – a female interlocutor – have been changed into a male one. Bannikov's afterword contains quite a few such quotations – some direct, some partly concealed, some which have been turned into free paraphrases of my diary. (For the most striking ones, see pp. 546, 551, 554.) Yet, there isn't a single reference to my work.

When I started to decode my entries in 1966, I didn't intend them to be for wide circulation. I persistently showed them only to people researching the life and works of Anna Akhmatova – K. Chukovsky and Academician V. M. Zhirmunsky, as well as a small circle of her close friends. However, one copy of the *Journals* managed to slip out of my control and for some time had a life of its own. Evidently, at that time, it fell prey to Bannikov; the author of the article "An Exalted Gift" had no qualms about using my work without my knowledge, against my will, being certain of only one thing: the name of the author of the *Journals* was banned in her homeland – and the author thus deprived of the chance to protest.

The publication of my *Journals* abroad (in 1976, 1980 and 1984) did not in any way hinder those who wanted to rob me at home. On the contrary, the predators were numerous and they were free to do as they liked.

For more about the ban on my name, see *Journals*, vol. 2, and also my book *The Process of Expulsion [Protsess isklyucheniya]* (Moscow, 1979 and 1990).

Regardless of the lifting of the ban, in 1989 Bannikov again forgot to mention my name in the foreword to the book: *Anna Akhmatova. Lyric and Narrative Poems [Anna Akhmatova. Stikhotvoreniya i poemy]* (Moscow, Molodaya Gvardiya).

gentle, so kind and careful with me today – God bless her! – that I even felt like a human being.

Alas, not for long.

26 June 1940

I phoned Anna Andreevna around four to discover the outcome of the director's visit; as usual she wouldn't tell me, but asked me over. I went. This time, she was elegantly dressed, her hair was done, the room was swept clean; she was expecting someone from the Moscow Art Theatre and Vladimir Georgievich that evening.

It turned out I was right: the director had come to remove only two poems, to ask Anna Andreevna to replace them and to show her the foreword. Those to be dropped are: "Everything is ravaged, bartered, betrayed" and "I am not with those who left their land".*

"The foreword is full of praise. I said that in my view it is embarrassing to publish praise of oneself in one's own book. He replied – 'Just wait and see what's coming next!' As for the withdrawal of the two poems, the motive for their withdrawal is incomprehensible: in that book they will not be noticed but in this one they will be ... Why? But I did not insist or argue, he was even surprised by the readiness with which I agreed to remove and replace them. He asked what 'Not a single solitary blow/ Did we try to deflect from ourselves' meant.† I replied: a poet cannot explain his words to tens of thousands of readers. If something is unintelligible, it is better not to publish it."

She had called me so that, in her words, we could choose the poems to replace the ones which had been cut. She put her glasses on, got her notebooks and began leafing through them.

Looking over her shoulder, I noticed that "Voronezh" was dedicated to N.Kh., and "You must celebrate our last anniversary ..." to V.G.‡ I

---

*   *FT, Anno Domini;* no. 40 and no. 41.

†   A line from the poem "I am not with those who left their land" – *FT, Anno Domini;* no 41.

‡   "Voronezh" – *FT, Reed;* no. 42.

   This poem, in which A.A. ostensibly tells N. Khardzhiev about her visit to a mutual friend of theirs, the exiled poet O. Mandelstam, subsequently acquired a different dedication: instead of "N.Kh." it became "O.M." and in the end four new lines were added. But in 1940, and in the volume *FSB,* the last four lines did not yet exist. I first heard them from Anna Andreevna in March 1958 (see *Journals,* vol. 2).

   "You must celebrate our *last* anniversary" – *FT, Reed;* no. 4. Many years later, in Moscow, A.A. saw, in my copy of *FSB,* above the poem "You must celebrate our last anniversary", the initials "V.G.", which had been pencilled in by me from memory. She became very angry and made me erase them at once: "This has nothing to do with V.G."

suggested she give the poems "On both sides/ The pillow has grown hot ..." (in the notebook it was called "Afterword") and "To a Friend" as replacements.*

Anna Andreevna agreed and asked me to copy them out. (Apparently, she never gives anything to publishers in her own hand.)

I copied the two out, considering earnestly the correct punctuation.

Anna Andreevna showed me a page with minor changes in the poem "Some gaze into affectionate eyes" (instead of "calm and double-horned" – "both watchful and double-horned") and later – the end of the extract "Dusk falls and in the dark blue sky".

"He wanted to put in my corrections, but couldn't find the poems ... I'm spoilt, I'm used to everyone knowing my poems by heart."

After that, she started talking about émigrés – about how indignantly they greeted the poem "I am not with those who left their land". Recently, she had been shown Bunin's lines, obviously written about her, although her name was not mentioned in them. She recited this poem to me by heart. There was a muff, pointed knees, a dissolute, sexless woman waiting for a prince. Pale, lifeless verse. Her outward appearance had been compiled from Altman's portrait of her and from "My uncurled fringe of hair/ Reaches almost to my eyebrows ..."†

I felt ashamed affirming her question: yes, it is about you. Ashamed for Bunin.

"Severyanin didn't like me either," Anna Andreevna said. "He criticized me viciously. My poetry is slanderous. Slanderous to women. Women are dreamers, like little budding flowers, luxuriant, proud, whereas mine are somehow wretched ... It's not right, it's not right ..."[70]

Then she suddenly asked: "Tell me, you know Pasternak so well – is it true that he cannot be divided into phases at all? I thought about this for the first time today. All his poems seem as if they were written on one day."

I said only that *Second Birth* is a very different book from all those that preceded it.

"I don't like that book," said Anna Andreevna. "It contains a great number of extremely unpleasant poems. 'Your fainting brought no

* I can't remember precisely which poem the title "To a Friend" referred to, maybe it was the working title. In any case, it is not about the one (from "Requiem") which is discussed in the footnote on pp. 78–9.

† Lines from the poem "A row of fine beads round my neck" – *FT, Plantain [Podorozhnik]*; no. 43.

peace...' Only certain lines in it are remarkable ... Do you happen to know, by the way, what a magneto is? You don't know either? No one knows."

I was not able to tell her what a magneto was, but asked her in turn what she found wrong with the poem – or line – "Your fainting brought no peace".

"I don't know, I don't know," replied Anna Andreevna, pulling a slightly wry face. "Maybe I find this book unpleasant because of Zina's presence in it ... Or maybe, you know why? Remember, you once told me that you don't like Mayakovsky's poem 'There are no flies on me, my dear', that you can hear in it the voice of a worldly-wise, smug old bachelor? Well, then, *Second Birth* is the poetry of a bridegroom. It is written by a flustered bridegroom ... And what unpleasant poems to his former wife! 'We do away not with life, not with spiritual union – but with mutual deceit.' He apologizes to one and runs to the other with a little nosegay – surely there you have a flustered bridegroom? You know which poems of his I like? The one about Irpen. 'Whence comes this sadness, Diotima?'"

30 June 1940

And today I got to know Annensky. Thanks to Anna Andreevna.

I called her during the day and went round. Vladimir Georgievich was there. All around there was disorder, dirty dishes, cheese rinds. She complained that her foot had swollen up. She complained that she had caught a cold – the temperature had dropped sharply during the night. Indeed, you could hear she had a blocked nose.

Vladimir Georgievich said goodbye, and I went to shut the door after him. On the way I asked what was the matter with Anna Andreevna.

"Oh, nothing," he replied a little irritably. "She's got a blister, that's all."

When he had already stepped out of the flat, he suddenly came back into the hall: "Only please don't tell her you asked me anything."

I couldn't think of a reply, and locked the door after him.

This request surprised and offended me. Did he really think I would inform Anna Andreevna of my question and his reply. But he had looked so tormented, upset, that I couldn't be angry.

I returned to Anna Andreevna. No news. Tanya is still in hospital. Vovochka is at his aunt's. I offered to go and buy something.

When I returned Anna Andreevna was already on her feet, in her dressing gown, combed, the table cleared. She switched the kettle on, and we sat down to breakfast. I asked whether she goes out for lunch, as Tanya is not there and there is no one to cook for her.

"I do go out sometimes, but rarely. A few days ago I ventured out and immediately met all those I didn't want to see. And now hunger battles within me against my aversion to going there."

She began to talk about Annensky. She has already mentioned him more than once as a remarkable poet. I had to admit my complete ignorance.

Anna Andreevna livened up.

"Would you like me to read you some?" She jumped up, and, first removing a mirror, opened the top of the dresser and started rummaging through the books. She couldn't locate Annensky. She showed me a group photograph: schoolgirls and her sister, Iya, amongst them. A beauty, with the face of a Greek empress. Resembling Anna Andreevna. Next a photograph of her father, her mother – no resemblance whatsoever to their daughters. The mother had a rather simple face. Next a picture of a slender, dark-eyed, young man with Anna Andreevna's mouth: her brother. Next she fished out a manuscript – her sister Iya's essay on archpriest Avvakum and with it her professor's laudatory remarks. Next an amateur photo of Anna Andreevna: she was half reclining in a garden, on a chaise longue, her face looked young, tranquil and very lovely – neither dramatic, nor fated, nor penetrating, but to be precise – lovely.

"Would you like me to give it to you?" asked Anna Andreevna and I joyfully accepted.

Annensky was found. Anna Andreevna sat down on the divan and put on her glasses.

"Now you'll see what a poet he is," she said, "how significant. I'm astonished you don't know him. For all poets are derived from him: Osip, and Pasternak, and I, and even Mayakovsky."[71]

She read me four poems, which really were most remarkable. I especially liked "Bow and Strings", "The Old Estonian Women" and "The Lyre-Clock". You really could hear her strongly, and Pasternak too.

Before I left she inscribed the photograph for me. On the stairs I read: "On the day we read Annensky".

There was a mistake in the surname – a letter missing.

5 July 1940

Today, on my return from the dacha, I called Anna Andreevna and heard the usual: "Come over now, please." I found Osmyorkin there and an extremely polite man I didn't know, who turned out to be Vsevolod Nikolaevich Petrov.[72] Anna Andreevna was wearing a new, white, very beautiful dress. The room smelled deliciously of paint: Osmyorkin was retouching or finishing her portrait. There were three bottles of wine and some glasses on the table. After making me sit down Anna Andreevna took up her place on the window sill. It was already half dark: the portrait was illuminated by bright lamps without shades directed at it.

The general conversation was about Repin, about Penaty (where Osmyorkin had been) and about Tatlin. Anna Andreevna begged Osmyorkin to stop working on the portrait for today and she moved over to the divan. As far as Tatlin was concerned, she declared that he was certifiably insane: once he had refused to let her into his studio, fearing – it later transpired – that she would trace his drawings. Petrov left shortly after that. Osmyorkin stayed a little longer, then also stood up. Anna Andreevna made me stay, she was most insistent. Osmyorkin promised to come tomorrow and definitely finish the portrait.

Having seen him out, Anna Andreevna said to me: "I sit only for him, I am very fond of him, he is very good to me, but in general it is not worth painting me, this subject has already been exhausted in painting and graphics. Besides, I have other things on my mind. My feet have swollen up again, this time both of them. Yesterday I could hardly drag myself to the House of Writers and, once there, I realized that I could not make it home. I only just managed to limp to the Rybakovs'. I walked down the street like Andersen's mermaid. I wanted to take my shoes off and go barefoot, but what gossip that would have started! I know so many people in that area, you see ... The Rybakovs rang Vladimir Georgievich, and he brought me home."[73]

9 July 1940

In the middle of the day I called Anna Andreevna and suggested going for lunch together at the House of Writers.

She agreed, but when I came to pick her up, it turned out that she would not go anywhere because she was waiting for Dr Baranov.

"I want to have a serious talk with you," started Anna Andreevna, after I'd sat down. (This put me on edge.) "About the book you brought me last time." (I felt relieved; I had brought her Mauriac.*) "I read it in

* *Thérèse Desqueyreux.*

one breath, in one gulp, as I always read books, and some parts even twice, in order to be better armed for my discussion with you. It is a very false book. Evidently, the author wanted to create something meaningful, but he didn't succeed. The heroine leaves me totally cold. Remember you spoke of the need for imagination. But where on earth was Thérèse's imagination when she fed her husband arsenic every night? And with no motive! She wanted to get out of the house, you see! But why? To end up in the arms of a housemaid? Her husband and her husband's mother, whom she hates so much, are much better than she is. They are simple, peaceful people, getting on with their own lives. The author is indignant because Maman de la Trave does not wish to live in the same house as Thérèse. But would you mind telling me, please, if some scoundrel had been poisoning your daughter every day would you then agree to share the same house? ... No, no, however you look at it, all this is false and incomprehensible."

I could find no objections, but asked in reply: "Why is it then that when you read the book everything seems truthful, natural, quite convincing? Why does one automatically sympathize with the heroine, and not with de la Trave? Why does this book hold a certain fascination for me – surely not because I am generally inclined to sympathize with poisoners?"

"It's all because the book is your contemporary," Anna Andreevna replied, after a pause. "It exudes contemporary art for you. It makes you feel as if some long-awaited friend has just greeted you over the phone. And you succumb to this familiar voice automatically."

This comment of hers – about contemporary art – interested me greatly. (More than her comments on Mauriac's book.) Because constantly in my thoughts and in our constant arguments about poetry, I myself maintain: if the soul is not moved by contemporary poetry it will not respond to classical poetry. The path to understanding classical poetry is through contemporary poetry, through that which is "about me". If you do not love Blok, Mayakovsky, Akhmatova, Pasternak and Mandelstam, do not hear them, you won't be able to hear Pushkin, you won't learn to apprehend him *personally*. He will remain a mere example, a model of cold perfection.

"Well, you hold on to that thought," said Anna Andreevna. "It is true and fruitful: only through contemporary art can one understand the art of the past. There is no other path. And when something new appears, do you know how a contemporary should feel? As if it is pure chance that it was not he who wrote it, as if he himself had just been about to write it, but somebody had snatched it out of his hands..."

Vladimir Georgievich and Dr Baranov arrived. I decided to go out for some food while Anna Andreevna was being examined. I headed for Nevsky. It was terribly hot. I bought sausages and a sweet loaf.

On my way back, as I was crossing the courtyard, someone suddenly called out to me from the little garden. It turned out that by chance the little garden had been left unlocked and it was V.G. – he was sitting on the bench waiting for the doctor to come out of Anna Andreevna's. I sat down next to him and we were silent for a while, enjoying the shade. Then I asked V.G. why it was that Anna Andreevna's feet kept swelling up.

"Oh, her feet are nothing!" he responded. "They swell a bit from the heat. She should wear wider shoes and low heels. That's all there is to it. But she doesn't want to: it can't be helped, *ewig weiblich!* Does that trouble you? You think I'm speaking in anger? I'm not, truly. But I do assure you that everything, everything with her is because of her nerves. Of course, that doesn't make it easier for her ... The trouble is that she doesn't want to do anything about it. First of all, it is vital that she move out of here, out of this flat. She is being tormented all the time, by both neighbours. But she refuses point blank. Why? Simply because she's afraid of the new. And there is her endless fear of losing her sanity: she saw Sreznevskaya ill and now she searches for the same symptoms in herself.* Have you noticed she always takes some very dubious fact as a premise and draws conclusions from it with the consistency of iron, with indisputable logic? ... And this terrible intensity of her spiritual and psychological life is burning her up!"

There was no sign of Dr Baranov so we decided to go up.

"It is difficult to help anyone," I said, catching my breath on the landing, "but especially her."

"Yes," replied Vladimir Georgievich in a sobbing voice and suddenly grabbed my shoulder, "but no matter what anyone says" (he pushed me away), "no matter what anyone says, these last two years I've been the one who's carried her in my arms."

We found Anna Andreevna and Dr Baranov in quiet conversation by the window. No sooner had we entered than Anna Andreevna asked the doctor to make an appointment for me.

* For more about Valeriya Sergeevna Sreznevskaya see note 90.

The doctor courteously agreed, wrote something down on a page of his notepad and handed it to me.

Respectfully, he bid us farewell. And left.

"What did he prescribe for you?" I asked Anna Andreevna.

"It seems he considers me beyond hope," she explained angrily, "because the only thing he prescribed is going to the country to get some fresh air."

And she started to explain to me and V.G. why she could on no account go to the country. V.G. tried to argue at first, then fell silent and, looking upset, took his leave. Anna Andreevna went to the kitchen to boil some sausages and, in the meantime, gave me some poems by Count Komarovsky, whose poetry I hardly knew.

"Well? Have you tasted them?" she asked cheerfully, on returning. And added: "He is one of my favourite poets."[74]

(After the argument about going to the country, she had once again become calm and collected.)

I asked her to let me take the Komarovsky and she agreed.

"So I didn't manage to convince you about Mauriac?" asked Anna Andreevna, showing me to the door. "No? Well, never mind, come back from the dacha soon and give me a call."

13 July 1940

Oh, I wish I could read her proofs with a clearer head.

My head aches, my legs are weak.

I came to town yesterday with the intention of rushing back today, right after seeing the doctor – to get butter and kerosene to the dacha as soon as possible. But at midnight Anna Andreevna rang: the proofs had arrived from Goslit, she asked me to go round in the morning. So I didn't leave, and straight after going to the doctor's, who saw me in the morning, I set off, not to the dacha, but to see her.

The doctor told me that I needed an operation and as soon as possible. I took this news rather calmly because I wasn't about to waste my time with all this now anyway.

On the way to Anna Andreevna's I stocked up on butter, sausages and bread.

I had hoped to have a rest in the little garden, but, no luck, the gate was locked again.

With great difficulty I climbed the stairs.

Anna Andreevna questioned me very earnestly in detail about what

Baranov had said to me. Evidently she put my poor state down to fear before the operation. But it isn't true: I am simply exhausted by the dacha. Anna Andreevna offered me Luminal and bromide and, out of sheer tact, said that she had to take some too. We swallowed the drops in turn.

I settled down to read the proofs. Oh no, they should be read with a clearer head! I spotted a few major misprints and, of course, corrected them, but on the whole I worked superficially, not profoundly, not the way Samuil Yakovlevich* demanded – "with fresh eyes" ... Anna Andreevna wandered about the room and, peering over my shoulder, again and again wondered at my proofreader's marks. In vain I swore that it was the simplest thing in the world and that I could teach her the proofreading marks in an hour.

"Not only am I not able to remember these marks which are child's play to you," she replied, "but I can't even write one of my poems down because I don't understand how to."

I laid down my pen and asked her to recite it to me.

She didn't know whether the word *nezvany* [uninvited] has one or two "n"s, and whether or not it is written as one word.†

Reading the proofs, I was surprised to find a new version of the poem "For me you are no woman of this earth".‡

"Can't I help you with anything?" asked Anna Andreevna. "I'm so ashamed of being a parasite."

"You can," I dared to say. "Allow me to ring Tamara Grigorievna, let her come and read the proofs instead of me while I lie down."

And that's what we did.

Anna Andreevna rang Tusya while I lay down on the divan. Tusya, bless her, came very quickly. Through the haze of semiconsciousness I heard their voices and watched them.

---

* Marshak.

† I think we were talking about the poem "Invocation" addressed to N. Gumilyov. It contains the lines:

> Uninvited,
> Not a bridegroom –
> Come and have supper with me.

The poem was published in *FT, Reed* with the censorial distortion "high gates" instead of "prison gates"; in *In Memory A.A.* without distortion; probably, however, it was written not in 1935, as indicated in both volumes and also in *My Voice*, but in 1936 for the 50th anniversary of Nikolay Stepanovich's birth.

‡ Now this poem begins like this: "He said I have no rivals ..." (*FT, Anno Domini*); but in the volume *FSB* and in publications until 1957 it was: "It is true, you have no rivals ...".

Tusya read the proofs very carefully and, unlike me, she talked to Anna Andreevna freely and with poise while doing so.

Anna Andreevna asked her advice on "The Cellar of Memory": should she publish it or not?

Then Tusya related Pertsov's article to us, that same man who, in his article of 1925, advised Anna Andreevna to die.*

"But that's nothing," said Anna Andreevna. "Take Kornely Zelinsky; he once wrote of me: 'Akhmatova pretends to have died, but in reality she lives in Leningrad.'"

I felt better. I got up and, despite Anna Andreevna's protestations, I read the contents page myself.

After finishing the work, we left. Tusya walked me right up to my house. On the way she recited Tyutchev's "Spring" to me ("However much fate's hand oppresses"), which, until now, I hadn't given the attention it deserved; and then together we recited Baratynsky's "Autumn", to which Shura had introduced us – the long "Autumn" in which:

> Winter comes, and the meagre earth
> Shows broad, bare patches of impotence [. . .]

I thought: This may be the best poem in Russian literature.

19 July 1940

During this time I went to Anna Andreevna's twice – on the 17th and yesterday, on the 18th.

She feels bad. Her face is grey, drawn, her feet are swollen. She doesn't leave the house. But the housekeeping has improved: Sarra has come (I couldn't gather from the conversations who that was) and she cooks and feeds her.† Anna Andreevna was planning to go to the Writers' Union House of Creativity in Detskoe on the 1st. She had agreed to it since repair work was starting on the flat and, the main reason, V.G. was going off to a dacha somewhere . . . But now it seems her good intentions would not be carried out.

On the 18th I was at her place at the same time as V.G. Anna

---

* About V. Pertsov's article, published in 1925, see footnote on p. 103. In the article of 1940, which appeared in *Literaturnaya gazeta* on 10 July, while acknowledging the poet's craftsmanship, he wrote: "Akhmatova's heroine and we are too unalike. This cannot help showing."

† On Sarra Iosifovna Arens, a relative of N. N. Punin's first wife, Anna Evgenevna Arens, see *Journals*, vol. 3.

Andreevna was called to the phone. She went to take the call and came back in a fury.

"Some secretary from Litfond called. To inform me that all the places in Detskoe have been taken and there is no room for me. I shouted (here she really did shout out each syllable) that 'I DO NOT WANT TO DEPRIVE ANYBODY OF THEIR VACATION, I would be glad not to go' . . . And she replied: 'Don't upset yourself, don't upset yourself, we'll manage to put you up somehow . . .' They have absolutely no idea with whom they're dealing! She expected me to start demanding 'Me, me, give me a place!' She expected me to take part in the communal scuffle!"

(Oh, how grateful I am to her that she understands so well who she is, that in preserving the dignity of Russian literature, which she represents at some invisible tribunal, she never takes part in any communal scuffles!)

2 August 1940

I returned from the dacha on the 31st, so that at night I could spend the anniversary at home, alone, in the very same walls, without casting gloom over the girls' lives.*

At seven o'clock I went to Anna Andreevna's. She was in a sad mood, didn't feel well.

"My foot is bad," she replied to my question, "my heart is bad. When I walk I keep feeling I'm about to collapse, you know how it is."

She was expecting the next reply on the 2nd. She was convinced it would be negative.

"But all the same," I told her (I said it carelessly, bluntly, cruelly), "you still have hope."

I shouldn't have compared Mitya's fate to Lyova's even in my thoughts . . . Lyova is alive.

(Is that worse? Better? Whatever, I shouldn't have done it. Several times already, during my previous visits, I thought I had heard – when Anna Andreevna had walked me through the kitchen along the corridor, or during the minutes of her long silences in the midst of our discussion – I thought I had heard Lyova's name, uttered by her, as if from a depth,

---

* On the night of 31 July into the early hours of 1 August 1937 our flat had been searched and I was served a warrant for Matvey Petrovich's arrest.

  At that time he was at his parents' in Kiev. I made several attempts to warn him but all proved unsuccessful. Matvey Petrovich was arrested in Kiev on the night of 5/6 August.

as if from the bottom of the sea ... "Lyova! Lyova!" she would repeat in one breath. Not even a sound, the shadow of a sound, a moan or a call ... Today I heard that moan several times.)

In came Vladimir Georgievich. He rinsed some grapes and put them on the table. He put the kettle on. Anna Andreevna told us that Sovetskiy pisatel had sent her ten more copies of her book – but not the one she'd asked for (I didn't quite understand what the difference was).

She asked me to pass one copy, with her dedication, on to Korney Ivanovich.

V.G. said goodbye. Anna Andreevna went to see him to the door and suddenly ran back into the room – nimbly leant out of the window and called him back up. He returned, she asked him for the phone number of the ambulance. It turned out Punin's maid had also been taken ill with haemocolitis, just as Tanya had previously.

So it was already the second case in this flat. Right next to Anna Andreevna.

I tried to persuade her to come and stay with me in Olgino. She did not give a positive reply, but neither did she refuse.

Tanya came in and in her characteristically direct, coarse language started telling us about the maid's illness. Anna Andreevna sent her to phone for an ambulance.

I asked Anna Andreevna whether she had any new poems.

"I've finished two old ones and started two new ones," she replied, put her glasses on and opened her book. She read me a new beginning to a poem which I had already heard ("I would like to find my little icon ..."). Now it begins like this:

> Little side road – little side ro...
> Tightened the noose about my throat.*

She read a new ending to the Terrifying House.† Then she asked: "Is it clear that "ro" is a cut-off, incomplete word?"

Next she read "My little curly-haired son I put to bed ...". It is unbearable to listen to these poems – what must it be like to write them?‡

The boys came in. She greeted them very tenderly. She took Vovochka in her arms. I've already noticed more than once how with a child in her arms she immediately takes on the appearance of a statue of the

---

* "The Third Zachatyevsky"; no. 44. In this case I will not give *FT* as a reference, as this poem was published with a two-line stanza missing and with minor inaccuracies.

† That is, the ending of the poem "In that house it was terrifying to live"; no. 36. Some lines at the start remained unfinished. I do not remember the previous ending of the poem.

‡ *BPL–A*, p. 289; no. 45.

Madonna – not her face, but her whole appearance, some humble and sorrowful grandeur.

She told me: "Vovochka's been playing with a kitten. He drags it by the tail, pulls its fur. It scratches him till he bleeds. But he is not angry. He came in today when Vladimir Georgievich was here: 'I'll show Volodya my figner.'"

The children left. Anna Andreevna took a letter from the chair and read it to me: a letter from an unknown woman reader.

"It is of the 'Dear Anna Akhmatova' sort," she explained, "although this one starts 'Dear Anna Andreevna'."

The letter was rapturous, provincial, a typical woman's letter. Enclosed were her own, bad, love poems. I tried to express my indignation at those female readers who imagine that Akhmatova writes for women, about some special kind of female sorrows, and that if she herself, the female reader, writes about how treacherous men are, she, the female reader, will become another Anna Akhmatova.

At that moment the doorbell rang; Anna Andreevna went to answer it and returned with her guests: Sreznevskaya had brought some gushing student-type along, who worked in the Public Library, who proceeded to settle down in the armchair and, without letting the hostess get a word in, started to explain how she adored Anna Andreevna and how happy she was to have the honour of making the acquaintance of such distinguished people as Sreznevskaya and Anna Andreevna. All in all it was amusing: as if the female reader, whose letter had just been read out, had suddenly materialized.

I soon left.

4 August 1940

Yesterday, before my return to the dacha, I paid a brief visit to Anna Andreevna to find out whether she was planning to go there with me next Friday.

Anna Andreevna was sad, anxious, pale. Her hair was swept up, which, in my opinion, doesn't suit her. When I entered she continued to tidy the room for a while: rolling up the bedding, sweeping the floor. After clearing the divan she settled in the corner, in her usual place.

As for Olgino, she couldn't say anything definite because she would probably have to go to Moscow again.

She had a call from Litfond saying that they would redecorate her room at their expense.

"That means that the new flat they promised me is a myth, and a second room in this one is also a myth. And my pension increase also turned out to be a myth – didn't you know? Yes, yes. But all this makes absolutely no difference to me, it doesn't upset me one bit. With me it's always like that, and only like that. That's my life, my biography. Who can renounce his own life?"[75]

She is very anxious. She may have to go to Moscow. And here they'll start doing up her room in her absence. Where should she put her stuff so that it won't be stolen? Vladimir Georgievich is leaving for the country with a heavy heart too, knowing that she'll be staying behind in town, in the oppressive heat ... But she can't stay with me, because she will probably have to go to Moscow ... And then there's the repair work ...

I didn't know what to advise her. That is, I did advise her, I made offers, but I didn't insist. If it hadn't been her I would have resolved all these questions in no time. As long as the trip to Moscow is not settled and it remains unclear when they'll start decorating she should go to the country. To get some fresh air and so that V.G. can go away without worrying. And when they do begin decorating, I can transfer her things to my flat in town and have locks put on Lyusha's and my doors ... I suggested all this to her, but she rejected it on the spot; and I didn't insist, because it was not someone else, but her, and behind all her reasons lies the overwhelming one, the reason of all reasons, which, it may well be, she won't even admit to herself, but which rules her emotional state and the climate of her soul.

I fell silent. Anna Andreevna was clearly glad that I hadn't tried to persuade her. She found an envelope under the armchair and handed it to me. Familiar handwriting; at first glance it looks so sprawling, wild, but a second look reveals its restraint, firmness and precision.

It was Boris Pasternak's letter about Anna Akhmatova's poems.

I settled down to read it. Two and a half large pages, writing on both sides.

Retelling Pasternak's letter, of course, is just as inconceivable as retelling his poetry. But I'll try to put down at least the basic points.

Congratulations on her victory, her triumph. Queues in Moscow for her book. We – Severyanin, Mayakovsky and I – owe you much more than I had previously thought. A new style in new poems, the birth of a new poet alongside the old one.

Then there followed a list of numbers referring to "clusters" and "constellations"; but at first I didn't understand what he meant, because it wasn't the lines of the poems that the numbers indicated, but the pages of the book.

"You read out the page numbers and I'll look for them," suggested Anna Andreevna, taking the book from the chair. "It'll be quicker."

To my amazement the poems mentioned by Boris Leonidovich were mainly from *Rosary* and *Anno Domini*, that is, old ones, which everyone, myself included, knows by heart.

I expressed my surprise aloud.

"I'll explain it all to you," said Anna Andreevna. "It's simply that he's reading my poetry for the first time. I assure you. When I started, he was involved in Tsentrifuga, and naturally, he was hostile to me and did not read my poetry. Now he's read it for the first time and, you see, he's made a discovery: he liked 'Her feather brushed the roof of the carriage...' very much. Dear, naïve, adorable Boris Leonidovich!"*

It was time for me to go. But how I didn't want to leave her alone, in the state of anxiety into which she would plunge the moment I had gone ... As she walked me to the door, she gave me a princely gift.

"I am reading the article you and Aleksandra Iosifovna wrote about commentators on the Russian classics.[49] It is a direct, honest, intelligent article. Nothing is there fortuitously: it is obvious that the authors thought and worked a great deal before writing it."

8 August 1940

Yesterday Anna Andreevna gave two most interesting monologues: first about Blok, then about her own poetry. And to finish off this feast – a new poem, completely new, different.

I called Anna Andreevna last night and, as always, heard: "Come as quickly as possible!" so I went. When she opened the door to me I had a shock at first, so strikingly distorted were her features, her cheeks had grown so grey, such terror – patient, steady, still, I would even say calm – gazed at me from her eyes.

But once we entered her room and she began to speak, sitting in her usual place, her voice sounded quite ordinary and tranquil, and I no longer saw the terror in her eyes.

Vladimir Georgievich has gone to the country.

The Punins' maid has come out of hospital.

---

* Boris Pasternak's letter of 28 July 1940 to Anna Akhmatova has now been published – see *Voprosy literatury*, 1972, no. 9. "Her feather brushed the roof of the carriage ..." is a line from the poem "The Ride" (*FT, Rosary*).

Vladimir Georgievich has persuaded Anna Andreevna not to give permission for the redecoration of her room until it's clear whether or not she'll have to go to Moscow.

After telling me this Anna Andreevna read me a new poem – about stillness in Paris – which was completed, but had a line missing, and which stunned me. I do not know whether it would be to the liking of the admirers of her feminine Muse, but I found it a work of genius. A moan from the depths of her soul, like the sigh "Lyova!" She senses the grief of the whole world.*

"Think what separations are taking place now!" Anna Andreevna said about France, Paris.

Whatever happens to her or near her, great or small, she always hears her country and the world in spite of her own problems.

Anna Andreevna put the kettle on. We had tea without sugar, with a stale roll.

Anna Andreevna said: "You know, today is the day of Blok's death. Nineteen years. A few days ago I reread 'Song of Fate'. Somehow I hadn't read it before. An unpleasant work, cold and tasteless. The sort of thing a 17-year-old would write, although he was already 28. It bears the stamp of bad times: the first decade of this century. The second decade was already quite a different period, a much better one ... But 'Song of Fate' is bentwood chairs, Art Nouveau, the northern modernist style. It is the spiritual contents of his flat, once more the familiar story of his relationship with Lyubov Dmitrievna and Volokhova. It's amazing that this was written in the same year as the magnificent 'Italian Poems'."

Then she suddenly mentioned an age-old article by Shaginyan about *Anno Domini*, which had appeared in *Zhizn iskusstva*.† She took a newspaper from the armchair and handed it to me.

"Read it. I'd be interested to know what you think," she said.

I read it.

As always with Shaginyan, valuable observations are jumbled with utter nonsense. Apparently there is mannerism, affectation – which for some reason is characteristic of classical lyric verse – and then there is style. Akhmatova still shows much mannerism, by which the author of the article for some reason means repetition of imagery; for example in Anna Akhmatova's poems the image of the Muse and the garden is often repeated ... Then it is pointed out that Akhmatova's true path is

*   "When they come to bury an age" – *FT, Seventh Book*; no. 46.
†   20 May 1922.

Narodnost, although the term is not defined . . . This conjecture certainly contains some truth; but one should not understand national populism as narrowly as Shaginyan does: from the examples she gives ("Cradle Song" and others), it follows that she understands populism as mere closeness to folklore. Whereas Akhmatova's poetry as a whole is deeply populist in character – and by no means only where a *chastushka* or song shows through.*

I told her what I thought.

Anna Andreevna seemed to agree with me, but then added: "All these pretensions to excellence, all these references to Goethe, but in reality it's all nonsense! And the underlying premise is wrong. Why is the repetition of garden and Muse imagery in my poetry mannerism? On the contrary, in order to get to the heart of it, one should study the clusters of constantly recurring imagery in a poet's work – it is there that the author's personality and the spirit of his poetry is hidden. Those of us who have been through the rigorous school of Pushkin studies know that 'a ridge of clouds' recurs in Pushkin's work dozens of times."

Then, I don't know why, the conversation turned to Kuzmin. I think it started because she asked me to get her a copy of *The Trout.*

"I only saw the book briefly, but it seemed to me to be a good book, and I'd like to read it through properly."

I promised to bring it. I said that it was only through this book that I came to understand and love Kuzmin.

"No, I am very fond of *Nets,*" Anna Andreevna interrupted. "And *The Guide* also contains a lovely poem about Tsarevich Dimitry. All in all, he is a genuine poet. But he was and is wrongly considered an Acmeist. I recently spent a whole evening trying to explain to Nikolay Ivanovich that Kuzmin belongs to late Symbolism and is not an Acmeist at all. He didn't see eye to eye with us on one single point; we don't even agree on the main thing – the question of stylization. We rejected it entirely, but Kuzmin is completely stylized."

I said that the lines:

> The wind from the lake is piercing,
> The road is winding uphill . . .
> The listing grey skiff
> Seems so simple, so touching,

sound just like Akhmatova.[76]

"That's not true," replied Anna Andreevna. "It was I who wrote like

* *BPL–A,* p. 179; no. 47.

him, not he like me. My poem 'The little boy who plays on the pipes ...'
is certainly written under his influence.* But that is accidental, basically
everything is different. We – Kolya for example – took everything seriously, but in Kuzmin's hands everything became a game ... He was
friends with Kolya only at the start, but then they quickly went their
separate ways. Kuzmin was a very nasty, malevolent and rancorous
person. Kolya wrote a review of *Autumn Lakes*, in which he called Kuzmin's poems 'boudoir poetry'. And he showed it to Kuzmin before publication. The latter asked him to change 'boudoir' to 'salon' and his whole
life he wouldn't forgive Kolya for this review ...[77] Kuzmin loved to say
bad things about everyone. He couldn't stand Blok, because he envied
him. Once Lourié[†] was playing his composition to Blok's words in front
of Kuzmin. Kuzmin knew perfectly whose words they were, but deliber-
ately asked: 'Is that Golenishchev-Kutuzov?' That's the kind of thing he
liked to say about everyone. He left a diary, which he sold to Bonch,
but Olenka, who was friends with Kuzmin, told me that it is something
monstrous. Future generations will get something like Vigel's diary. He
loved no one, was indifferent to everyone, except his latest boy. There
was a real cult of gossip in his salon. This salon had the most pernicious
influence on young people: they took it as the height of intellect and art,
but in reality it was the perversion of intellect, because everything was
considered a game, everything was mocked or jeered at ... No, Mikhail
Alekseevich didn't have an ounce of kindness in him. My Olenka used
to fall in love very often. Once she fell in love with a young composer
and brought his works to show Kuzmin. Kuzmin knew perfectly well of
her love, but chose to mock the young composer's efforts mercilessly.
Tell me, why did he have to do that? He could have said something
vague, something human, like 'It is alien to me ... my interests lie
elsewhere,' but he would never miss an opportunity to upset a person.
He couldn't stand me. Anna Dmitrievna[‡] reigned in his salon.[78] And I
can still recognize people from Kuzmin's salon unerringly – one phrase
is all I need."

From the chair she took a copy of *Literaturny sovremennik*, in which
her "Cleopatra" had been published, and offered to read me some poems
from it. "They are all on a rather high level," she said, putting her glasses
on. "You tell me when you get bored with listening ... Simonov is
good."

* *FT, Evening*; no. 48.
† For more about A. S. Lourié see note 84.
‡ Radlova.

After Simonov she read Braun, who, contrary to my expectations, was not too bad.[79] After Braun, Shefner; I could not listen to it all the way through without laughing.

One poem begins like this:

> I do not dream of nights with you,
> I'd only like a photo taken with you,

Maybe it's not as bad as all that, but I couldn't help laughing, so Anna Andreevna put the journal down. As an excuse I explained: "Those 'nots' are very treacherous. When you read: 'I did not roam with a bludgeon in the dense forest' – then you imagine a forest and a robber with a bludgeon, and when you read: 'The drum did not beat before the restless regiment' – then you hear the beat of the drum.

> I do not dream of nights with you,
> I'd only like a photo taken with you,

there the "not" makes the poem semi-obscene, whereas the rhyming pun *snyatsya* [dream] – *snyat'sya* [to be photographed] makes it semi-comical."

Anna Andreevna cheered up for a minute . . .

"It would have been better if he had just dreamt of them," she said, laughing, "it might have been more modest."

"And how must the young lady to whom he presented this poem have felt!" I said.

"Oh, come on, L.K.! There was no young lady! Do you think one could really present such a poem to a real woman? Just imagine: an acquaintance comes to you and presents you with a scroll containing a poem like that. You would throw him down the stairs at once, regardless of the word 'not' . . . No, no, he invented all this."*

The cheerful moment passed. Anna Andreevna became sad and weary once more.

She told me the story of Annensky's death: Bryusov had rejected his poems for *Vesy*, but Makovsky had decided to publish them in issue no. 1 of *Apollon*; he praised these poems highly and generally promoted Annensky as a counterweight to the Symbolists. Annensky didn't understand this whole game, but was happy . . . And then Max and Vasilieva

---

* V. Shefner's poem actually begins like this:

> Oh, I don't even dream of nights with you,
> I'd only like a photo taken with you,

A.A. subsequently changed her attitude to Shefner: she spoke of his poetry with interest and praise. (See *Journals*, vol. 2.)

invented Cherubina de Gabriak; she started writing Makovsky perfumed letters, making herself out to be Spanish and so on. Then Makovsky went and published Cherubina in no. 1 instead of Annensky . . .

"Annensky was stunned and dejected," Anna Andreevna recounted. "Later on I saw his letter to Makovsky; it contained the line: 'Better not to think about it.' And one of his terrifying poems about anguish is dated the very same month . . . And a few days later he fell and died at Tsarskoe Selo railway station . . .[80] In that respect I am fortunate: I've been praised a great deal and criticized a great deal in my life, but it never seriously got to me. I never concerned myself with numerical order – whether first or third, I couldn't care less. Only once did I really get upset; that was when Osip called me 'a stylite on a pillar of parquet'. But that was because it was Osip, only because it was Osip . . ."

13 August 1940

Yesterday morning I rang Anna Andreevna and asked when it would be most convenient for me to come round. She replied: "As soon as possible would be most convenient."

I went. This time she didn't say anything of a historical-literary nature to me. She was sad, ill. Her heart was troubling her. She often lapsed into complete silence and once, during a long silence, I heard a whisper, I think it was a line of poetry. I asked her to recite to me – it was impossible to find a topic of conversation and I only wanted to hear some poetry. She recited "August, 1940", already complete, including the missing line; then "A Contemporary"*; then a short, incomplete one, "Were I a Painter",† reminiscent of Kuzmin's "Alexandrine Songs".

"Perhaps I will make something of it," said Anna Andreevna pensively. "For now, only the lower banks are right; the rest is only there by chance."

17 August 1940

In the morning I rushed to the post office and the baker's. I was carrying a loaf of bread in one hand; in the other, in my clenched fist, some stamps.

---

* "August 1940" is the poem "When they come to bury an age"; no. 46. "A Contemporary" – no. 49; on first publication of this poem in *Literaturnaya gazeta* in October 1960, A.A. was forced by the publishers to change the title (it was explained to her that "A Contemporary" is not her but *our* contemporary). Then she called the poem "A Shade", and the new title stuck; *FT, Seventh Book*.

† ?

Suddenly someone called out to me so unexpectedly that I dropped the stamps.

"Where are you off to now?"

I looked round – it was Vladimir Georgievich.

"I'm going home."

"Let me come with you, please!"

He picked up my stamps and we set off. We climbed the stairs in silence. We kept silent while I unlocked the door.

He came back from the country yesterday. He has been to Anna Andreevna's and believes she is on the verge of insanity. The hair.* He again complained of the falseness of her premises and the iron logic of her conclusions. He asked me to be sure to go and see her, not to contradict her, but to try to influence her. Then he suddenly started to cry the most genuine tears. Embarrassed, I went to the kitchen to put the kettle on. When I came back he was no longer crying, but one large tear remained half-way down his cheek.

I poured him some tea. He took a sip and sobbed.

I asked: "What hurts you the most? Her condition? Her anger?"

"No," he replied. "I myself. I understand that right now, at this moment I must be with her, totally with her, only with her. But, to be honest, without mincing words, I can only go to her by committing a transgression. Believe me, these are not just words. All right, suppose I take that step, suppose I go. But if I did, then she wouldn't want me anymore."

And again about her: about her philosophy of poverty, about her inaptitude for domesticity, about the fact that she won't do anything, that she is not trying to combat her neurosis.

"Couldn't it be," I asked, "that we simply lack the imagination to understand that she is right? Maybe it's not her neurosis, but our thick skin?"

He shook his head.

In the evening I rang Anna Andreevna and went to see her, buying all sorts of food and a bunch of lilacs on the way.

Anna Andreevna was gloomy and distracted. Her face was sallow, her eyes animated, shining. She complained that Tanya was beating Valya hard, in a frenzy and in hysterics.

---

* Having the feeling that she was being watched, A.A. placed a hair in the notebook containing her poems, and it disappeared. She was convinced that during her absence her place had been searched.

"I can't bear to hear it. I can't take it anymore. Yesterday I went up to their door and started pounding it with my fists."

The phone rang. Anna Andreevna went to answer it and returned white as a sheet.

"Just think, what a call! That's them. It was definitely them. A female voice: 'I'm speaking to you in the name of your admirers. We thank you for your poems, especially for *one*.' I said: 'Thank you' and hung up. I have no doubt..."*

I tried to say that some doubt was still possible, but Anna Andreevna wouldn't let me finish: "Excuse me, please!" she shouted, unrestrained. "I know how admirers talk. I have the right to judge. I assure you. It is not like that at all."

Over tea she continued: "You understand, she spoke to me in a cold voice, as if she were reprimanding me: 'You did not return my ten roubles.'"

Once again I tried to say that it is we who took the "one" poem to refer to "And the stone word fell...", but it may well be she had liked "The Tale of the Black Ring" or something else. But my words brought forth only fury.

"V.G. said to our mutual acquaintance about me: 'Madame is cracking up.' Wouldn't it be right to assume that it is not me who is cracking up, but that those who can't confront the very simplest facts are insane..."

She began to tell me in a whisper about the hair, which, it turns out, hadn't disappeared from the page, but had moved further to the right, while she was out at lunch and then I understood at once why V.G. had cried. I had never seen her more agitated, anxious, lost and inaccessible to reason.

19 August 1940

Last night I visited Anna Andreevna again.

She was calmer than on the previous day, her hair more neatly combed, she wasn't so agitated or irritable.

A letter from K., which touched her deeply.†

"When she was young K. was as beautiful as a houri," Anna

---

*   A.A. suspected that the "admirer" had in mind the poem "And the stone word fell" from "Requiem". It was published in the journal *Zvezda* (1940, no. 3–4) and in her just published collection *FSB*. (The title "The Sentence", of course, was omitted from the manuscript submitted to the publishers. Both in the journal and in the book); no. 3.

†   K. –?

Andreevna said. "She was the most beautiful woman I have ever seen."

Then I brought up the subject of Moscow, having already prepared arguments in favour of the trip on my way there. I hid the main argument: maybe the trip would be fruitless, but at least, even if only briefly, Anna Andreevna would be out of this room. Anna Andreevna disagreed with me on every point and proved to me with iron logic that there was no need to go, but after all that, she ended with a request to drop into Litfond to book a ticket. I was jubilant.

And then a discussion began, which it will be very hard for me to reproduce – actually it wasn't a discussion, but a monologue by her. I saw that she was in the mood for reminiscing, and I tried not to interrupt her, only sometimes throwing in questions.

Oh yes, before her monologue she recited something new to me:

The neighbour from pity might go two blocks*

What a noble spirit dwells within her! With what power she turns into pure gold the broken fragments which life throws her way! Indeed "from what rubbish verses grow, knowing no shame". There is Tanya, beating Valya, and helpless V.G., but in the poems it is no longer a cesspit of a communal flat, but a solemn and touching funeral hour.

And then, throwing her hands behind her head, sitting straight and majestic in one corner of the tattered divan, looking very beautiful, she said: "I'm reading Vyacheslav's *Following the Stars*. What articles! What insight, what revelations. It's a vital book. He understood everything and anticipated it all. But the strange thing is: in spite of such profound understanding, he himself wrote bad poetry. He was, of course, a poet, an outstanding poet, but his poems were often bad. No, no, there is no contradiction here; one can be a remarkable poet, but write bad poems. You read his articles and you think: A person who understands poetry *so well* must write extraordinary poems. And in fact the same profundity

---

*   In contrast to the text published in *BPL–A* on p. 290, the version I remembered went as
     follows:
              A neighbour from pity might go two blocks,
              The old women, as is their wont, to the prison gates,
              But he, whose hand I used to hold,
              Would go with me to the pit itself.
              And would stand over it, alone in the world,
              Above the black, crumbly native soil,
              And would call . . . But no longer would my voice
              Reply to him, as once it did.

     Now this poem is published correctly. See *My Voice*, p. 265.

of understanding, the same subtlety and charm of the image is there in his poetry, but – but the rhythm is listless, Balmontesque. Of course some of his poems are also beautiful, but these are rare."

She reached over to the chair, took Vyacheslav Ivanov's book and read me two poems. I cannot remember which ones: on the way home, I realized that I had forgotten them instantly and completely, although while Anna Andreevna had been reading them I had liked them. I think one of them was something to do with a funeral, the other with an icon lamp and a moth.

Then, putting down the Ivanov, she got a copy of *To the Blue Star* and recited a poem about a forest – "At that time I was tormented by a woman" – austere, pure and powerful.[81]

After a pause, she said: "Right now I have the opportunity to see how memoirs are created. When I was at the Gymnasium in Tsarskoe, two years above me there was a young girl. I remember she was swarthy and slender and in winter used to wear a muff. That's all I remember about her. Whereas she now dictates memoirs about me to some club at the Youth Theatre. What can she remember? I was 15, the most unremarkable, quiet, ordinary schoolgirl."

"Fifteen isn't that young," I said.

"Come on now, please, don't go imagining it was my Lycée period."

Pausing and lighting a cigarette, she continued: "That's probably what happened to Lermontov too. He had a very short life. Nobody noticed him. Nobody glimpsed his life, nobody understood what kind of person he was. And then everyone rushed to write their memoirs. Those people were nearly 60. They couldn't remember a thing and copied each other ... That's exactly why working with Lermontov's biography is so boring. The late Shchyogolev suggested that we make a montage of memoirs on Lermontov together, rather like Veresaev's. I started and immediately realized: it's very dull."

I said that in my childhood and youth I hadn't understood Lermontov at all and had only come to like him about five years ago; and that as a child I had loved Zhukovsky very much.

"Yes, I'm rereading *Undine* right now," responded Anna Andreevna. "How lovely it is, simply delightful. In Zhukovsky's poems, in all of them, there is such a remarkable, unusual, special *sound* ... It is sometimes hard to find a way into Lermontov because there is a great deal of graphomania there. Much of his lyrical work lacks definite form, definite content; and one flows into the other without sufficient justification." She smiled at her own words. "Then towards the end came a whole string of masterpieces."

"You know what I want to tell you," she began anew, "I can't stand it when today's 50-year-old ladies claim that in their time young people were better than nowadays. Don't you believe them. It's not true. In our youth, young people neither liked nor understood poetry. There was no way of getting through to them. Poetry had been forgotten and was no longer loved. Because our fathers and mothers, influenced by Pisarevism, considered it utter rubbish, not useful for anything; or, at worst, they were content with Rozengeym. I remember very well how I took *Poems on the Beautiful Lady* to school and the pupil who was top of the class said to me: 'Gorenko, how can you read this nonsense all the way through!' A chubby, blond, little girl, with a little white collar and a huge bow in her hair – her whole future mapped out ... There was no way of getting through to her. And that's what all of them were like."

I said that perhaps all the girls who went to that school came from the same background.

"Not at all. We had rich girls, who were served breakfast at midday on silver trays brought by a lackey from home, and we had poor ones, daughters of tailors, or orphans. But neither one lot nor the other liked or knew any poetry ... Just to think that Tyutchev's work spanned almost half a century, but their mothers and fathers missed it ... No, the Modernists did a great thing for Russia. This should not be forgotten. They handed back the country in a completely different shape from that in which they'd received it. They taught people to love poetry once again, even the technical standard of book publishing went up."

I asked whether she thought that many people in our country love and understand poetry now.

"Yes, undoubtedly. In fact, I don't know any other country where people love poetry more than in ours, and where there is a greater need for it than here. While I was in hospital, the attendant once asked me – not even an attendant, a cleaning lady: 'They say, citizen, that you write poems ... Could you write me a little verse, I'll send it to my village ...' It turned out that she ends each of her letters with a poem and that the person who writes back from her village does the same. Can you imagine!"

It was already late, around midnight; I wanted to go, but she insisted that I stay. We started talking about specifically women's poetry. I said I didn't like it.

"Yes, there is something unpleasant about it ..." Anna Andreevna reached for some book on the armchair and showed me some poems by Shaginyan – bad ones and, on top of that, somehow unchaste.

"Shameless," I said.

"But, you see, a poet ought to be shameless," Anna Andreevna slowly pronounced. She held her hand in typical Akhmatova fashion: thumb under her chin, three fingers – holding a cigarette – extended along her cheek, little finger sticking out. (And just then I was struck once again by how inaccurately portrait painters have depicted her hand: in reality, she does not have long bony fingers, her palm is childlike and her fingers are slender, but small.) "A poet ought to be shameless. But, somehow differently, not the way she is."

Then, with no transition, she began talking about Blok and Lyubov Dmitrievna.

"What a terrible life they had! That was made clear by the *Diary*, and even before that it was apparent. Real bedlam, there is no other word for it. He has one affair after another. She keeps packing her cases all the time and going off somewhere with her latest young man. He sits alone in the flat, angry, missing her. He writes in his *Diary*: 'Lyuba! Lyuba!' She returns – he is happy – but by that time he's having an affair with Delmas. And so it went on. Why didn't they divorce? Perhaps she would have found ordinary female happiness ... No, I am generally and always in favour of divorce," she concluded meaningfully.

The coincidence of our views made my mouth drop open and I told her about my perpetual arguments with Tusya, who has been explaining, in a very complicated, clever, interesting and yet, for me, unconvincing way, why one can and should "preserve the family" regardless of another love.

"No, no, I am always for divorce," repeated Anna Andreevna. "It is very difficult to stay together once it is over. What you get is bedlam, like we have in the flat" – and she tapped lightly on Nikolay Nikolaevich's wall.

I asked whether Lyubov Dmitrievna had been beautiful.

"Come on, L.K., with a back like that! Not only was she not beautiful, she was hideous! I met her when she was 30. That woman's main feature was her back – immensely broad, round-shouldered. And her bass voice. And thick, large arms and legs. Inwardly, too, she was hideous and malevolent, as if something had broken her ... But he, always, all his life, saw in her the girl with whom he'd fallen in love ... And he loved her ... Incidentally, they say there are some terrible things in the *Diary* about her – Orlov didn't publish them, but people who've read the manuscript told me ... I saw Delmas at the very height of their affair; she appeared at the Army and Navy House, together with me. Decent, kind, but not clever. She had freckles, red hair, an unattractive, flat face, but beautiful shoulders and she was plump ... (Apparently he liked his women to be well covered.) Valentina Andreevna* was enchanting, I was very friendly with her, she was not exactly beautiful, but charming ... Volokhova had beautiful black eyes ... Blok's love letters are very noble; Valentina Andreevna showed me one: 'All that remains of my youth – is yours ...'"[82]

I commented on how many of Blok's love poems are terrifying in their lack of love – if by love one understands kindness, tenderness; the very root of the word, the very essence of it, is missing from his feeling. "It is tempting for me to insult you ..." – there is no love in this temptation.

"Yes, perhaps," agreed Anna Andreevna. "Do you remember: 'Again you called me inhuman'?[83] And this absence of love which you speak of is most apparent of all in 'The Snow Mask' ... There you have only the rattling of bones ...[84] I believe Blok generally treated women badly, disrespectfully. I never had even a trace of an affair with Blok" (I was surprised, I had always thought that "my celebrated contemporary"[†] referred to him), "but by chance I know a bit about his affairs ... Two women at different times told me about their relationships with him – essentially, it was the same story ... Both were young and beautiful ... One visited him late, in his empty flat ... the other at The Stray Dog ... Both were the *femme fatale* type ... But he pushed them away at the last moment: 'My God ... It's dawn already ... farewell ... farewell ...'"

"Well these stories show them, rather than him, in a bad light," I said.

"Yes, of course ... But through constant encounters with that type of lady, he began to think with disrespect of all women."

I started expounding my favourite theory on the necessity of divorce. Anna Andreevna agreed, with certain reservations.

"Sometimes there are chance infidelities and then everything rights itself again, but that is rare ... And, sometimes, people do not divorce because of children ... But I think that for the children, their parents' divorce more often benefits than harms them. But such an accumulation

---

* Shchyogoleva.
† A line from the poem "My imagination, obedient to me" – *FT, Rosary*; no. 50.

of wives" – once again, she tapped Nikolay Nikolaevich's wall lightly – "is utter nonsense."

I told her about a woman, a dressmaker, whose husband can't leave her because she attempts suicide the moment he reaches for his suitcase.

"That's fairly common," Anna Andreevna commented contemptuously. "And believe me, now he won't ever get rid of her. I know such women: she throws herself into a pond, walks around all wet, dries off, then throws herself in again . . . That's for life, nothing can be done . . ."

She spoke impassively and drily but I immediately recalled Vladimir Georgievich's recent words about the transgression which he does not have the strength to commit.

"Nikolay Stepanovich and I lived together for seven years. We were friends and spiritually owed each other a great deal. But I told him that we had to separate. He did not object at all, but I could see that he was deeply hurt. That poem I read to you about the forest was about me. At the time he had just returned from Paris, after his unrequited love for the Blue Star. He was full of her – yet my wish for a separation stung him all the same . . . We went to Bezhetsk together to see Lyova who was staying at his grandmother's. We were sitting on the divan and Lyovushka was playing between us. Kolya said: 'And what did you start this for?' That was all . . . You must admit, you can't build anything on that," she added sadly, "that's not enough, is it?" And, after a pause: "I believe we were engaged for too long. I was in Sebastopol, he was in Paris. When we got married in 1910, he had already lost his passion . . ."

I did not interrupt, I was silent and, stubbing out her cigarette, she started to speak again: "Strange that I lived with Nikolay Nikolaevich for so long after it had ended, isn't it? But I was so depressed that I didn't have the strength to leave. I was very low, because I hadn't written any poetry for 13 years, just think: 13 years!* I tried to leave him in 1930. Sr.† promised to get me a room. But Nikolay Nikolaevich went to see him and said that for him, my leaving was a matter of life and death . . . Sr. believed him, grew scared and didn't get me a room. I stayed.

---

* This statement can be explained by her vehemence: there were no such periods in her life when A.A. didn't write any poetry at all. True, some years she wrote less than usual. During her marriage to Punin, Akhmatova wrote approximately 30 poems, including: "And you'll forgive me all", "Here Pushkin's banishment began", "If the terror of moonlight dances", "That city, loved by me from childhood", "Wild honey smells of freedom", "The Last Toast", "They led you away at daybreak", "Some gaze into affectionate eyes"; the poem "Russian Trianon" and others had also been started and almost completed. For more about this see vol. 2 of my *Journals*.
† Vyacheslav Vyacheslavovich Sreznevsky? Valeriya Sergeevna's husband?

You can't imagine how rude he could be ... during these ... flirtations of his. He had to keep showing how bored he was with you the whole time. He would sit playing patience and would keep repeating each minute: 'God, how boring ... Oh, what boredom ...' Meaning: feel how his soul is trying to fly elsewhere ... I spent the whole year going over and over all this in my mind and he didn't notice a thing ... And you know how it all happened, how I left? I said to Anna Evgenevna in front of him: 'Let's exchange rooms.' This suited her very well, and we immediately started moving our things. Nikolay Nikolaevich said nothing; then, when we were alone for a minute, he uttered: 'You could have stayed with me for just one more year.'"

She laughed and so did I. She laughed lightly and good-naturedly. As if she hadn't been talking about him, about herself.

"Then he quoted: 'He shall not forget the King's daughter' – and left the room. And that was it. You must admit, nothing can be built on that either ... Since then I haven't thought of him even once. When we meet, we talk about newspapers, about the weather, about matches, but, as for *him*, I haven't thought about him even once."*

It was already two. We agreed that tomorrow I'd ask for a ticket for her at Litfond and then ring her. I left, happy that at last, for a while, I had managed to distract her from her greatest anguish.

22 August 1940

On the 20th, I went to Litfond and ordered a ticket for Anna Andreevna for the 24th. I phoned her from there and told her about it, and then left for the dacha. Today I brought her my coat from the dacha, because she has nothing to wear for the trip. She thanked me, but, in her own words, she has decided to decline the ticket: it would be pointless to go. I left her the coat and went.

---

* During the war, in Tashkent, where she'd been evacuated, in spring 1942 A.A. received a long letter of repentance from N. N. Punin in Samarkand (where he'd been evacuated with the Academy of Arts). She read it to me on 22 April 1942, saying that she would reply with forgiveness.

    N. N. Punin's letter to Akhmatova has now been published. See *Akhmatova. Ardis*, p. 78, and also the magazine *Nashe nasledie* (1988, no. 4, p. 108).

    Judging by one of the "Northern Elegies" ("So here it is – that autumn landscape"), in Lermontov-style, Nikolay Nikolaevich used to call Anna Andreevna: "the sea princess". (She was an exceptional swimmer, see pp. 30 and 171–2). That's why at their moment of separation, on parting, he recited the last line of Lermontov's poem "The Sea Princess": "He shall not forget the King's daughter".

25 August 1940

On my return from the dacha, I phoned Anna Andreevna. It turned out she had gone to Moscow after all.

31 August 1940

This morning, I got a phone call: "Akhmatova speaking. Lydia Korneevna, I am back already and desperate to return your coat."

I set off in a torrential downpour.

She was lying down – lying down again! Again the heavy blanket without a sheet, her hair spread across the pillow, and then her Chinese dressing gown – splendid, but torn along the seam . . .

Before telling me about her troubles, Anna Andreevna told me that she had visited my relatives in Peredelkino, that K.I. had read her his translations of Whitman.

"They are magnificent," Anna Andreevna said.

She had had great luck, according to her, on her journey there: she had ended up in the same compartment as Fedin's wife, who gave her a lift to Peredelkino straight away. She was surprised and, of course, glad that Fadeev received her most cordially and immediately did all he could to help. (The last days before her departure she had kept saying: "Fadeev won't even let me into his sight.") To her surprise she learnt that Fadeev and Pasternak had entered her book for the Stalin Prize.

"I stayed at the dacha for two days.* When I had to go to Moscow, K.I. arranged for me to get a lift with Viktor Fink. There we were: Fink, the driver, a young woman, an editor from Detizdat, who was visiting K.I. on some editorial business, and I. And all the way to Moscow she told me how a few years ago she'd stolen my books from some acquaintances of hers and how she'd recently spent six hours queuing for my book and everyone had been given a number. I know that story by heart already, I have heard it from so many lips that it feels as if it were branded on me.

"K.I. was telling me about Lyubov Dmitrievna's *Diary*. He says it's such muck that you have to wear galoshes. And there I was feeling sorry for her, I thought it was a diary from her youth. Not at all, it contains recent recollections . . . Just think, she writes: 'I cast aside the blanket

---

* Whose? One can't tell from the entry. But according to M. S. Petrovykh it was at Pasternak's.

and he admired my voluptuous body.' My God, how awful! And she is so petty, so nasty about Blok, all his illnesses are listed."

I asked how Boris Leonidovich was.

"Not too good. Worse than when I went to Moscow last time. Then he was euphoric over the success of *Hamlet*. But now he is gloomy. He says that he was almost ready to write some poems, but it didn't work out. 'First, Zina was preparing to go to the Crimea (the eldest boy had something wrong with his lungs) ... then the cucumbers ripened ... barrels had to be found ... barrels had to be steamed ...' I swear, that's what he said: barrels steamed."

I asked if he was still angry with K.I.

"Yes, I think he's still angry. All because of *Hamlet*, of course. I've told you before: no writer is free of the occupational disease. Including him. I am the only one who is indifferent to what people think of my poetry. Nikolay Ivanovich had this to say about my book: 'Oh, what kind of book is that?! And why do you need it?! It's good for nothing!'" She laughed. "But I didn't love him any the less for it."

A photograph of her was lying on the table, a new one, one I hadn't seen before. From the latest Moscow batch. Superb. A tormented face with lowered eyes.

Anna Andreevna also liked it.

"Here everything is already present, it says it all," she repeated a few times, "whereas others force me to put on a cheerful face – a kind of mask ..."

When I got up she suddenly said: "I'm not sure how to let Vladimir Georgievich know that I'm back. Maybe you would be so good as to ring him ..."

And in response to my promise she added: "I don't phone there myself."

I asked her if her journey back had been good.

"Delightful. Well, it goes without saying that I fell asleep two hours after the others and woke up two hours earlier, but I did sleep, all the same. Usually, I have a nonstop white night on trains."

She was delighted with the toys I'd brought from Lyusha for the children. She studied them earnestly and at length, working out how to wind the frog up and make it jump on the floor, wondering aloud what was for whom: what is for Malayka,* what is for Vova and what is for Valya.

* Malayka is a childish nickname for Anya, Nikolay Nikolaevich's granddaughter, daughter of Irina Nikolaevna Punin.

5 September 1940

I behaved so boorishly. Anna Andreevna called me on the 2nd and asked me to come over, but I had already made arrangements with Tatyana Aleksandrovna and so I promised Anna Andreevna that I'd come on the 3rd.[85] But on the 3rd I didn't go either. Tanechka had a fever and I got stuck at the dacha. Today, she rang again and caught me in town. And we made arrangements for this evening.

She greeted me rather listlessly, pale, tired, with Vovochka in her arms. His parents had gone to the cinema; he was wet, she couldn't find another pair of shorts. According to her, her thyroid condition had worsened and her foot was hurting ... Valya came, found some shorts and carried Vova away. She livened up a bit.

"Recently, an admirer visited me. You should have seen her! A model admirer, one could say. A delightful, pretty, 17-year-old girl, from some literary circle in Kiev. The things she said! My God, the things she said!"

"Surely not more stupid than the one from the Public Library?" I asked.

"And how! The other one seems like Immanuel Kant by comparison. She asked me two stunning questions. The first was: 'You probably led a very interesting life ... in your youth?' I replied that I can't judge my own life. The second question was this: 'Is it true that there are two statuettes of you and both are in Paris, as you are an Acmeist?' What gibberish! They were told something about Acmeism there and she got all confused."

"Did she recite any poems? Any good?"

"She did. No good. A 17-year-old's."

I asked Anna Andreevna whether she had liked *The Trout.*

"Everything in it is derived from German Expressionism. We didn't know it, and that's why it sounds stunningly new to us. But, really – it's all from there. However strange it may seem, much of the book sounds official, like captions under pictures ... I liked 'Lazarus' and certain poems, for instance, the one which you also like so much: 'The ship is flying over the joyful sea'. The ending is unpleasant though – about two-year-olds.* The salaciousness leaves one with a very heavy heart ... I'd like to have put ellipses in many places ... It's too exclu-

* A.A. means the lines:

> Soon people will turn into two-year-olds,
> The hobbyhorse will gallop like clockwork ...

See "Panorama with Footnotes", "Footnote Three" (*The Trout Breaks through the Ice*).

sively for those with peculiar tastes: 'practising nincompoops'. Kuzmin has always been homosexual in his poetry, but here he has gone beyond all reasonable bounds. Previously, he could not have got away with this: Vyacheslav Ivanov would have turned up his nose ... But in the '20s there was no longer anybody to be wary of ... Maybe Villon would have managed to carry it off somehow, but Mikhail Alekseevich could not. It's most repulsive."

Then Anna Andreevna gave me some bad news: Tanya had warned her that as from next month she'd no longer prepare lunch for her.

Seeing my upset face, she said: "Perhaps the Punins will allow their domestic help to cook lunch for me."

Perhaps! Damn this flat!

10 September 1940

Late last night, when I was already going to bed, the phone rang suddenly: Vladimir Georgievich. In a distraught voice he said hurriedly: "Anna Andreevna begs you to come over. It is very, very important. Can you? Will you come? Oh, thank God!"

I went. It was around eleven o'clock. Rain; the wet, black asphalt was shining autumnally and cinematographically.

Anna Andreevna was in the armchair by the table, wearing a white shawl over her dressing gown, stern, tranquil, quiet and gloomy. I marvelled once again how a person could be so exquisite and so perfectly defined. As if ready to be cast in bronze, embossed on a medal, mounted on a pedestal. A statue of pensiveness, if she were pensive – of fury, if she were furious.

When I entered, anguish personified was sitting before me. But this soon changed.

"The other day, A. and his wife were here;* he is now Director of the House of Cinema. He offered to arrange a recital for me. You understand how attractive I find this offer, for all kinds of reasons. I said: I can't do it now, I'm ill, but I'll agree to do it at the end of October, but I myself will recite only in homeopathic doses. Chernyavsky will recite – have you heard him? He recites superbly! Only we'll have to make a selection of poems not in the feminine gender for him.[86] Then someone will sing, then I'll recite five or six things."

I asked if she usually had enough voice for readings.

* A.?

"When well listened to, everyone has enough voice," she replied.

I told her about B.'s* obsequious article.

"That's exactly why I stopped working on Pushkin ... Besides, I couldn't stand the backbiting among the Pushkinists. In the evening, you'd go to sleep safe, but in the morning you'd discover that during the night your hand or foot had been bitten off ... Even Tsyavlovsky banged his fist on the table at me. I was lucky when I worked on *The Golden Cockerel*: the book turned up in Pushkin's library. If not for that, they would never have believed me. Tsyavlovsky shouted at me, claiming it is a Russian tale, but in doing so only proved his ignorance, because the plot of every Russian tale has been well known for a long time, you can count them all, like beads on a string ... And there is no such plot amongst Russian folktales."†

The conversation turned to Dostoevsky.

I said that I love him very much, but rarely reread him: he's too heavy.

"But lately he seems almost idyllic to me," said Anna Andreevna. "When I was in Moscow just now I reread *A Raw Youth*. Oh, what a work! But all this is not frightening at all. It has nothing to do with reality. These are all aspects of his soul – and that's all. In reality, there never was or will be anything like it."

I said that I don't like Turgenev.

"Everything is shallow with him, people and events are shallow, he himself is shallow," said Anna Andreevna.

Then: "When I was at Korney Ivanovich's he was called away on some matter. He apologized and went for about 20 minutes, giving me Goncharov to read in the meantime. Do you remember Goncharov's story about how Turgenev robbed him? Of course, there is a lot of ranting in it, but when you read it, you understand that it is fundamentally true, after all."

After this, having told me very solemnly and meaningfully that Lozinsky was already translating Canto xx of the *Inferno*, she said: "You know, the original will of Beatrice's father has been preserved in Florence. From this will it is clear that she was not called Beatrice at all, but Bice. For ages scholars couldn't understand why Dante gave her a different name. But it turned out to be a chivalric custom of the Middle Ages to extol a lady under a veiled, invented name. For, if you used her real name, you might have got your face slapped with an iron gauntlet."

---

* ?
† The article by A.A. referred to here is "Pushkin's Last Tale" – see *OP*, p. 10.

I got up, but she said pleadingly: "I'm putting the kettle on now. You can't imagine how quickly it'll boil!"

She jumped up from the chair and put the plug into the socket with an extremely quick and deft movement.

"True, I only have one rusk to go with the tea, and even that is stale. Nobody treats their guests as badly as I do."

While we had tea she told me about Moscow again, in particular about Nikolay Ivanovich.

"He is currently in a new orbit ... Now he is shaven, smart and has even stopped fearing the Metro escalators, whereas before it was such a torment ... The lady in whose orbit he was before has now been excommunicated from his bed and board. It was my job to give her psychological first aid. I advised her to erect a mausoleum in her heart to deceased feelings and simply to step aside ... I know from my own experience that this is *the only way* to act in such cases. He is undoubtedly in a new orbit: he is even different towards me. He was very glad to see me, he was attentive, but quite, quite different from before. There is nothing to be surprised at – we live in different cities, we rarely see each other."

Nikolay Nikolaevich knocked and entered. Scratching his head, he asked: "Anya, do you happen to have 15 roubles?"

"I have 50."

"Fine, give me 50. I tried to sell some books, but it didn't work out."

"Nowadays everybody tries to sell books but it never works out ... Olga came today, took 50 roubles: she had tried to sell some books but it hadn't worked out ...* Here, please, take it."

Nikolay Nikolaevich took it, thanked her, scratched his head and left.

Anna Andreevna told me she was planning to buy her book back from Tanya for 100 roubles.

"What? You mean she won't give it back to you just like that? After all, she got it from you for nothing."

"She didn't get it, she simply came into the room and took it herself, when there was a pile of books on the chair. And now she says that perhaps she would let me have it back for 100 roubles."

What a flat!

* *Olga:* Olga Fyodorovna Berggolts. For more about her see *Journals*, vol. 2.

17 September 1940

Last night I rang Anna Andreevna and asked permission to come over. On the way I bought some cakes. Lotta was with her. She was trying to convince Anna Andreevna at length that she was scared senseless by her. But judging by her familiarity and witticisms you couldn't tell.

She soon left.

Anna Andreevna told me: "He covered his face with his hands." And about Racine: "Racine died because the King did not respond to his bow. He was in favour, but then someone pushed him aside. In order to ascertain his status he went to Mass and stood in his appointed place. He waited for the King to appear. He bowed to him, but the latter did not respond. After that, Racine went home, went to bed and, towards evening, passed away."*

The whole of last night she had been reading Dante, comparing it to the literal French translation.

"That is, it's not a literal rendering; contemporaries probably took it to be a magnificent translation. I learnt a lot that I previously had no idea about. For example: as everyone knows, Hugo was filled with indignation at Dante calling his poem 'Divine'. But it turns out that he never called it that. Simply a *Comedy*, and it was others who called it 'Divine' ... Italians think that all Italian poetry derives from the *Comedy*, which is true, of course. But the interesting thing is this: with Dante everything was domestic, almost familial. But with Petrarch, with Tasso everything became general, abstract, lost its domesticity. Our Mayakovsky was of the same ilk – domestic, familial."

We sat in semidarkness, and from the other side of the wall a drunken voice could constantly be heard. Gradually, I realized that this drunken voice was tutoring, was teaching a child to write. It was Zhenya[†] teaching Valya. An inhuman, dark voice ...

Anna Andreevna recited three poems by S.[‡] to me. I told her that it was very strange to hear her reciting somebody else's poems, that they acquired the intonation of her poetry.

"Yes, yes, I've been told that before. At the Poets' Guild they used to make me recite Nekrasov, for fun:

---

* Who covered his face with his hands and to whom something happened, similar to what happened to Racine, I do not recall.
† Smirnov, Valya and Vova's father.
‡ S.?

> Your captivating glances he
> [...]
> Will give up anything for flat springs ...

Nekrasov, naturally, recited quite differently. Everybody laughed a lot."

I liked S.'s poems: they were pure, Tyutchevesque. It turned out the author is over 40. I asked whether he'd been writing long: because people rarely start writing poetry at a mature age (prose – many do). In connection with this, we discussed Lermontov's extremely early development.

"As a boy, he wrote 'The Angel' and 'The Mermaid'," said Anna Andreevna, "'The mermaid was swimming down the blue river.' Just imagine! ... 'If I had had such a son, I would have cried...'"

She put the kettle on, unwrapped the cakes and continued: "My aunt said something of the sort to me once."

"Would she have cried for happiness?" I asked.

"No, for sorrow, of course. She said to me: 'If I were your mama I would cry nonstop.'"

"How did you manage to upset her so much?"

"I was about 13 at the time. I used to wear shoes on bare feet and a dress on my naked body – with a tear here, all down the thigh ..."

(I thought to myself that I've also often seen her in her 50s wearing a dressing gown with a tear all down the thigh.)

"... right down to the knee, and, to hide it, I used to hold my dress with my hand like this ... Of course, it wasn't very effective. And also I used to throw myself into the sea off anything – off a rock, off a boat, off a boulder, off a beam ... You know what reply I gave my aunt? I must admit I was awfully cheeky! I said: 'It is better for both of us that you are not my mama.'"

The conversation turned to Mandelstam. I recited a stanza:

> The child who has not slept his fill
> Will yet take offence from the saucer,
> But I have no one to sulk at,
> And wherever I go I'm alone ...

saying how much I love it, that in these lines there is something unusually precise.

"Yes, yes," replied Anna Andreevna, "delightful lines – and so like him! For he was so strange: he couldn't touch a cat, or a dog, or a fish ... But loved children. And wherever he was living, he would always talk about some neighbour's baby..."

We sat down to drink tea. Over tea Anna Andreevna started telling me that Lotta had tried to convince her that everyone is afraid of her, of Anna Andreevna.

"I can't understand what causes it. But I'm often told this. Why? I never say anything unpleasant to anyone. Sologub, for example, he liked and knew how to say unpleasant things, and that's why he was feared. But I've never said anything to anyone. All the same, Lotta does swear that once, at the Writers' Club, when I walked through the billiard hall, everybody in it stopped playing out of fear. I think there's something offensive about that."

I asked about her domestic situation. Loathsome. Tanya had gone to Vyborg, and anyway she'd already refused to feed her. The Punins wouldn't let their domestic help look after her either. And the House of Writers canteen is closed.

"Soon they'll put me in hospital," said Anna Andreevna, "and then I'll eat three times a day."

Vladimir Georgievich arrived, totally exhausted. He sat down in the armchair, covered his face with his hands and started to complain. After five minutes I left.

18 September 1940

Last night Anna Andreevna rang and came round – it was late, about ten o'clock. Her face seemed irritated to me, angry. She wore a black silk dress and a silk shawl, beautiful, majestic. The conversation turned to Kseniya Grigorievna. Anna Andreevna spoke of her with fury, her face distorted by hatred.* Then she recited to me again the magnificent "A Contemporary" – a beauty of 1913. Then she enquired about my work. I complained that when I have just written something – be it poetry or prose – I am not at all able to judge its quality.

"Well, nobody is able to ... You are sailing with no rudder or sail ... Only later do you notice that everybody reacts similarly to the same lines, and then you yourself begin to understand. Take, for example, 'The Way of All the Earth'. Everyone, absolutely everyone, said the very

---

* Kseniya Grigorievna irritated Anna Andreevna and me no end with her reasoning about arrests. Her point of view can be expressed by two inappropriate but face-saving sayings, to which people clung fiercely in those days: "You can't make an omelette without breaking eggs" (meaning, if they are to get the guilty, they must sometimes also accidentally get the innocent) and "There is no smoke without fire" (meaning, people are not imprisoned for nothing). These sayings served to justify the Terror and therefore could not fail to enrage Anna Andreevna.

same thing about this poem: 'It's a magical work' and 'It's a new art'. Well, of course, except for Ks. Gr., who honestly admitted that she didn't understand a thing. But then she is not supposed to understand."

She stayed at my place until two. I set off to walk her home. It took ages for the yardkeeper to unlock the front entrance for us, and we gazed at the dark city through the glass. Occasional cars swam past soundlessly, like fish. And the trams clanged by: "gone astray". Then the yardkeeper unlocked it for us, we set off, and again she was afraid to cross Nevsky.

24 September 1940

Yesterday I realized that I would have a gap in my work at the House of Entertaining Science and would therefore be able to go up to Anna Andreevna's for an hour.* I phoned her from downstairs. "Of course, come up!" she said. However, when I arrived, it turned out that she had been invited out to lunch and it was already time to go. She asked me to accompany her, and I set off, hoping that I'd be back at the HES on time.

We came out onto the Fontanka. It was a warm, sunny, golden day – "Quite your 'autumn in spring'" said I. We walked towards the Neva. She brought up Kolya Davidenkov's wife, how she torments him, a real, contemporary Carmen or Manon Lescaut.

"But when she has three children by three different men, what then, will they wander from daddy to daddy like a horde of gypsies?" said Anna Andreevna. "And all, unlike Carmen, for an extra hundred roubles, believe me."

I said that such a woman, who loves no one and is mercenary, will always be loved.

"Not at all. She's still fresh, but this will pass. Kolya will leave her, and the next husband too. They say Kolya is already fed up with her. How many times in my life have I seen this happen."

We crossed Simeonevskaya Street, which was all dug up, and walked down Mokhovaya.

"Recently I had a visit from Valeriya Sergeevna again," said Anna Andreevna. "Can you imagine, she's a completely different person, new, I don't know her. A total change of personality. Even in little ways she is different. Once, in her youth, it was very hard to get her going. When

---

* At that time I would occasionally edit manuscripts at the House of Entertaining Science, which was in the former Sheremetev Palace; Akhmatova lived there too, at Fontanka no. 34, not in the main building, but in the annexe.

she was getting ready to go out she would change dresses three times, change her hairdo three times then stay home. Now when I renewed our acquaintance I must admit I was counting on that a bit: well, I thought, she'll come here twice during the winter, and that's it. But no! Now she is perfectly happy to go out! As much as you wish! Without any difficulty whatsoever! ... But this is only half the problem. She's changed spiritually. The other day she borrowed my Pasternak, to read it. And she returned it. She was terribly indignant: 'Vulgar ... talentless ... conceited ... convoluted ...' We could easily have read all this 20 years ago in *Novoe vremya*. 'He is promoting his friend Neygauz.' My God! Neygauz is a famous musician and has no need whatsoever for promotion. Everything about 'Ballad' incurred her wrath; she didn't have a clue that Podol is part of a town, she thought he was talking about the hem of a woman's skirt. And the cynicism infuriates her."

"Did you explain it to her?"

"Of course not ... I would like her to meet Kseniya Grigorievna at my place someday. Neither of them have any inkling how very alike they are."

"Did Valeriya Sergeevna used to be so like Kseniya Grigorievna?"

"Not a bit – I'm telling you, she underwent a total personality change."

We reached the Neva. It was slightly foamy, but still a light blue.

"This river always flows backwards. Always," said Anna Andreevna.

29 September 1940

Three evenings ago Kolya Davidenkov told me that in an article on literature in *Leningradskaya pravda* there was a very unfavourable comment about Anna Andreevna. I wanted to go and see her at once, but couldn't because I had flu. Yesterday morning, when I felt a little better, I rang her and went round. I found her still in bed. Valya was sitting next to her doing his homework. It turned out she knew nothing about the article. She took the news indifferently but still sent Valya to the Punins' for the newspaper. I read her the whole article. They came down on her not like a ton of bricks but, let's say, a couple of hundredweight ...* On the other hand, the phrases criticizing Z. upset her very much and she returned to the injustice of these several times during the conversation.†

---

* *Leningradskaya pravda*, 27 September 1940. The article "To Activate Creative Work among Writers" mentioned Anna Akhmatova's "decadent" and "dull" poems which had been included in the volume *FSB* through the fault of careless editors.

† I have confused something here. I can't tell whom I have hidden behind the letter "Z.".

Then she asked me to get a batch of letters from the chest of drawers and, putting on her glasses, read out a letter to me from some citizen of Novosibirsk, which had moved her deeply. And the letter, in spite of not being very cultured, really was a good one. It contained these words: "And for this, Comrade Akhmatova, I offer you my gratitude."

"Doesn't 'Comrade Akhmatova' sound very sweet here?" said Anna Andreevna. "Yesterday, I was at Pushkin House attending a Blok Committee meeting. There, in the break, a young man approached me and handed me a note containing a poem."

Anna Andreevna read this poem aloud to me, having warned me: "The rhythm has been lost in one line due to an excess of emotion."

I switched the kettle on and unwrapped the cakes. Anna Andreevna gave Valya two and told him to go home and give one to Vovochka.

While we were waiting for the kettle to boil, Anna Andreevna recited some poems to me. She recited one about dark souls, one about Shakespeare, then, apologizing for reciting something unfinished, one about hands and about Pavlovsk.*

I said about the first one: it has the same tonality as "The Way of All the Earth".

She was surprised: "But to me, it feels quite old, as if it is from *The White Flock* ... The only one which feels new to me is the third one."

She had already achieved the complete "mastery of form" whereby the constant, ancient dream of poets is manifestly realized:

> Oh, if only without words
> It were possible to express one's soul!

You listen and it seems as if there are no words, metres, rhythms, rhymes, but simply – simply! – the soul itself speaking, bypassing form, of its own accord, by a miracle.

All the time she was reading, from the next room Tanya could be heard, shouting: "You beast, you bastard, just you wait, you little bastard!"

That was Tanya teaching Valya to do his homework.

1 October 1940

This morning, tragicomedy with the bookbinder. Two weeks ago, when giving him Akhmatova's book, I asked him to be especially careful with

---

* A.A. recited "Thus dark souls take flight", no. 19; "To Londoners", no. 51 (*FT, Seventh Book*); "Sixteen-year-old hands" – subsequently became "Fifteen-year-old hands" and finally "My youthful hands", no. 27.

the inscription. He promised he would be. And today he handed me the book, very smartly bound, but with the inscription cut off – only the tails of some of the letters remained. I stamped my feet and yelled. "What are you getting so upset about, citizen?" he said phlegmatically. "Big deal, an inscription! It's not as if it's Lev Tolstoy." On parting, he joked, "If you like, I can inscribe it for you myself."

I decided to go to Anna Andreevna's and ask her to inscribe the book for me again. I dropped in with Lyushenka, on the way back from her English tutor's. We arrived at an inopportune moment. Anna Andreevna was in disarray, unkempt, her face was haggard. I could not refrain from telling her immediately about my mishap with the bookbinder. Without asking about her health, without finding out why she looked so bad.

She told me,* and I felt ashamed of myself.

All the same, she sat down to inscribe the book anew. The pen didn't work and Lyusha was sent to the Punins' for another one.

During the night, Anna Andreevna had had a heart attack.

She was trying to be pleasant to me and affectionate to Lyusha, but it didn't come easily to her.

She asked me to get her a copy of yesterday's *Literaturnaya gazeta*; evidently there had been an article about her.[87]

Lyusha and I said goodbye. Anna Andreevna saw us to the front door. When she noticed the light in the kitchen, she said sharply to the Punins' domestic help: "Put it out at once. This is a communal flat and I don't want to be sent to a labour camp because of you." It was the first time I had heard her speak to anybody in such a sharp and irritable tone.

At the door, bidding farewell to Lyusha and me: "Today is his birthday."

3 October 1940

Last night Anna Andreevna called to say she was coming over. Kolya Davidenkov was at my place, we were working on his manuscript. When we raised our heads it was 1 a.m.: Anna Andreevna hadn't come.

This morning I set off to her place to find out what had happened. A man was sealing the window in her room with putty. Anna Andreevna was lying on the divan under a thick blanket, sallow-faced – she looked somehow small, withered.

"Forgive me. Last night I set out to your place, reached Nevsky and

---

* Some bad news about Lyova.

turned back: I had seen a clock and it said twenty to twelve. And I had thought it was seven."

"Did you sleep today?"

"No."

I apologized for still not having been able to get her the newspaper.

On the chair next to Anna Andreevna was a volume of Bagritsky, part of the Poet's Library (small series) edition.

She asked me if I was familiar with Bagritsky's poetry and what I thought of it.

I replied: "I am familiar with it, but I don't think anything because it somehow passes me by without touching or affecting me."

"It's not in the least interesting," agreed Anna Andreevna. "This is the first time I've read any. I was flabbergasted by the poem 'February': the most ignominious vilification of the Revolution."

And, in her own words, she very methodically, in detail, slowly recounted the plot and contents of this narrative poem.[88]

"I'm surprised at the book's editor. Why publish this? And the introduction by Grinberg! How irresponsible! He claims that Acmeists dominated all journals in 1915. Every schoolboy knows that 1915 was the year of Blok, Sologub, Bryusov and Bely. In 1915 Acmeists could not publish anywhere."

I was ready to go but the sirens started wailing, the radio started blaring – the air raid alert had begun.

"The voice of doom," said Anna Andreevna.

She asked me to switch the kettle on. In the cupboard I found a piece of ossified bread; I located the sugar and washed the cups and spoons. I told her my idea for an article on Zoshchenko: the article would be about Zoshchenko as a moralist writer, who is mainly concerned with ethical problems, and about how he poses these problems in children's stories.[89]

Anna Andreevna interrupted me.

"How strange that is! Khlebnikov once expressed to me that very same idea concerning ethics, a moral strain, about myself . . . Can you imagine? Khlebnikov saying this about me!"

The siren sounded the all clear. These cheerful sounds went very well with the golden leaves outside the window, the bright sun and the blueness of sky.

I said goodbye.

8 October 1940

Yesterday I visited Anna Andreevna. I got the impression she was gloomy and troubled. When I came in she was kneeling in front of a trunk, taking out some books and drawings and laying them on the floor. She explained that she was looking for a small landscape which she wants to give Vladimir Georgievich. She found the drawing: a little boat, a lake, the reflection of a hill in the water . . . (I couldn't make the artist's signature out properly; it could have been Voinov.) And only once she had got up off her knees, and sat down in her usual place, did I notice that her face was distorted, somewhat puffy and drawn. Her face had been like that last year in August, when she was seeing Lyova off.

Soon a guest arrived – someone from the Hermitage. He told us about Orbeli's illness: Orbeli has sinusitis, the doctors insist on an operation but he refuses.

"What will happen?" I asked.

The whole time, Anna Andreevna had been listening very absent-mindedly, sitting in silence, thinking her own thoughts. But she responded forcefully and angrily to my question: "Death – that's what will happen. That's the punishment for cowardice!"

13 October 1940

Anna Andreevna phoned me last night and very insistently asked me to come round. I set off for her place in pouring rain.

The room looks empty, spacious, carefully tidied. Anna Andreevna's eyes are white and her lips blue. Her eyes are sunken, sockets like hollows. She sat me down on the divan.

"I received a letter. Today. At eight o'clock in the morning. Not getting letters is horrible – not a single letter in three months – but getting them is even worse."

She read me the letter. Her voice was strained: "Life, it appears, is hanging by a thread." When she had finished, there were tears in her eyes.

And now she has to inform Lyova of another failure!

I asked what other news she had.

"Oh, just some funny trivia" – and she held out a slip of paper to me. It was a typed invitation, with a blank space for the surname to be filled in by hand, to submit poems for some collection – "Poems from 1939–40". It was a standard slip. At the same time I was pleased even with that: it would not have been sent had the name Anna Akhmatova become entirely odious.

Anna Andreevna put the kettle on. Then I realized my stupidity: I hadn't bought anything on the way and there was absolutely nothing to have with the tea. I went to buy something.

When I returned with the shopping, Sreznevskaya[90] was sitting on the divan next to Anna Andreevna. She was wearing Anna Andreevna's famous azure shawl. We drank tea. Valeriya Sergeevna launched into reminiscences, in her resonant voice, with her strong, Russian dialect. She speaks well, colourfully, sometimes her remarks are subtle, but she peppers her speech with the words "know what I mean" much too often and overuses "exceptionally" and "remarkably".

She was saying: "Now old ladies try to attach themselves to Anya. Only the other day I heard about one who took your book off somebody because, as she put it, she has 'such memories' of your book and you: you both loved the same man and she gave him to you."

"That's Vladimir Kazimirovich," laughed Anna Andreevna. "How absurd."

"He was exceptionally, inexpressibly handsome," exclaimed Valeriya Sergeevna enthusiastically. "Tall, slender. The shape of his head was simply classical. And what a genius he was."

I was worried at first that Anna Andreevna would find this chatter unpleasant – but no, she listened willingly and put in a few words.

They started talking about the unreliability of memoirs. Sreznevskaya: "Take Gollerbakh, for example. What can he remember and understand? It is we who clearly remember his mother's pâtisserie. She had a whole crowd of children, and Erka ran around – *schneller!* – his galoshes falling off. Isn't it true, Anya, in those days we never imagined that that was a future art historian?[91] I ask you, what can he remember? ... We used to buy fruit drops there – do you remember, Anya?"

"This is what he did," said Anna Andreevna, "he married the second wife of my late sister's husband. And appropriated my letters and my sister's diary."*

Then they went on to reminisce about the coachman at Tsarskoe, who had turned around and said something funny to them;† then, about

---

* This refers to Anna Akhmatova's letters to S. V. Shteyn. These were first published abroad in 1977. See *Akhmatova. Ardis*. In the Soviet Union – in the journal *Novy mir* (1986, no. 9). Publication by E. G. Gershteyn.

† The coachman said: "You've got a jealousy upset, miladies" (as told to me, in Anna Andreevna's words, by M. S. Petrovykh in 1968).

Valeriya Sergeevna's nanny, who spoke fabulous Russian, wore a hair shirt and was friends with Fedka the Eunuch; then, about Anna Andreevna's mother.

"Your nanny," said Anna Andreevna, "couldn't get over the fact that Kolya married me: hooknosed, skinny, nothing special about her. Whereas Kolya was the most eligible bachelor in Tsarskoe. That's understandable. For she, like all the rest there, had great respect for Kolya's mother. Anna Ivanovna was a real mistress of the house, not like our mothers."

"Oh yes, your mother wasn't able to do a thing in her life. Imagine, Lydia Korneevna, she belonged to the nobility, but went off to study. How she intended to live is beyond me."

"Not only to study," corrected Anna Andreevna, "she joined a circle of the People's Will. What could be more revolutionary?"

"Imagine, Lydia Korneevna, a small woman, rosy, with an exceptional complexion, fair-haired, with exceptional hands."

"Lovely white little hands!" interjected Anna Andreevna.

"A marvellous command of French," continued Sreznevskaya, "her pince-nez continually falling down, and she wasn't able to do anything, not a thing . . . And your father! Handsome, tall, slender, always immaculately dressed, his top hat slightly tilted, as worn in Napoleon III's time, and he used to say about Napoleon's wife: 'Eugenie was not bad-looking . . .'"

"He had seen her in Constantinople," put in Anna Andreevna, "he considered her the most beautiful woman in the world."

For some reason the conversation then turned to Nikolay Stepanovich's hands: "Immortal hands!" said Valeriya Sergeevna.

They spoke about the countryside, then about peasants, Ukrainian and Russian.

"Only the Ukrainian peasants behaved subserviently," said Anna Andreevna. "They had been corrupted by Polish landowners. With my own eyes, I saw an estate manager there, driving around in red gloves and women of 70 kissing those gloves. Disgusting! Whereas in the province of Tver it was quite a different story – absolute dignity."

> And the critical glances of
> Calm, sun-tanned peasant women . . .

pronounced Valeriya Sergeevna.*

---

* Lines from the poem "You know, I languish in captivity" – *FT, Rosary.*

They returned again to reminiscences and to some future biography.

"I know a lady who, as confirmation of the legend of your romance with Blok, cited the lines 'Do not crumple, my dear, my letter,/ Read it, my friend, to the end./ I am fed up with being a stranger,/ An alien on the path of your life.'"*

Valeriya Sergeevna couldn't restrain herself and added with a sigh: "That is how *our* biographies will be written."

I glanced at the clock – it was two. We left together. As we walked through the courtyard, Valeriya Sergeevna continued talking about memoirs and biographies.

"Gollerbakh is writing something, but he doesn't have a clue about me – what material I have. After all, Anya and I went to school together, she stayed with me when she left Kolya ... Ah, what an exceptional, perfectly special friendship I had with Kolya ... But I am not available to anyone, Gollerbakh won't get to me. I am not available to anyone except the most first-rate people."

We took leave of each other.

17 October 1940

Last night Anna Andreevna came to visit me. She wore a black silk dress, a white necklace, she looked elegant. But sad and very distracted.

Musya was with me.†

Anna Andreevna sat very straight on the edge of the divan, not settling further back as usual, smoked in silence and drank her tea in silence.

On the shelf she spotted a little book of poems by Simonov and asked me to read some out. I read two poems: "Trans-Siberian Express" and "The Suitcase". I asked her why it was that although the "Express" seemed to contain all the requisite elements it was still a bad poem. She pulled a wry face: "It's shallow ... shallow ... and what an abundance he reaped from Pasternak!"

I read aloud Zoshchenko's "The History of an Illness". To my surprise, she didn't laugh, but when I had finished she said: "Very good. Splendid."

I asked her to explain why she didn't like Chekhov.

"First of all, I don't like his plays. Theatre is spectacle. Whereas Chekhov's plays epitomize the disintegration of theatre. But that's not the point. I don't like him because all his people are pathetic, they know

---

* *FT, Rosary.*
† Musya: Mariya Yakovlevna Varshavskaya. For more about her see note 92.

nothing of heroic deeds. And everybody's situation is hopeless. I don't like such literature. I do understand that these characteristics of Chekhov's works are conditioned by the times, but all the same – I don't like them.

"And the same goes for the Art Theatre. Especially when they do Shakespeare. They shouldn't even go near Shakespeare. They don't understand how to approach him, he's not for them. Even Mikhail Chekhov, an actor of genius – I can't forget his Erik – was bad in *Hamlet* ... I never liked the Art Theatre. Volodya Shileyko and I once went to see some Chekhov play. During the interval he said to me: 'Did you see? A little mouse jumped on to the stage over there. Did it happen by chance, I wonder, or was it part of the director's intention?'"

Anna Andreevna was very taciturn that evening. She spoke only in response to a question. I asked whether it was true, as Korney Ivanovich had told me, that when she was young she had gone in for gymnastics.

"No, I never went in for gymnastics. K.I. probably meant the acrobatics I used to do. I could bend backwards and touch the floor with the back of my head. I could lie on my belly and touch my feet with my head. Without the least bit of training I was able to do things which are usually only achieved by constant, daily practice. Circus people used to say that, had I gone to train in a circus as a child, I would have become world famous."

Silence again. Then Musya confessed that she was trying to read *Ulysses* but could not understand it.

"A wonderful book. A great book," said Anna Andreevna. "You don't understand it because you don't have enough time. Now I had plenty of time. I used to read five hours a day and I've read it six times. In the beginning, I also felt I couldn't understand it, but then everything gradually fell into place – you know, like a photograph being developed. Hemingway, Dos Passos descended from him. They all feed on crumbs from his table."

"Do you like Hemingway?" asked Musya.

"Very much. His best work is "The Snows of Kilimanjaro".

She got up, went into the hallway, put her coat on and then, after searching through her pockets, found she'd left the keys to her flat and room at home. She rang Nikolay Nikolaevich ("Akhmatova speaking") and asked him to open the front door for her.

I walked her home, accompanied her up the stairs and waited until the door was opened for her. On my return, I rang her to check that she had managed to get into her room. She had; they had used a master key to unlock the door.

In response she asked whether she hadn't left her keys on my divan. That's exactly what had happened.

At about one o'clock today I went to take the keys round to her.

She was lying down; dishevelled hair, a thick blanket without a sheet – everything as usual. But today she was livelier, more cheerful than yesterday. She shoved an armful of underwear off the chair and offered me a seat.

"Was there something else upsetting you yesterday?" I asked.

"Yes," she replied without explanation.

She invited me to take a look at Pushkin's notebooks which she had just received. A beautiful case, and then Pushkin's handwriting. Leafing through the notebook of commentaries, I came across one by her.

"I must read it," I said.

"No, no, you absolutely must not!" cried Anna Andreevna. "It's utter nonsense! Rubbish!" (I do love hearing her say such words.) "Such eccentrics, those Pushkinists! Take Bondi, he based the whole of his commentary on a polemic with Izmaylov. Tell me, who needs it? They've sunk their teeth so deep into each other that they don't understand anything anymore."

Then she told me about Puts' visit.* He really does seem a most unpleasant gentleman.

"He's supposed to phone me today," continued Anna Andreevna. "I'll tell him that I've changed my mind about sitting for him. I'll tell him that my friends don't advise it: I'm too old for it."

"But he will protest gallantly."

"He'll do no such thing. I'll hang up."

I said that fame evidently has its drawbacks.

"Oh yes!" Anna Andreevna confirmed cheerfully. "When you're travelling in a soft landau, under a little umbrella, with a big dog next to you on the seat and everyone says: 'There goes Akhmatova', that's one thing. But when you're standing in a courtyard, wet snow falling, queuing for herring and there is such a pungent smell of herring that your shoes and coat reek of it for ten days and suddenly someone behind you recites: 'On the dish the oysters in ice smelled of the sea, fresh and sharp ...' – that is something else entirely. I was gripped by such fury that I didn't even turn around."

* ?

I asked whether Baranov had recovered and if he had examined her. (She was to undergo treatment, to go into hospital.)

"I don't know. But I'm not going for more treatment. It is too much of a strain."

"But you yourself, Anna Andreevna, scolded me and assured me that being in hospital is even pleasant!"

"But now I'm not going to go for treatment. After they refused me I decided not to go."

22 October 1940

Evening. Anna Andreevna is looking a bit better and is lying on her divan in a white dress. She greeted me affectionately, joyfully. She showed me an unpublished volume of Khlebnikov, which she had just been given by Nikolay Ivanovich.

"An excellent job, a superb one. But you know what: more and more I come to the conclusion that the history of literature is nothing but hypothetical nonsense! It is evident even here, in this excellent work by Nikolay Ivanovich. Khlebnikov vilifies Sologub, Artsybashev and Blok. Nikolay Ivanovich explains that this was nothing but a battle with the Symbolists. Rubbish! What kind of a Symbolist is Artsybashev? And Khlebnikov never engaged in a conscious battle with the Symbolists. They fought anyone of renown in order to clear a space for themselves ... By the way, Khlebnikov also attacks Korney Ivanovich here. And this, of course, is also in the framework of a battle with fame. Take Mayakovsky. Nowadays they say and write that he liked my poetry. But publicly he always berated me ... They had to clear the woods, so they chopped down the trees that were a little taller."

She told me indignantly about Maksimov's speculations.[93]

"It's utter nonsense! Rubbish! And this is a specialist speaking. No, such things could no longer occur in Pushkin studies. Pushkin studies really do involve accurate knowledge. There is a letter from Pushkin to Dmitriev, for example, a very courteous one. But we have already learnt what this courteousness means, Pushkin scholars know perfectly well that Pushkin considered Dmitriev dirt."

I've often complained to her about my inability to understand the attraction of Khlebnikov. She remembered this, bent over to get her glasses from the chair and an old volume of Khlebnikov, and, looking stern in her glasses, propped up on the cushion, slowly recited two poems: "I shall not be a ruler" and "But the singing and the tears". Then she gave me the third to read aloud myself: about mountains, a journey, a train conductor.[94]

"Did you understand it?"

"Yes," I replied unconvincingly and dared to remark that the lack of a definite rhythm disturbed my ear, that the alternation of the words and the movement of the lines seem arbitrary to me. I said that I didn't feel them to be obligatory; it seemed to me that these were drafts of poems, as yet unfinished, and that, in my opinion, either Zhukovsky's poetry is poetry, or this is poetry.

"Oh, come now! How can you say that! All this is being viewed as if for the first time, afresh. Poets know how difficult that is: to write, as Boris Leonidovich says, 'free from poetic mud'..."

"I like Khlebnikov very much," she continued, "though not in all his phases. He had many phases, you see, not like Pasternak. I can't stand the early, Slavonic Khlebnikov. Do you like Remizov? No? Neither do I. What lack of taste, what nonsense! Whenever I read *Lel* I feel sick. What is Lel, where does it come from? Khlebnikov, likewise, has a Lel phase, which I don't like."

We sat down to tea. The conversation turned to the Crimea, to the sea. Anna Andreevna said: "Recently I reread 'By the Seashore' and I wondered whether it was clear that the heroine is not a young woman, but a girl?"

"I thought she was a young woman about 16 or 17."

"No, she's just a girl, about 13 ... You can't imagine what a monster I was at that time. Do you know what young ladies used to wear to the beach in those days? A corset, with a bodice on top, and two petticoats – one of them starched – and a silk dress. They would put on little rubber shoes, and a special little cap, they would go into the water, splash some on themselves and then back to the beach. And then this monster would appear – me – in a dress over my naked body, barefoot. I would jump into the sea and would swim off for about two hours. I would return, put the dress on my wet body, the dress would be as stiff as a board because of the salt ... And like that, hair dishevelled, wet, I would run home."

"You probably miss the sea a great deal?"

"No. I remember it. It is always with me ... Even then I had a very nasty character. My mama often used to send us children to the market in Khersones, for melons and watermelons. Actually it was a risky thing to do; we had to go out into the open sea. So once, on the way back, the children insisted that I should row too. But I was very lazy and didn't want to row. I refused. First they scolded me, then they started to make fun of me, saying to each other: We are transporting watermelons and Anya. I took offence. I stood on the side and jumped into the sea. They didn't even look back, just went straight on. Mama asked them: 'And where is Anya?' – 'She threw herself overboard.' But I managed to swim back, although all this happened very far from the shore . . ."

27 October 1940

Anna Andreevna asked me to come and see her. I went with Lyusha. She was asleep, but Nikolay Nikolaevich, who opened the door to us, told us that she had asked to be woken without fail as soon as we arrived.

She was very affable and affectionate, although she did not seem to me fully awake.

She asked about Lyusha's marks for that term and then about what Lyusha was reading. Lyushenka is rereading *Uncle Tom's Cabin*. I asked Anna Andreevna if she liked the book.

"I couldn't finish it," Anna Andreevna replied earnestly. "I felt too sorry for the Negroes."

I asked her what she was currently reading.

"The Acts," she replied somehow unwillingly.

I asked whether she had decided to move in with me.*

"No. Nikolay Nikolaevich reminded me in no uncertain terms of my promise not to give my room over to people he doesn't know."

I did not insist. We left.

7 November 1940

Anna Andreevna has bronchitis, a runny nose and during the night she had suffered a heart attack. I went to see her. She was composed, calm and sad. Tanya, who wanted to exchange her room, decided not to; Anna Andreevna is glad that the children aren't going to be taken away. She asked me to bring a copy of *Wash Them Clean* for Vovochka.

I enquired what she was reading.

"Khlebnikov," she replied. "You know, his naïveté is astounding. He actually believed that as soon as people had read his poetry they would

* By that time Katyshev (NKVD) was no longer living in Matvey Petrovich's room; ordinary students were living there, with whom it was possible to exchange rooms legally.

understand it all immediately and everything would change at once. That's why he was so eager to be published."

We turned to Bely's memoirs. She spoke of them, not for the first time, with indignation.

"They are mendacious, consciously mendacious memoirs, in which everything is distorted – the roles people played as well as events."

I said that I always found everything Bely wrote about Blok highly unpleasant: he appears to revere him, but in reality he condemns him. She replied: "It used to be considered improper to write about someone if your relationship with the person was that of Bely to Blok ... After all, they would not have published D'Anthès's memoirs of Pushkin, would they?'

(I didn't grasp her remark at once. Only on the way home did I understand it.)

She recited three poems to me, two of which were short and terrifying: "But I give you solemn warning", "No, it's not I, someone else is suffering",* and the third was "Thus dark souls take flight", by now with no omissions.

I put the kettle on. There was nothing apart from tea – absolutely nothing. "Tanya is not well and hasn't been shopping," explained Anna Andreevna. We drank plain tea.

13 November 1940

I found Anna Andreevna on her feet. She looked drawn, aged. Her left foot had swollen up noticeably. She had a nagging cough.

Valya was sitting at the table and trying to locate the river Indigirka on the map.

Anna Andreevna stood by the well-stoked-up stove. Valya soon left. Now and again, Anna Andreevna would sit down on the divan, closer to me.

"At the moment I'm rereading Pasternak a lot," said Anna Andreevna. "And it seems to me that at last I've found what I've been searching for so long: phases. They do exist. At the beginning he wrote without caution, he was in a ferment, foaming, boiling, overflowing. But then he limited himself, appeared to become more pensive. His poem dedicated to me as well as the one to Marina Tsvetaeva, all this was written with

---

* "But I give you solemn warning" – *FT, Seventh Book,* no 52; "No, it's not I, someone else is suffering" – "Requiem", 3; no. 53.

a certain restraint, and from then on he became more contained."

I said that as a child I couldn't understand the meaning of Blok's poem dedicated to her.

"I don't understand it even now. And nobody understands it. One thing is clear, that it was written like that" – with her palms she made a warding-off gesture: "Do not touch me."

"Do you like 'Retribution'?"

"I can't stand the first canto. On the whole, I don't like any of it, except the 'Prologue' and 'Warsaw'. Magnificent Warsaw, Pan Frost . . . If there is someone who has clear-cut phases it is Blok. 'Unexpected Joy' and 'The Snow Mask' – that is something entirely new. In 1916 he stopped writing. Then came 'The Twelve', 'The Scythians', and that was it. What he wrote for World Literature and the Bolshoy Dramatic Theatre – these are not the works of Blok anymore."

She went to the chest and pulled an envelope out of one of the drawers.

"I haven't read you Boris Leonidovich's letter, have I? Sit here. I'll read it to you."

We sat side by side on the divan.

"Ornate handwriting," I said, studying the address on the envelope.

"Not ornate – ornithic," Anna Andreevna corrected me. "It takes flight."

She read it aloud to me, holding the paper well away from her face and sometimes indicating to me with her little finger a word she could not make out. A splendid letter, typical of Pasternak, and very moving – particularly one passage in which he tells her that she is the creator of what makes life precious for others, and that therefore it cannot and must not be the case that she does not love life.

"How kind, how sweet he is, how much he wants to help me," said Anna Andreevna. "But how wild he is! In the first place, he compromises me as a woman. Yes, he does!" she laughed. "I can just see the idiotic mug of some commentator who will make God knows what of this letter. No, don't laugh, just listen: 'By coming here, you so categorically reminded me how dear you are to me,' and he goes on to explain why he hadn't been able to spend whole days with me and so on. There is no doubt that something will be made of it. We can already see what commentators have made of other letters."[95]

She recalled how, on one of her visits to Moscow, Boris Leonidovich had visited her at Nina Antonovna's.

"Nina Antonovna later said to me: 'You were showing him out, but he got stuck in the hallway. You were edging him towards the door, but he still wouldn't leave and continued to utter words of genius.'"

"Do you like *The Year 1905*?" she asked, after a pause.

"Yes."

"Do you like all of it?"

I said that I liked all of it with the exception, perhaps, of "Peasants and Factory Workers".

"I really don't like *Schmidt*, except certain, short passages. In fact, he wrote about nothing but the weather there. What I do like is 'Fathers'. Oh, that's so good!"

I said that I really liked "Childhood". She agreed.

She took an envelope from the chair.

"I want to show you some poems and a letter which I received yesterday from two young ladies. They are seeking my opinion. Vladimir Georgievich sent them a postcard in my name, asking them to come over on Sunday. To no avail, I think. Read them and tell me what you think."

I read them. The letter was colourless. The poems by one of them were rather facile, those by the other were angular and a little better. We began to speculate what each of them might look like, and Anna Andreevna suggested that the one whose poetry was sadder and more angular would be unattractive.

Anna Andreevna put the kettle on, then suddenly, as if she'd just remembered something, stopped before me, almost touching me.

"You know, these last few days I've understood that I myself am to blame for everything. For everything that happened with the book. The Central Committee is absolutely right, it is me who is to blame. Yes, yes. They wanted to publish my poems. The publishing house selected some poems and took them to Moscow. There they were approved. Then, out of the blue I took it upon myself to add new ones, and, as if that weren't enough, I put the saddest poem in pride of place* and, on top of that, used the title of the poem for the whole section. Then the editor added about another 30 old poems. And in the end it turned out to be an entirely different book from the one which had been approved and which they wanted to see. Please don't argue. This is exactly how it all happened."

In vain I tried to remind her that it was not she who had added the new poems, that the editors had begged, had pleaded for them, that

---

* "The Willow"; no. 10. In the volume *FSB* there was a section called "The Willow", which opened with that poem. Subsequently (in *FT*) this same section was given the title: "The Reed".

nobody had known precisely what kind of book *they wanted* to see, that everyone had been living on rumours and so on – she would not budge and became angry. Here I had come right up against that iron logic that Vladimir Georgievich had told me about, founded on the basis of some unknown or even nonexistent fact.

"And if I had not done this," concluded Anna Andreevna, "Lyova would be at home."

I fell silent.

We sat down to tea. I cursed myself for not being able to convince her otherwise.

Anna Andreevna started talking about something else.

"Every time L.* comes, she manages to say something wrong. She was here yesterday. We talked about the poem 'Flight'.† L. said that this poem was very Petersburgian. And she suddenly added: 'Actually, it has been said for a long time that your poems are more evocative of Tsarskoe Selo than of Petersburg.' And because of the fact that she did not wish to reveal the name of the person who had been saying that, it was clear: it was someone I know. I think it is R.‡ A little snob from Kuzmin's salon. Things far worse than that were said there . . . Anyway, it is the opinion not of a literary circle but of a pseudoliterary circle. I can tell by the smell."

She proclaimed all this with great anger.

"What they mean to say is that my poetry is provincial. They do not understand that living in Tsarskoe Selo was considered much more metropolitan than living in Roty or on Vasilievsky Island. But that's not the point."

Then she took a sheaf of papers out of the drawer and asked me to sit next to her on the divan.

"I haven't read this to you, because it didn't seem intelligible enough to me. It is not finished. But I wrote it a long time ago – on 3 September."

She read something on Dostoevsky.

"Tell me, isn't this like 'Fathers'?"

"No. It has an entirely different sound," I replied.

"That's the main thing, the sound should be different," said Anna Andreevna.§

* Probably Lotta.
† "Flight" – *BPL–A*, p. 100.
‡ R.?
§ Evidently it was the beginning of the elegy "Dostoevsky's Russia. The moon", which subsequently acquired the title "Prehistory". Although in *FT* the elegy is dated 1945 (*Seventh Book*), it was started in Leningrad before the war, and completed in Tashkent.

Then she read about the doll and Pierrot. My mouth fell open in wonder, so unlike her was this.

"And between these two, there will be 'Fifteen-year-old hands'," explained Anna Andreevna.

"It seems you've entered a completely new phase," I said.*

"Fathers" is the title of one of the cantos in B. Pasternak's poem *The Year 1905*. It was placed first in the poem for a reason – it deals not with 1905, but, like Akhmatova's "Prehistory", with the period of the '70s and '80s – the period which preceded the birth of both Akhmatova and Pasternak, and coincided with the youth of their mothers and fathers.

* In fact, what I noted down as "The Doll and Pierrot" was the first shoot of the impending "Poem without a Hero".

Later, in the introduction to the "Poem", Akhmatova says: "It came to me for the first time on the night of 27 December 1940, after sending me *like a messenger, back in the autumn, one small passage*" (*Italics mine. – L.Ch.*). On the basis of my entry of 13.11.40 about "The Doll and Pierrot", I assume the passage I heard was that autumnal "messenger".

In the final text of the "Poem" the passage underwent some transformations. But in the first version of the "Poem", in the manuscript given to me by Anna Andreevna in Tashkent in the autumn of 1942, it corresponded exactly to what I had heard in Leningrad on 13 November. I quote:

> From nowhere you came into Russia,
> O my flaxen-haired wonder,
> Columbine of nineteen hundred and ten!
> Why is your gaze so troubled and so keen?
> Doll of St Petersburg, actress,
> You are one of my doubles.
> One must add to your other titles
> All these. O friend of poets!
> I shall inherit your glory.
> Here, to the music of the marvellous maestro,
> The wild wind of Leningrad,
> I can see the court dance of the skeletons.

> * * *

> The wedding candles are guttering,
> The kissable shoulders are veiled,
> The temple thundered: "Come, innocent dove!"
> Mountains of violets from Parma in April –
> And meeting in the chapel of Malta,
> Is like a poison in your breast.
> The house is gaudier than a circus wagon,
> Cupids with peeled-off paint
> Keep watch over the altar of Venus.
> Your bedroom you adorned like a bower.
> The merry Pskovian would not recognize
> The village wench – his neighbour . . .
> And the golden, golden candlesticks,
> And the saints on the azure walls –
> Half stolen are these goods.
> Decked in flowers like Botticelli's *Primavera*,
> You would receive your friends in your bed,
> And Pierrot, on sentry-go, would pine.

From the text of my entry it becomes clear that, speaking to me on 13 November 1940 about the future cycle and indicating a proposed sequence of poems, A.A. herself still did

She was no longer sitting on the divan but in her tattered arm-chair, arms spread out, sad and touching. For some reason we began to speak of Mickiewicz. I said that Mickiewicz's poems of wrath directed against Pushkin are actually justified, and Pushkin, so that he might respond with dignity, had no choice but to respond from the astral heights.

"You are wrong," said Anna Andreevna. "Pushkin behaved much better than Mickiewicz. Pushkin wrote as a Russian, whereas Mickiewicz called the Poles to battle but all the time sat around in Germany, indulging in affairs with German maidens. And all that during an uprising!"

I said that progressive Russians, after all, did not sympathize with Pushkin's poems about Warsaw. Vyazemsky, for example.

"On that score, I am myself more on the side of the Poles than of Pushkin," replied Anna Andreevna, "but from his own point of view, Pushkin was right. And Vyazemsky is not a good example, Vyazemsky secretly rather disliked Pushkin. And so he jotted it down in his old notebook on the quiet – for posterity."

I got up. Seeing me out, Anna Andreevna went on to say: "I wrote a whole study of Mickiewicz, about Pushkin portraying *him* as the improviser in his 'Egyptian Nights'. That is undoubtedly the case. After all, Pushkin never described his heroes' physical appearance. 'An officer with a black moustache', and that's all. The only ones whose physical appearance he described were Pugachov and Khlopusha, and these descriptions were authentic, historically accurate. And in the case of the improviser, he was given the looks of Mickiewicz. And the third, unclear theme at the recital is proposed by the improviser himself, by Mickiewicz."*

I asked why she didn't publish this work.

"Now is not the time to offend the Poles. Nor was it the time when I wrote it."

---

not know that she was continuing to work on "Northern Elegies" and was starting to work on the "Poem".

   (In the notebook she gave me, after many crossings out, deletions and erasures, what it says is: "The temple thundered". I believe this is a slip of the pen; it should say "thunders".

* The final version of Akhmatova's article "Pushkin and Mickiewicz" was lost during the blockade. Working on her article "Two New Tales by Pushkin", Akhmatova included her comments on the Polish and Russian poets. For more details see *OP*, p. 265.

22 November 1940

"Valya has gone mad. I sat there with her for three days" – these are the words with which Anna Andreevna greeted me yesterday, on opening the door. And in her room, without sitting down, she continued: "We sent her to hospital."

Anna Andreevna recounted to me in detail Valeriya Sergeevna's ravings and all the ups and downs of her illness.

"She was lying on her bed, naked, in a torn nightshirt, her hair matted. Now I understand why, in paintings from the Middle Ages, lunatics were always depicted as so dishevelled. She had been to the bathhouse, but instead of washing her hair, had then smeared it with Vaseline. She tells me: 'You know, Anya, Hitler is Feuchtwanger, and Ribbentrop is that gentleman, you remember, the one who courted me in Tsarskoe. Just look closely and you'll see for yourself.' I have known Valya since the age of twelve, but only now do I understand her fully. This is a woman of exceptional, infernal power, and of awesome pride. I understood from a few words of her delirium that she has been tormented by pride all her life. How she resisted! The doctors would come and go, fooled by her. In their presence, she was a woman of the world. No ravings whatsoever: calm, refined, caustic conversation. She told one of the female doctors: 'As a woman, you should take more care of yourself.' When the male nurses came for her, she spoke to them in a steely voice: 'I haven't bitten anybody. You have no right to take me from my bed.' Poor thing, poor thing. Just before that, I had said goodbye to her and left. She had not known what was going to happen to her within the minute. Now she considers me a traitor."

Anna Andreevna took a small volume of the *Divine Comedy* from the chest and handed it to me.

"She gave me this recently. Look at the inscription."

I read it: "To dear Anya on the threshold of hell. V.S."

So as to divert Anna Andreevna's attention from Valeriya Sergeevna's misfortune, I asked her whether she had finished reading the book of Pasternak's translations. (I had brought it for her a few days ago, coming up for a minute from the House of Entertaining Science.[96])

Anna Andreevna took two identical books from the armchair, and we sat down on the divan.

"I'm returning your copy with gratitude. Boris Leonidovich has sent me the book as a present. Look: the inscription has been glued in on a separate sheet – and not permanently – so that I can unstick it if it's not to my liking. Just imagine that! What can you do with a man like that?"

The inscription went something like: "To dear Anna Andreevna, who has forgiven people so much that perhaps she will forgive this book too."[97]

"This reminds me of the time I was in Vilna," said Anna Andreevna. "I had gone there to see Kolya off to the front. In the morning, I go up to the hotel window and what do I see: the whole street is on its knees. All these people crawling uphill on their knees. It turned out that they have this custom: crawling on their knees to the icon on its saint's day ... When I saw this half-stuck-in inscription and read it – I immediately recalled Vilna."

I enquired if those young ladies with their poems had been to see her on Sunday.

"Yes, they did come," she replied, laughing. 'And you know, L.K., you and I made complete monkeys of ourselves (sic!). The one we thought would be unattractive is as pretty as an angel from heaven. Fair-skinned, with rosy cheeks and dark eyes, slender and with a little girl's laughter – I said something which really made them laugh."

Lidiya Yakovlevna arrived. During tea, Anna Andreevna praised her book on Lermontov, in particular those passages where she deals with the difference between Pushkin's and Lermontov's language.[98] Then Anna Andreevna showed her some drawings for children from 1837, amongst which she had found a Russian Mayoshka.[99]

We drank vodka. But for once the table was abundantly laden: bread, butter, sugar and even sausage.

Anna Andreevna once again picked up Pasternak's book and read out what she liked best: Shakespeare's "Music" and "Winter" and Keats' "On the Sea". She spoke unfavourably about the translation of "Stanzas to Augusta": "'a bald hump' – this doesn't sound at all Byronic"; she was indifferent to the translations of Verlaine, whereas she said about Keats' "On the Sea": "The Byronic intonation is already fully embodied in Russian poetry even without Pasternak. But this sound – the sound of Keats – has now been heard in Russian for the first time" – and once again she read aloud the sonnet "On the Sea".

I ventured to comment that the word "nonsense" [*drebeden*] is pure Pasternak, and not Keats ["uproar rude"] at all. Anna Andreevna found the original and we read the poem in English. It turned out I was right.

In the Interim

June 1967

With the entry on the previous page my diary of 1940 breaks off. The last notebook has been lost. I only discovered further entries about Anna Akhmatova in my notebooks dating from the war years.

The loss is upsetting. It was precisely in the autumn of 1940 that Anna Andreevna started work on the "Poem without a Hero". In the lost notebook of my diary there were certain to be entries about the "Poem".

The notebook may yet turn up, if I didn't destroy it, that is, in one of my recurrent bouts of terror: right at the end of 1940, an overt investigation started, forcing me to leave Leningrad in spring 1941, and preventing me from going near my diary for a few months before my departure.

At about the same time as I was reading *Sofia Petrovna* to Anna Andreevna, I read the novella to some of my friends. I invited eight people to my place, a ninth turned up uninvited, almost against my will. No, he wasn't a traitor and he didn't rush off to the Big House to inform on me. But he did talk too much. He told someone the interesting piece of news, and that someone told someone else, and by the end of 1940 this news, in a distorted form, "on the grapevine", found its way *there*; it became known there that I was harbouring some "document about '37" – that is how the interrogator who interrogated those closely or distantly connected with me referred to *Sofia Petrovna*.

Even now, 30 years after the Ezhov Terror, as I write these lines the authorities still will not tolerate any mention of '37. They fear memory. This is what it is like now. And what was it like then? The crimes were still fresh; the blood in the offices of the interrogators and in the cellars of the Big House had not yet dried; the blood demanded words, the torture chamber demanded silence. Where are you, cranes of Ibycus, where are you, talking reed?

To this very day I still don't understand why I wasn't arrested and shot as soon as they found out about my novella. Instead they began to conduct a preliminary investigation. (Anna Andreevna told me once: "You are like a glass which has rolled under the bench during an explosion in a china shop.")

It goes without saying that for a long time already I hadn't been keeping either *Sofia Petrovna* or the diaries at home. After reading it to my friends, I placed my only copy – a thick school exercise book with pages numbered by Lyusha – in reliable hands.

I didn't tell Anna Andreevna anything about my new misfortune. Even without my misfortunes she was tormented by worries about Lyova, about herself, worn out by her work: again she wrote through the night and each time we met she would read me new passages from the "Poem".

(The passage created first was "From nowhere you came into Russia...", which ended with the line: "And Pierrot, on sentry-go, would pine." I don't remember the order of what came next. I recall that once Anna Andreevna read out the "Poem" at my place to Aleksandra Iosifovna, Tamara Grigorievna and me.

Tamara Grigorievna said: "Listening to this work, one gets the feeling that you climbed to the top of a high tower and, from that height, looked back..."

These words subsequently gave birth to the following lines in the 'Introduction' to the "Poem":

> From the year nineteen-forty,
> As if from a tower I survey everything).

I continued to see Anna Andreevna from time to time and listen to the "Poem". But the more obvious the interest of the Big House in me became, the less often, under various pretexts, did I try to see her.

The intensive searches for the "document about '37" began like this.

One day a policeman came to our flat: Ida – Lyusha's nanny – was urgently summoned to the police station. At that time, that was where passports were being renewed, and we both decided that Ida had been summoned for that purpose.

However, she only returned 24 hours later and on the verge of a nervous breakdown.

It turned out that she had immediately been transported from the police station to the Big House, where they had interrogated her solidly for six hours.

They questioned her about me and about my friends. Who came round? What did we talk about? Did we talk loudly or in a whisper? What kind of documents was I keeping and where?

Crying, Ida told me that the interrogator had given her the code name "Petrova", and as she was leaving, he had instructed her: "On Tuesday, Petrova, you will take the girl to school and on the way back you'll meet me at the tram stop. You will tell me who came to see your employer in the last few days."

And thus began our life under surveillance. At that time some friends and I were compiling a reader for younger schoolchildren. We worked mostly in the evenings at my place, selecting and editing fairy tales, short stories and poetry. While we busied ourselves with fairy tales, downstairs, in the main entrance hall, the "agentry" kept watch. In the morning the interrogator, meeting up with Ida at the prearranged place, would ask her: "Who came to see your employer yesterday?"

"So-and-so, and So-and-so."

"What did they do?"

"They read fairy tales."

"When did they leave?"

"At eleven."

"That's not true," said the interrogator, glancing at his notebook, "it was at 11.20."

Fortunately, the interrogator didn't ask about Anna Andreevna. I lied to her, saying that my flat was being redecorated, and she did not come to see me.

Not content just with meetings at the tram stop, the interrogator would ask Ida to go and see him in his office about three times a month. The questions became more and more absorbing, and became, to my amazement, more and more concerned with my family: "Does your employer tell anyone that her husband was not guilty of anything? Does she keep his photograph on her desk? What does she want her little girl to be when she grows up?"

This last question surprised me greatly, and I asked Ida about it again and again. Lyusha was nine years old then. What did they mean? Did I want her to become an engineer, a doctor or a teacher? And why did this interest them?

I did not yet know, and found out only much later, that according to a plan drawn up by the NKVD, the families of "enemies of the people" were supposed to be nurturing "avengers" in their bosoms; the children of these families were being kept under precautionary surveillance; the interrogator was not in the least interested in Lyusha's future career – no, he was interested in how we were fostering the memory of Matvey

Petrovich; he would have liked to hear Ida admit: "My employer wants her husband avenged by her daughter when she grows up."

"Avengers"! . . . Having shot the fathers, the torture chamber was taking revenge for its villainy on the children of those it had murdered.

Ida's distress grew. At home she never stopped crying, convinced that soon both she and I would be arrested.

In order to give her a break, in the middle of February 1941 I went to the Uzkoe sanatorium near Moscow. And they really did stop calling Ida in for a time. Nobody paid the slightest attention to me either, in Moscow. But no sooner had I returned home than everything started up again and what is more, ten times worse. Ida was threatened that if she did not find the "document", she would be severely punished. They also promised to come during the day when Lyusha and I would not be at home to search the flat.

Even though I had nothing compromising, I was still afraid of a search: they could plant and find anything they wanted.

Friends advised me to go away – to go away for a long time. To go to hospital. To have an operation which the doctors had been insisting on for a long time already.

On 10 May 1941, a month and a half before the war broke out, I gathered a few essentials together, locked the flat and went to Moscow with Lyusha and Ida.

A week later, I was in the hospital attached to the Institute of Endocrinology. About ten days later I was operated on. And another week later in Korney Ivanovich's new Moscow flat, to which I had been transferred from the hospital, I was visited by Anna Andreevna, who had come from Leningrad to Moscow on business.

We hardly talked; I didn't have the strength either to speak or to listen. Anna Andreevna sat for about an hour at my bedside. I recall her compassionate, sympathetic face, with its mournfully raised eyebrows, leaning over me. "You looked as though you'd just been taken down from the cross," she told me several months later, referring to that visit.

She was planning to go home to Leningrad. Whereas I was supposed to be moved to the dacha at Peredelkino: the wound hadn't healed yet, I still could not walk and I needed further treatment.

During the first air raids, I was still at the dacha – I was weak, my throat was still bandaged. To try to make it to Leningrad in that condition was out of the question.

On 28 July 1941, together with the families of some Moscow writers,

Lyusha, Ida and my four-year-old nephew Zhenya, I was sent by steamer to Chistopol.*

It was there that I lived through the newspaper editorial "The Enemy is at the Gates of Leningrad", and my meeting with Tsvetaeva and the death of Tsvetaeva.

And it was there, in October 1941, that Anna Andreevna, having been evacuated by plane from Leningrad to Moscow, came to join me. From there, we made the journey to Tashkent together.

About Anna Andreevna's arrival in Chistopol and about our journey together, only a few occasional and brief entries in my diary survive.

Here they are.

---

* Zhenya (b. 1937): son of my younger brother Boris, a hydro-construction engineer. During the first month of the war, Boris Korneevich joined the Moscow volunteer corps and was killed in fighting near Moscow in the autumn of 1941.

1941

15 October 1941. Chistopol. *

I have just received a telegram from Korney Ivanovich: PASTERNAK FEDIN ANNA ANDREEVNA LEFT FOR CHISTOPOL ... The rest was about money and a fur coat.

And so I am destined to see Anna Andreevna again. Unless she decides to stay in Kazan.

Akhmatova in Chistopol! This is just as hard to imagine as the Admiralty spire or the Arch of the General Staff headquarters in Chistopol.

October 1941 †

In the evening, after we had already gone to bed, there was a knock at the gates of our hut. Swearing, our landlady went to open it, carrying a lantern. I followed her.

Anna Andreevna was standing by the gate with somebody whom I could not make out in the darkness. The light of the lantern fell on her face: it was desperate. Just as if she were standing in the middle of Nevsky, unable to cross. In a borrowed unbuttoned fur coat, a white woollen shawl; clutching a bundle to her breast, petrified.

She seemed about to fall or break into a scream at any moment.

I grabbed the bundle, took her by the hand and led her to the house, along the plank over the mud.

There was nothing in which to boil water for tea, so I just gave her something cold.

Then I put her in my bed, and I lay down on a little mattress on the floor.

At first we seemed to talk about everything at once. I tried to find out

---

* No. 20, Rosa Luxemburg Street.
† The original has been damaged.

in more detail about Tusya and Shura. (Anna Andreevna had brought me letters from them.)

Then I asked: "Are people in Leningrad afraid of the Germans? Might they really break through?"

Anna Andreevna raised herself on to her elbow.

"Come on, L.K., who cares about the Germans? Nobody's giving the Germans a thought. People are starving in the city, they are already eating cats and dogs. There'll be a plague there, the city will become extinct. Nobody cares about the Germans."

19 October 1941

Anna Andreevna read me a poem about Leningrad. About artillery shelling.*

20 October 1941

Today, Anna Andreevna told me: "I have made up my mind. I am going with you."†

Ida is already buying meat, eggs, honey and bread for the journey ... I would like to know how long our journey will last. And – will we survive it?

21 October 1941

Anna Andreevna questions me about Tsvetaeva.

I read her what I wrote on 4 September, right after the news of the suicide.

Today, Anna Andreevna and I were walking along the Kama, I helped her over the plank, over the same puddle-ocean which I had helped Marina Ivanovna cross not much more than 50 days ago when I had been taking her to the Shneyders'.[100]

"Very strange," I said. "The same river and puddle, and the same little plank. Two months ago, at this very place, I helped Marina Ivanovna cross this very puddle. And we were talking about you. And now she's gone and you and I are talking about her. In the very same spot!"

---

* "First Long-Range Shelling of Leningrad" – *FT, Seventh Book*; no. 54.
† From Korney Ivanovich I received papers, money and a request to leave at once for Tashkent, where he himself had already gone from Moscow.

Anna Andreevna gave no reply, just looked attentively at me. But I didn't tell her what we'd been talking about then.*

28 October 1941 [On board the Kazan-Tashkent train]

Anna Andreevna doesn't leave the window.

"I'm glad to be seeing so much of Russia."

In Kazan everything was very arduous. If it hadn't been for Ida, I doubt we would have managed to get off the steamer on to the pier and then to fight our way into the town through the crowd. We headed for the House of Publications. We kept asking passers-by. A Tatar said to me: "Because you are young but grey, I'll take you there." The huge hall of the House of Publications was crammed with refugees from Moscow. They were sleeping on chairs. The chairs were lined up back to back. There were no empty seats. Ida and I got a table for Anna Andreevna to sleep on and for Lyusha and Zhenya to sleep underneath, while we ourselves sat down on a window sill. Anna Andreevna lay straight, stretched out, with sunken eyes and mouth, as if dead. Towards morning, a serviceman gave up his place on the chairs to me. I lay down but couldn't sleep. When dawn came, it turned out that, sleeping right beside me, on the other side of the chairs, was Fadeev.

I knew Samuil Yakovlevich's Kazan address† and, taking the children, I went off in the morning to find him. I found the house but he wasn't in. I left a note. In the evening, he came to see us at the House of Publications. He told us that two carriages for writers, on a train headed for Central Asia, had been assigned to him, Marshak, and that he would try to take us.

The next day L. M. Kvitko visited us, and in reply to my question as to whether we'd be let on the train he said: "If there isn't enough room, my family and I will stay behind and you'll go. Chukovsky's grand-children must join him."[101]

---

* I had been expressing my joy to Marina Ivanovna: A.A. is not here, is not in Chistopol, she is not in this alien, semi-Tatar village, buried in mud, rejected by the world. "She would certainly have died here ... The local existence would have killed her ... After all, she can't do anything for herself."

"And you think I can?" Marina Ivanovna interrupted me sharply.

(In 1981, I described in detail meeting Tsvetaeva in Chistopol in the sketch "On the Threshold of Death". See the journal *Vremya i my*, no. 66, 1982. Now, in 1988, the sketch has been published in Moscow in the journal *Sobesednik*, no. 3 (Moskovskiy Rabochiy).

† Marshak.

Fortunately, we all managed to get on.

Boarding was difficult. For about four hours we sat on the platform in total darkness, on our belongings, waiting for the train which was supposed to be arriving at any moment. Anna Andreevna stayed silent throughout – it was a heavy silence, like in the prison queue. Samuil Yakovlevich came up to us often. Seeing our feeble crew, he offered to lift Zhenya into the carriage. Ida was to carry the belongings and I would help Lyushenka and Anna Andreevna. While waiting for the train, Samuil Yakovlevich walked up and down the platform with Zhenya in his arms. I asked Zhenya: "Do you know who this is? It is Marshak ... *Fire, Post* ... You remember those books, don't you?"

"Have you gone completely mad, Lida?" Zhenya answered me very distinctly. Then burred: "Magshak died ages ago!"

When at last the train pulled in, Ida boarded it first with our things. Then me, holding Lyusha by the hand. Ida grabbed her, and I helped Anna Andreevna on. Then Samuil Yakovlevich passed Zhenya to me and ran off to his carriage. (We were travelling in different ones.)

Our carriage is over-crowded.

It keeps jolting, it's hard to write.

I read Anna Andreevna the letters she'd brought for me from my Leningrad friends. I wept as I read. Anna Andreevna said nothing. We were both thinking back to it, to our native city.*

26.9.[41]

Dear Lidochka,

I have just found out that Anna Andreevna is going to Chistopol.

It is very hard for me to write, and I haven't written a single line to anyone for a long time. But now I feel the urge to send you at least a line or two.

It may be, my friend, that we will never see each other again. I thank you for the long years of friendship. I thank you for the fact that I am now living surrounded by good, dear and lofty memories.

Do not think that things are very bad for me now. I don't

---

* I have lost A. I. Lyubarskaya's letter. I will insert the letter Anna Andreevna brought me from T. G. Gabbe into the text, as an exception: it speaks of besieged Leningrad, and prisons, and is a testament for the future.

allow myself to think about myself, and therefore things are not only not bad but often even good.

I just can't write letters though, it is too painful.

My friend, the greatest anguish in my life is Iosif.[102] I can do nothing for him now and I'm so afraid of leaving him to his fate.

This is what I would like to ask you: if I do not live to find him and look after him, you try to – maybe you will be luckier. If not now, then later, when it becomes possible.

Just in case, here is the essential information for making enquiries. Date of birth: 1901. Place of birth: the Mayaty settlement. Place of last employment: Architectural workshop LQM (Red Army Living Quarters Maintenance Service). Last day of work: 22 May 1941. He was in Lefortovo prison. It was there that they accepted the clothes and money I brought. The money which I sent him from Leningrad in July does seem to have reached him. (It was not returned to me.) The money I sent on 4 August was returned on 4 September with a note on the postal order: (Returned due to incorrect address.) I had sent it to post box 686 at the main post office, as they had instructed me to at the reception office on Kuznetsky.

The note, as you can see for yourself, is not very intelligible.

At the prosecutor's office they told me that his file is in the 3rd Directorate of the NKO.

My applications and enquiries to the People's Commissariat remained unanswered.

I think that is all you may need to make enquiries.

Dear Lidochka, I hope you have enough strength to live on for a long time, I hope that Lyushka will grow big and that someday people will find out how we lived.

If you are able and would like to write, let me know how you are. About your health, whether you have found work, what your everyday life is like – yours and your daughter's.

It will give me great pleasure to find out something about you at first hand, and not from other people's letters.

I will try to answer too, although that is the hardest thing of all for me.

I send you my love.

Be happy.

Tusya

30 October 1941

At one station, where the train stood for a long time, Marshak and Kvitko came to see us. They offered to transfer Anna Andreevna to their carriage – it was warmer, softer and more spacious.*

"Captain!?" Anna Andreevna asked me pathetically.

"But of course!"

And I jumped out to accompany them there.

Since then I've been going there about twice a day. Sometimes, when the train stops for long and it is safe to run back and forth, I take Lyusha or Zhenya with me to warm up a bit.

She keeps calling me "my Captain."†

I take Anna Andreevna some food.

She is reading *Through the Looking Glass* again – the book K.I. had given me to read to the children on the journey.

"Don't you think," Anna Andreevna asked me, "that we too are now through the looking glass?"

2 November 1941. Novosibirsk.

Blue carriages of the Moscow metro, buried under the snow.

Eagle-eyed Anna Andreevna pointed them out to me.

3 November 1941

Another conversation with Anna Andreevna about Marina Ivanovna's demise. By the way, Anna Andreevna told me that Mandelstam's poem "Not Believing in the Miracle of the Resurrection" is dedicated to Tsvetaeva.

Then: "Osip tried to fall in love with me twice, but both times it seemed to me to be such an insult to our friendship that I immediately put a stop to it."

---

* Into the international carriage in which S. Marshak, M. Ilin, the Kukryniksy, L. Kvitko with their families, and also Lina Shtern were travelling to Alma-Ata. When they arrived in Alma-Ata, Anna Andreevna returned to us.

† A.A. subsequently inscribed one of her Tashkent photographs as a memento of our journey: "To my Captain".

5 November 1941

A trainload of Volga Germans. There was nowhere for it to stop. Freight carriages; the doors had been slid open; you could see children, women, washing on lines. We heard they've been travelling for over a month, and no one will accept them.

At the stations, on the platforms, there were women, children, bundles in heaps. Eyes, eyes ... When Anna Andreevna looks at these women and children, her face somehow starts to look like their faces. A peasant woman, a refugee ... Looking at them she falls silent.

I told her that today, on my way to see her, when I passed a troop carriage, I had heard somebody from the upper bunk say: "I would've left those Yids to Hitler, let him bury 'em all alive in the earth!"

"Such people should be shot!" said Anna Andreevna quickly.

8 November 1941

The desert.

We have been stuck a long time between stations.

Camels in the distance. I've realized for the first time that they are beautiful, not ugly: the caravan is swaying along with a harmonious, stately motion.

Anna Andreevna is animated, interested; she notices far more than I do. She keeps pointing things out to me all the while: "An eagle!" she said. "It's landed on that mountain over there! Look – a river, it's yellow!"

She doesn't believe that I can't see it. She has stopped reading, conversing, she's watching, watching.

9 November 1941

I pushed Anna Andreevna away from the window – some Uzbek boys are throwing stones at our train, shouting: "Here's an air raid for you!"

A stone hit the side of the carriage.

We are somewhere very near Tashkent. Everything is in bloom.

The windows are open.

9 November. Tashkent. The hotel.

K.I. met us at the station by car. He drove Ida and the children to his place, then drove Anna Andreevna and me to the hotel.

The Poems of
Anna Akhmatova

Those without which my entries
would be hard to understand

1   *see pp. 11, 87*

Boris Pasternak

He, who compared himself to the eye of a steed,
Looks askance, glances, sees, recognizes,
And lo! Like melted diamonds
Ice wastes away and puddles shine.

Backyards, platforms, beams and leaves
Repose with clouds in lilac mist.
Engines' whistles, the crunch of melon peel,
A timid hand in a fragrant glove.

Ringing, thundering, grinding, the crash of waves
And sudden quiet – all means he
Treads over the pine needles with trepidation
So as not to disturb the fragile sleep of space.

And it means, he counts the grains
In the empty ears; it means he has come
From some funeral once again
To visit the cursed, black Daryal grave-stone.

And once more the languor of Moscow burns,
The sleigh bells of death ring out afar off . . .
Who has got lost two steps from home,
Where the snow is waist deep and an end to everything?

For comparing smoke to Laocoon,
For singing of graveyard thistles,

For filling the world with a new song
In the new space of reflected verses,

He is endowed with eternal childhood,
With the generosity and sharpness of the spheres
And all the earth was his inheritance,
And he shared it all with everyone.

19 January 1936

2   *see p. 22*

Creativity

It happens thus: a kind of languor;
A ceaseless chiming is ringing in my ears;
Far off, a dying peal of thunder,
I seem to hear the plaints and groans
Of unrecognized and captive voices,
A secret circle draws in round me,
But amongst this host of chimes and whispers
One all-pervading sound mounts up.
And all around is so incorrigibly quiet,
That one can hear the grass growing in the wood,
And evil with its knapsack treading the earth . . .
But already I can hear the words
And little signal sounds of easy rhymes –
And then I start to understand,
And simply lines as if dictated
Nestle down on the snow-white page.

[5 November 1936]

3   *see pp. 27, 142*

The Sentence

And the stone word fell
Upon my still living breast.
Never mind, I was prepared for this.
Somehow I shall stand the test.
Today I have many things to do:
I must kill my memory quite dead,
My heart must turn to stone,
I must learn to live ahead.
Otherwise ... I feel the warm rustle of summer,
Like a feast day, outside my window.
Long since I foresaw all this,
The bright clear day, the deserted house.

[22 June] 1939

4   *see pp. 27, 121*

You must celebrate our last anniversary –
Understand that the snowy night
Of our first diamond winter
Is exactly repeated today.

From the Tsar's stables steam billows forth,
The Moika canal plunges into the dark,
As if on purpose, the light of the moon grows dim,
And where we are going I cannot conceive.

Between the tombs of grandson and grandfather
The tangled garden has gone astray,
The funereal streetlamps are ablaze,
As though emerging from the madness of prison.

Menacing icebergs cover Marsovo Square
And Lebyazhya Kanavka lies smothered in crystals . . .
Whose fate can compare with my own,
If joy and fear lie in my heart?

And over my shoulder your voice
Quivers like a wondrous bird,
And warmed by a sudden shaft
The snowy dust sparkles like silver.

1938

5   *see pp. 28–9*

How is this age worse than those that went before?
Is it because in the fume of sorrows and alarms
It has touched the blackest ulcer,
But could not heal it?

In the west Earth's sun still shines,
And in its rays the roofs of towns yet gleam.
But here Death already chalks crosses on the houses
And calls the ravens and the ravens fly.

1919

6   *see p. 33*

The Muse

When at night I wait for her to come,
It seems that life is hanging by a strand.
What are honours, what is youth, what is freedom
Before that dear guest with shepherd's flute in hand!
Now she is here. Throwing back her veil,
She glanced attentively at me.
I say to her: "Did you dictate to Dante
The pages of the *Inferno*?" She answers: "It was I."

1924

7   see p. 36

To Death

You will come in any case – so why not come now?
I am waiting for you – I cannot bear it any longer.
I have turned out the light and opened wide the door
For you, so wondrous and so simple.
Take whatever form you choose to visit me –
Break in like a poisoned shot,
Or creep up, with a club, like a hardened bandit,
Or poison me with typhus fumes.
Or use the little fairy tale of yours,
So sickeningly familiar to all –
So that I should see the blue policeman's cap
And the caretaker's face, so pale with fear.
I don't care anymore. The Enisey swirls on,
The polar star shines bright.
And the blue gleam of the eyes I love
Is shrouded by the final horror.

19 August 1939
Fontanny House

8   see p. 43

"Sister, I have come to take your place,
By the woodland, by the high forest fire.

Your hair has grown grey. Your eyes
Have grown dim, misted over with tears.

You no longer understand the song of birds,
Or notice the summer lightning or the stars.

For long now the tambourine has not been heard,
Yet I know you are frightened of silence.

Sister, I have come to take your place,
By the woodland, by the high forest fire."

"You have come to bury me.
Where is your shovel, where your spade?
In your hand you have only a flute.
I shall not accuse you,
Only a pity that sometime long ago
My voice forever fell silent.

Put on my clothes,
Pay no heed to my alarm,
Allow the wind to frolic with your curls.
You smell like the scent of lilac,
But you've come by a difficult path,
To be illumined here."

And away she went
Down an unknown and narrow path,
Yielding place to the other,
And faltered, like someone blind.

And all the time, it seemed she saw
A flame close by . . . in her hand a tambourine.
Like a white banner,
Like the light of a beacon she seemed.

                                        1912

9   *see p. 53*

To the New Year! To New Grief!
Here he dances, mischief-maker
Above the smoky Baltic Sea,
Bandy-legged, bent and wild.
And what fate has he in store
For those who have eluded torment?
They've gone to the fields to die.
O stars of heaven, shine on them!
Earthly bread they will not see
Nor the eyes of those they love.

[January 1940]

10   *see pp. 56, 175*

The Willow

And a copse of ancient trees.
PUSHKIN

And I grew up in patterned silence,
In the cool nursery of our young age.
I had no fondness for the voice of men,
But the voice of the wind was clear to me.
I loved the burdock and stinging nettles,
But most of all I loved a silver willow.
And, in gratitude, it lived with me
For all my life, and with its weeping branches
Entwined my sleeplessness with dreams.
And – strange to say! – I did outlive it.
There now a stump stands out, and other willows
With other voices whisper something else
Under our skies, under those skies.
And I am silent. As when a brother dies.

[18 January] 1940

11   *see p. 56*

> I have no need for a host of odes,
> Nor the charms of elegiac conceits.
> Things in poetry should, I think,
> Be out of place, not tidy, everyday.
>
> If you did but know from what rubbish
> Verses grow, knowing no shame,
> Like the yellow dandelion by the fence,
> Like burdock and goosefoot.
>
> An angry shout, fresh smell of tar,
> On the wall mysterious mould . . .
> And the verse already sounds lively, tender,
> To your joy and my joy.
>
> *[21 January 1940]*

12   *see p. 56*

> When a man is dying,
> His portraits undergo a change.
> The eyes acquire another look, and the lips
> Wear a different smile.
> I noticed this when I returned
> From the funeral of a certain poet.
> Since then I have often tested this,
> And my surmise has been confirmed.
>
> *[21 January] 1940*

13 *see p. 57*

It was only then that the dead
Used to smile – to be at peace were glad.
And like a useless ornament
Amongst its prisons swung Leningrad.
Then, grown frenzied by torment,
Regiments of condemned were marching,
And the engines' whistles sang
The brief song of parting.
Stars of death stood above us;
Under the wheels of Black Marias,
Under the heel of blood-stained boots,
Writhed innocent Russia.

14 *see pp. 60, 63, 64*

Cleopatra

A sweet shade enveloped
Alexandria's palace.
PUSHKIN

She had already kissed the dead lips of Antony,
And on her knees shed tears before Augustus . . .
Servants had betrayed her. Trumpets of victory rumble
Under the Roman eagle, and the mist of evening spreads around.

There enters the last of her beauty's captives,
Stately and tall, and whispers, disturbed:
"He will send you ahead, as a slave, in triumph . . ."
But her swan-like neck stayed quietly inclined.

The children will be clapped in chains tomorrow. How little
Remains for her in the world – a joke, perhaps, with a peasant
And then to place with a careless hand on her dusky breast
A black asp as a parting gesture of pity.

[7 February] 1940

15   *see p. 65*

Dedication

Mountains bow before this sorrow,
The great river cannot flow,
But strong are the bolts of prison gates,
And beyond them are "convicts' burrows"
And hopeless deathly anguish.
For someone the wind blows fresh,
For someone the sky glows warm at dusk –
We know not, we are everywhere the same,
We only hear the hateful crunch of keys
And heavy marching steps of soldiers.
We would rise up, as though to early mass,
And walk through the capital, grown wild,
And meet, more breathless than the dead themselves – .
The sun was lower, the Neva more misty,
But somewhere hope still sang from afar.
Sentenced . . . And at once her tears pour forth,
Cut off already from all around,
As though life were wrenched from her heart with pain,
As though they'd rudely flung her down,
Yet she walks on . . . Swaying . . . Alone . . .
Where are now those women, my unwitting friends,
From those two hellish years of mine?
What do they see in a Siberian blizzard?
What do they sense in the haze of the moon?
To them I send my farewell greeting.

March 1940

16   *see p. 65*

Quietly flows the quiet Don,
Yellow moon slides through the door.

With cap askew the yellow moon
Sees a shadow in the room.

It's a woman on her own,
Sick woman, woman alone.

Son in prison, husband dead,
Let your prayer for me be said.

17   *see p. 66*

Mayakovsky in 1913

I knew you not in your time of glory,
I remember only your stormy dawn,
But now, perhaps, I have the right
To recall a day from those far-off years.
How sounds would strengthen in your verses,
And ever new voices swarm . . .
Your young hands were not left idle,
Threatening scaffolding you raised,
Everything that you touched did not seem
What it had been up till then,
That which you tried to destroy – was destroyed.
In every word there breathed a judgment.
Alone and often in dissatisfaction,
Impatiently you hastened fate,
Knowing that soon you would emerge
Joyful and free for your valiant struggle.
And already the answering roar of the rising tide
Could be heard, when you read to us,
The rain slanted its eyes in wrath
And you argued fiercely with the city.
And your name, as yet unknown,
Like lightning flew round the stuffy hall,
So that now, protected by all the land,
It might ring out like a clarion call.

1940

18   *see pp. 69, 75*

[To Boris Pilnyak]

All this you alone will guess . . .
When the sleepless gloom seethes round about,
That sunny, lily-of-the-valley wedge
Bursts into the darkness of the December night.
And I am on my way to you along the path.
And you laugh a carefree laugh.
But the fir-tree forest and the rushes of the pond
Answer with some weird echo . . .
Oh, if by this I waken you from death,
Forgive me – for I cannot otherwise:
I mourn for you, as for my own,
And envy every man who weeps,
Who at this fearful hour can weep
For those who lie in the depths of the ravine . . .
My tears have not reached my eyes,
They are scalded dry, quite unrefreshed.

1938

19   *see pp. 70, 72, 161*

Thus dark souls take flight . . .
"I shall wander in my mind, but do not listen.

You dropped in by chance, without warning –
For you are not bound by time.

Stay with me but a while longer.
Remember we were together in Poland?

In Warsaw that first morning . . . Who are you?
Are you the second or the third?" – "The hundredth!"

"And your voice is just the same as before.
You know, I spent years in the hope

That you would return, and now – it's no joy.
Nothing at all do I need on earth –

Not the thunder of Homer, nor the wonder of Dante.
Soon I shall be treading the blissful shore:

And Troy has not fallen, Eabany still lives,
And all has been drowned in a fragrant mist.

Under a green willow I would like to doze off,
But that ringing gives me no peace.

What can it be? A flock coming back from the mountains?
But no cooling breeze blew in my face.

Or is it a priest bearing gifts?
And the stars are in heaven, and night over the hills . . .

Or are the people summoned to council?"
– "No, this is your last evening!"

1940

20   *see p. 75*

The Way of All the Earth

Sitting in a sleigh, departing
by the way of all the earth . . .
VLADIMIR MONOMAKH'S HOMILY
TO THE CHILDREN

Right in the path of bullets,
Casting aside the years
By Januarys and Julys
I shall make my way . . .
None shall see my wound,
None shall hear my cry,
I, who am from Kitezh,
Have been called home.
A hundred thousand birch trees
Have chased after me,
In a wall of glass
Frost has streamed by.
Fires of long ago
Are but a charred heap.
"Here's your pass, comrade,
Make your way back . . ."
Calmly the soldier
Turns his bayonet aside.
How lushly and sultrily
That island rose up!
And the red-coloured clay,
And the orchard of apples . . .
O Salve Regina! –
Blazes forth the sunset.
Steeply, all atremble,
The pathway climbed up.
Here I must give
A greeting to someone . . .

But I don't hear the groan
Of the hoarse hurdy-gurdy,
The young maid from Kitezh
Heard the wrong chime.

2

Trenches, all trenches –
Here you'll get lost!
Out of old Europe
But a rag has remained,
Where towns are ablaze
In a thick pall of smoke . . .
Here the Crimean ridge
Already grows dark.
A flock of mourners
Behind me I lead.
Oh, the blue mantle
Of my peaceful homeland! . . .
Above a dead Medusa
In confusion I stand;
Here I met with the Muse
And made her a vow.
But she laughs out loud,
Disbelieving: "What, you?"
April, all fragrance,
Is dripping in drops.
The high threshold of fame
Is already at hand,
But a voice, very sly,
Gives warning to me:
"You will come back,
Return many times,
But stumble again
Against adamant diamond.
You had better go by,
You had better go back,
Lauded, disparaged,
To the home of your fathers."

3

The mist grows much thicker
At evening tide.
Let Hoffmann walk with me
As far as the corner.
How hollow a muffled cry
Is, he knows,
And whose double
Has crawled into the lane.
For it's surely no joke
That for twenty-five years
I have seen only one
Fearsome silhouette.
"So it means, to the right,
Right here, round the corner?
I thank you!" – There's a ditch
And a very small house.
I wasn't to know that the moon
Was aware of it all.
From the rope ladders
He comes hurtling down,
And quietly goes round
The abandoned house,
Where at night on the wane,
At the round table
I glanced at a fragment
Of mirrors all shattered,
And in the depths of the darkness
A slaughtered man slept.

4

A sublime power resides
In the purest of sounds,
As though separation
Was sated with pleasure.
Familiar buildings
Glance out from death –
A hundred times sadder

A meeting there'll be
Than all that did ever
Happen to me . . .
Through the crucified city
I make my way home.

5

A bird-cherry tree
Stole by like a dream.
"Tsushima," someone said
Over the phone.
Quickly, quickly,
Time is running out:
Ships *Koreyets* and *Varyag*
have sailed to the East . . .
There, like a lark,
Hovers ancient pain . . .
Further on in the dark
Looms Fort Chabrole,
Like a ruined crypt
From a century ago,
Where an aged cripple
Became deaf and blind.
With rifles at the ready,
Severe and sullen,
The Boers keep watch.
"Go back, go back."

6

A long time I waited
For the great winter to come,
And I took it upon me,
Like a nun's white veil.
Quietly I climb
Into the light sleigh . . .
I shall return before night
To you, people of Kitezh.
There's one way across

By the old ferry stage . . .
No one will go now
With the woman from Kitezh,
Neither brother, nor neighbour,
Nor the first bridegroom –
Only the branch of a fir
And a sunbaked verse,
Tossed off by a beggar
And gathered by me . . .
Lay me to rest
In my last dwelling place.

March 1940
Fontanny House

21 *see p. 76*

From you I hid my heart,
As though I'd hurled it in the Neva . . .
Wingless and quite tamed
I am living in your home.
Only . . . I hear creaks in the night.
What's there in the unfamiliar gloom?
The Sheremetev linden trees . . .
The calls of household spirits . . .
There creeps up warily,
Like the babbling of water,
Nuzzling hotly against my ear,
A black whisper of disaster –
And mumbles, as if it was its business
To fuss around all night:
"So it was comfort you wanted,
Now you know where it is – your comfort."

[30 October] 1936

22   *see pp. 28–9, 77*

> We thought we were beggars, and possessed nothing at all,
> But when we began to lose one thing, then another,
> So that each day turned into
> One of remembrance –
> We began to compose songs
> About God's great generosity,
> And about our former great wealth.

1915

23   *see pp. 77, 105*

> Fear, which picks out objects in the dark,
> Guides a ray of moonlight to an axe.
> From behind the wall comes an ominous knock –
> What is there? A spectre, a thief or rats?
>
> In the stuffy kitchen fear splashes in water,
> Counts up the shifting floorboards.
> It darts past the attic window
> With its black and glossy beard.
>
> It grows quiet. How evil and cunning it is,
> It has blown out the candle and hidden the matches.
> Better the gleam of gun barrels
> Levelled against my breast.
>
> It were better on some green square
> To lie down on the bare boards of a scaffold,
> And to the sound of groans and cries of joy
> Let red blood flow out to the end.
>
> I press the smooth cross to my heart –
> O God, bring back peace to my soul.
> The nauseating sweet smell of decay
> Comes wafting from the chilly sheet.

1921

24   *see pp. 56, 77*

The Cellar of Memory

But it's arrant nonsense that I live in sadness
And that remembrance nags at me.
Not often am I guest of memory,
And it always leaves me confused.
When I go down with a lantern to the cellar,
It seems to me once more a landslip
Thunders down the narrow stairway after me.
The lantern smokes, I cannot now return,
But I know I go there to the enemy.
And I pray as if for mercy . . . But there
It's dark and quiet. My feast day has come to an end!
Thirty years have gone since bidding the ladies farewell,
That joker is dead from old age . . .
I have come too late. As if it matters!
I may not show myself anywhere,
But on the walls I touch the paintings
And by the fire I warm myself. Is that not a miracle?
Through this mould, these fumes, this dust
Two sparkling emeralds flashed,
And a cat mewed. Well, let's go home!

But where is my home and where my reason?

1940

25 see pp. 49, 77

Wild honey smells of freedom,
Dust – of the rays of the sun,
A maiden's mouth – of violets,
But gold – has none.
Mignonette smells of water,
Love smells of apples
But we have learnt for ever
That blood only smells of blood . . .
In vain the Roman governor
Washed his hands before the people
To the threatening cries of the rabble;
In vain the Queen of Scots
Washed from her slender palms
The gory blood-red drops
In the stifling royal chamber . . .

[Mid-1930s]

26 see p. 77

About Poetry

To Vladimir Narbut

It's – the residue of sleepless nights,
It's – the snuff of crooked candles,
It's – a myriad white bell towers
And the first peal of morning . . .
It's – the windowsill all warm
In the moonlight of Chernigov,
It's – sweet clover, it's the bees,
It's – dust and murk and sultry heat.

27   *see pp. 77, 161*

My youthful hands
Signed that agreement
Amongst the flower kiosks
And crackle of gramophones,
Under the drunken, squinting gaze
Of streetlamps lit by gas.
And I was older than the century
By exactly ten years.

Against the sunset was laid
The white mourning of cherry trees,
That came tumbling down
In a fine, fragrant, dry rain . . .
And the clouds were riddled through
With the gory foam of Tsushima,
And landaus smoothly bore the people
Who have died long since . . .

That evening would have
Seemed to us like a masquerade,
Would have seemed like a carnival,
Like a scene of magic, grand gala . . .

Not a splinter remains of that house,
That avenue of trees has been felled,
Those hats and little shoes long since
Have gone to rest in museums.

Who knows how empty the sky is
On the spot of the fallen tower,
Who knows how quiet the house is,
Where the son has not come home?

You are always there, like conscience,
Like air, you are always with me,
Why then do you call me to account?
Your witnesses I know:

The dome of the Pavlovsk Station,
All glowing red with music,
And the waterfall, white-maned,
By the Palace of the Babolovs.

1940

28   see p. 78

The Last Toast

I drink to my ruined home,
To my cruel life I drink,
To the loneliness we shared
And to you I drink –
To the lie on the lips which betrayed me,
To the deathly cold of your eyes,
To the cruelty and crudeness on earth,
To the God who forsook me.

1934

29   see p. 78

Already madness with its wing
Has spread itself over half my soul
And gives me fiery wine to drink
And lures me into the black valley.

And I understood that I have
To cede victory to it, whilst
Hearkening to my own delirium
As if someone else were raving.

And it will not permit me
To take anything away of mine
(However much I may implore,
However much I do entreat it) –

Neither the petrified eyes of my son –
Which have turned to stone from suffering,
Nor the day, when the storm arose,
Nor the hour of prison meeting,

Nor the dear, cool touch of hands,
Nor the agitated linden shadows,
Nor the distant gentle murmur –
The final words of consolation.

4 May 1940
Fontanny House

30   *see p. 85*

To M. Lozinsky

The heavy amber day drags on for ever!
How sadness is impossible, how expectation vain!
And with its silvered voice the deer in the park
Speaks of the Northern Lights yet again.

I then believed that there exists cool snow
And a blue font for those who are poor and ill,
And such an unsteady ride of small sleighs
To the sound of ancient chimes from distant bells.

[1913]

31   *see p. 85*

"Tall woman, where is your little gypsy boy,
He, who would cry under your black shawl,
Where is your tiny first-born child,
What do you know of him, what recall?"

"A mother's fate is a joyous torment,
And I was not worthy of that fate.
The gates to white Paradise opened wide,
And Magdalene took from me my little son.

My every day was fine and joyous,
And in the long springtime I lost my way,
But for their burden my arms still mourn,
And in my sleep I hear his cries.

My heart grows languid and anxious,
And then I remember just nothing,
I keep on wandering through the dark rooms,
I go on searching for his tiny cradle."

1914

32   *see p. 85*

We shall not drink from the same glass
Neither water, nor sweet wine,
We shall not kiss of a morning early,
Nor glance through the window at evening time.
You breathe with the sun, I breathe with the moon,
But love for each other keeps us alive.

With you, you always have your gay companion,
With me I have my loving, faithful friend.
But in your grey eyes the fear I understand,
You are the cause of my malaise.
We never try to increase our brief encounters.
Thus is our peace ordained to be kept.

Your voice alone sings in my poems,
In your verses my breath breathes.
Oh, there is a fire, which neither fear
Nor oblivion dares touch.
And if you did but know how I love
Your dry, rose-coloured lips.

1913

33   *see p. 101*

Epilogue

The hour of remembrance draws near.
Once more I hear, I feel, I see you here:

You, whom to the window they barely led,
You, who this earth no longer tread,

And you who, shaking your beautiful head,
Came here as though home, you said.

I would like to name each one in turn,
But they've taken the list; there's nowhere to learn.

From the poor words you used, which I overheard,
I have woven for you a burial shroud.

I shall remember them everywhere, always,
I shall not forget them come fresh evil days,

And if they shut my tortured mouth,
Through which a hundred million shout,

Then may you too remember me
On the eve of my remembrance day.

If they think someday in this country
To raise a monument to me,

To this solemn gesture I consent,
But with the condition that it be put

Not by the sea where I was born
(My last bond with the sea is torn),

Nor in the park by the hallowed tree
Where an inconsolable shade seeks me,

But here where three hundred hours and more
I stood and no one unlocked the door.

Because even in blessed death I'm afraid
I'll forget the noise Black Marias made

And the ugly way the door slammed shut
And the old woman's howl like a beast that was hurt.

And from my motionless bronze lids
May the thawing snow stream down like tears

And the prison dove coo from afar
And the boats go quietly down the Neva.

1940
March

34   *see p. 105*
see p. 105

All the souls of those I loved are on distant stars.
How wonderful that there is none to lose
And one can weep. The air of Tsarskoe Selo
Was made for songs to be repeated.

The silvery willow standing by the shore
Touches the brilliant September waters.
Resurrected from times of long ago, silently
My shadow comes towards me.

Here so many lyres are hanging on the branches,
It seems for mine as well there is a place.
And this fine, sunny, scattered shower
Brings me consolation and glad tidings.

1921

35   *see p. 105*

The fifth act of the drama
Lies in the autumnal air.
In the park each flowerbed
Seems to be a fresh-dug grave.
A quiet wake has been held,
And there is nothing more to be done.
Why then do I linger, as though
A miracle may soon occur?
Thus it's possible, with a frail hand,
To hold a heavily laden boat
By a pier whilst bidding farewell
To those who have remained on shore.

[1921]

36   *see pp. 105, 132*

In that house it was terrifying to live,
And neither the patriarchal heat of the hearth,
Nor the tiny cradle of our child,
Nor that both of us were young
And brimming with ideas . . .
. . . . nor that good fortune
For all of seven years dared not depart
One single step from our threshold –
Did not diminish this feeling of fear.
And I learnt to laugh at it
And would leave a tiny drop of wine
And crumbs of bread for him who by night
Would scratch at the door like a dog
Or peer through the narrow little window,
Whilst after midnight we would endeavour not to see
What was transpiring through the looking glass,
Under whose most heavy pace
The dark steps of the staircase groaned,
As though begging dolefully for mercy,
And you said, with a strange smile:
"Whom are *they* carrying down the staircase?"

Now you are there, where all is known –Tell me:
What lived in that house apart from us?

1921
Ts. S.

37   *see p. 108, 111*

Dusk falls and in the dark blue sky,
Where not long since the Temple of Jerusalem
Shone in mysterious majesty, only
Two stars gleam above the tangle of branches,
And from somewhere the snow is scurrying, not from above,
But seemingly rising from the ground,
Lazily, caressingly and carefully.
I had a strange walk that day.
When I left home a transparent light
On things and faces dazzled me,
As though everywhere petals lay
Of those yellow pink-tinged roses,
The name of which I have forgotten.
The dry, windless, frosty air
Preserved and nurtured each sound in such a way,
That it seemed to me: there is no silence.
And on the bridge, through rusty railings
Children thrust their hands in mittens
To feed the variegated, greedy ducks,
Which were tumbling in the black ice-hole.
And I thought: it cannot be
That someday I should forget this,
And if a difficult path lies ahead of me,
Here is a light burden, which I have the strength
To take with me, so that in old age or illness,
May be in penury, I could recall
That violent sunset and the fullness
Of my spiritual strength and the charm of a sweet life.

1914–16: [1940]

38   *see p. 116*

> On both sides
> The pillow has grown hot.
> Now the second candle
> Burns out, and louder grows
> The cawing of the crows.
> I did not sleep that night,
> It's late to think of sleep . . .
> How unbearably white is the blind
> Against the white window.
> Good morning!
>
> *1909*

39   *see p. 116*

Little Song

> At the rising of the sun
> I do sing of love,
> In the garden on my knee
> Goosefoot I do weed.
>
> I pluck it out and throw away –
> May I be forgiven.
> Sobbing by the fence
> A barefoot girl I see.
>
> Of the voice of trouble
> The resounding cries do frighten me,
> The warm smell is stronger still
> Of the dead goosefoot.
>
> There will be stone in place of bread,
> My reward of evil.
> Above me is the sky alone,
> And with me is your voice.
>
> *1911*

40   *see pp. 28–9*

To Natalya Rykova

Everything is ravaged, bartered, betrayed,
The black wing of death has hovered nearby,
Everything is gnawed through by hungry gloom,
Why then did we feel so light of heart?

By day the matchless forest near the town
Is sweet with the breath of cherry trees,
The depths of the limpid skies of July
Are aglitter with new constellations by night –

And the miraculous is drawing so close
To the dirty, tumbledown houses . . .
Not known, not known to anyone,
Yet desired by us from olden times.

1921

41   *see p. 121*

I am not with those who left their land
For enemies to tear apart.
No heed I pay to their gross flattery,
My songs I will not give to them.

But I feel pity for the exiled,
As for prisoners or the sick.
Obscure is your road, O wanderer,
Bitter the taste of alien corn.

But here, in the dense fumes of the fire
Destroying what's left of one's youth,
Not a single solitary blow
Did we try to deflect from ourselves.

And we know that in the final count
Each hour will have its reckoning . . .
But the world knows no people more tearless,
More proud, more simple than we.

1922

42 *see p. 121*

Voronezh

To O.M.

The whole town stands covered in ice.
The trees, the walls, the snow are as though under glass.
Tentatively I walk over the crystals.
The decorated sledges bump along.
Crows flying over Peter's statue in Voronezh,
And poplar trees and the bright green vault,
Eroded, dulled in the dust of the sun,
And the slopes – are redolent of Kulikov Battle,
In the mighty, victorious land.
And the poplar trees, like clinking beakers,
At once will sound more loudly over us,
As though a thousand guests are drinking
To our triumph at the bridal feast.

But in the room of the poet in disgrace
Fear and the muse keep watch in turn.
The night presses on,
Which knows no dawn.

[4 March 1936]

43   *see p. 122*

[In the Mirror]

A row of fine beads round my neck,
I hide my arms in a large muff,
My eyes gaze absentmindedly
And never again weep tears.

And my face, it seems, is paler
From the silk which grows more violet,
My uncurled fringe of hair
Reaches almost to my eyebrows.

And my halting, sluggish gait,
In no way resembling flight,
As though a raft lay under my legs
And not little squares of parquet floor.

And my pale mouth is slightly opened,
My laboured breathing is uneven,
And the flowers of a meeting I missed
Lie trembling on my breast.

1913

44   *see p. 132*

The Third Zachatyevsky

Little side road, little side ro . . .
Tightened the noose about my throat.

A breeze of freshness from the Moscow River.
In the windows lights are aglimmer.

A rotten lamppost leans awry –
A bell-ringer leaves the belfry . . .

Wasteland lies to the left,
A monastery to the right,

On the other side a tall maple tree
Crimsoned by the ruddy glow.

On the other side a tall maple tree
Listens to long groans at night.

I would like to find my little icon,
For my time is near its end,

I would like once again my black kerchief,
And a taste from the River Neva.

[1940]

45   *see p. 132*

My little curly-haired son I put to bed
And I went to the lake to draw water.
Singing songs I went, and I was happy.
I scooped up some water and listened:
And I heard a familiar voice,
The chiming of bells
From beneath the blue waves,
Thus our bells were tolled in Kitezh city.
The great bells peal in Saint George's,
And the small bells ring from Annunciation Tower,
And in threatening tones they speak:
    "Oh, alone you left the attack,
    Our groans you did not hear,
    Our bitter destruction you did not see.
    But the everlasting candle burns bright
    At the throne of God for you.
    Why then did you tarry on earth
    And don't hasten to don your martyr's crown?
    Your lily has blossomed at midnight,
    And the bridal veil is woven down to your feet.
    Why then do you sadden your warrior brother
    And your innocent sister, the nun,
    And cause your little child to sorrow? ..."
No sooner had I heard the last word,
Than everything went dark before my eyes,
When I looked back – the house was plunged in flames.

March, 1940

46   *see pp. 136, 140*

When they come to bury an age,
And no psalm rings out above the grave,
Only thistles and nettles
Are doomed to adorn it.
Only the gravediggers toil apace.
The work cannot wait!
And Lord, it's so quiet, so quiet,
That the passing of time can be heard.
And later it floats to the surface,
Like a corpse on the river in spring –
But the son won't know his mother,
And the grandson turns away in despair.
And heads bow ever lower,
Like the toing and froing of the moon.

Thus – over fallen Paris
Such a silence now reigns.

[5 August 1940]

47   *see p. 137*

Cradle Song

Far away in a large, large forest,
By the blue river waters,
Lived a poor woodcutter with his children
In a small, dark hut.

His youngest son was as tall as a thumb –
How can I calm you,
Sleep, my quiet one, sleep, my son,
I am a bad mother.

News does arrive but seldom
At our hearth and home,
They have given to your father
A little white cross.

There was grief, there will be grief,
There is no end to grief,
May Saint George watch over,
And keep your father safe.

48   *see p. 138*

The little boy who plays on the pipes,
And the little girl who weaves a garland,
And two footpaths crossing in the forest,
And in the distant field a distant light –

I see it all. I remember it all.
I keep it lovingly gently in my heart.
There is only one thing I never know
And cannot even remember anymore.

I ask neither for wisdom nor for strength.
Only grant that I be warmed at the fire!
I feel the cold ... With wings or without wings
The God of Joy will not be visiting me.

1911

49   *see p. 140*

The Shade

What does a woman alone know
about the hour of death?

O MANDELSTAM

Always more elegant than all, rosier and taller,
Why do you float up from the depths of the lost years,
Why does grasping memory wave before me
Your transparent profile behind carriage windows?
How arguments ran then – were you angel or bird?
Solóminka a poet used to call you.
Equally upon all through your black lashes
The gentle light of your Daryal eyes would fall.

O shade! Forgive me, but cloudless weather,
Flaubert, insomnia and the late lilac
Made me think of you – the beauty of the year '13 –
And your cloudless and untroubled day
I recalled . . . But such memories as these
Do not become me. O shade!

[9 August 1940]

50   *see p. 147*

My imagination, obedient to me,
Portrays your grey eyes vividly.
And in Tver, when lonely, I recall
Bitterest memories of you.

Happy captive in beautiful arms
On the left bank of the Neva,
My celebrated contemporary,
It happened just as you desired,

You, who gave me orders: it's enough,
Just go off and kill your love!
And now I melt, I lose my desire,
But ever stronger beats my blood.

And if I should die, then who will write
And send on to you my poems,
And who will help to make sure that my
As yet unspoken words ring out?

Slepnyovo
1913

51   *see p. 161*

To Londoners

Time is now writing the twenty-fourth drama
Of Shakespeare with a passionless hand.
Ourselves participants in the awful feast,
We had better read *Hamlet, Caesar* or *Lear*
Over the river laden with lead;
We had better follow fair Juliet this day
With torches and singing to where she will rest.
Better to glance at Macbeth through the window,
Tremble together with the hired assassin,
Only not this, not this, not this,
We no longer have the strength to read this.

1940

52 *see p. 173*

> But I give you solemn warning,
> I am living for the last time.
> Not as a maple, or a swallow,
> Not as a star, or a reed,
> Nor water from a source,
> Nor the peal of bells –
> Shall I trouble people
> Or visit others' dreams
> With an unrequited groan.
>
> *1940*

53 *see p. 173*

> No, it's not I, someone else is suffering.
> I could not suffer thus, and as for what happened,
> May black cloth cover it and let
> The lights be taken away . . .
>   Night.

54   *see p. 188*

First Long-Range Shelling of Leningrad

And all the motley bustle of the crowd
All of a sudden changed.
But this was not a city noise,
Nor yet a country sound.
It was rather like the brother,
To a peal of distant thunder,
But thunder has the moisture
Of lofty fresh-formed clouds
And the longing of the meadows –
News of happy showers.
But this, like torrid heat, was dry,
And our hearing, in confusion,
Had no wish to believe
That it was growing and spreading,
And that, quite without concern, it
Was bringing ruin to my child.

[September 1941]

"...But strong are the bolts of prison gates"

Lev Nikolaevich Gumilyov (1912–92): son of Gumilyov and Akhmatova; Orientalist, specialist in the history of the peoples of Central Asia. Arrested in 1935, but freed after Akhmatova's letter to Stalin; rearrested in 1938; in 1944, from exile in the Turukhan Region (where he had been sent after the labour camp) he went as a volunteer to the front.

After the war, in 1948, he defended his candidate's dissertation on the subject of "The Political History of the First Turkic Kahnate (546–659)". Arrested again in 1949; freed and rehabilitated only in 1956. Four years later, in 1960, he published the book *Khunnu. Central Asia in Ancient Times* [*Khunnu. Sredinnaya Aziya v drevnie vremena*] (Moscow: Izd-vo. vostochnoy lit.); in 1961, he defended his doctoral dissertation on "The Ancient Turki of the 6th and 7th Centuries". This, however, was not Gumilyov's only doctoral dissertation. In the mid-'70s he also defended a doctoral dissertation on physical geography science, "Ethnogenesis and The Earth's Biosphere" [Etnogenez i biosfera Zemli].

Lev Nikolaevich worked on the history of the Ancient Turkis and other Eurasian peoples of the Steppe; he studied and made classifications of historico-cultural ethnic types according to a people's relations to the character of its geographical surroundings; he worked on the history of Tibetan art of the Middle Ages, on problems in the interpretation of *The Lay of Igor's Campaign* and on many other topics. His other published books are: *The Discovery of Khazaria* [*Otkrytie Khazarii*], with a foreword by Prof. M. I. Artamonov (Moscow: Nauka, 1966); *Ancient Turkic Peoples* [*Drevnie Tyurki*] (Moscow: Nauka, 1967); *The Search for an Imaginary Kingdom: The Legend of "the Realm of John the Presbyter"* [*Poiski vymyshlennogo tsarstva: Legenda o "gosudarstve presvitera Ioanna"*], with a foreword by Professor S. Rudenko (Moscow: Nauka, 1970); *Hsiung-Nu in China: Three Centuries of China's Wars with the Peoples of the Steppe from the 3rd to the 6th Centuries* [*Khunny v Kitae: Tri veka voyny Kitaya so stepnymi narodami III–VI vv*] (Moscow: Nauka, 1974); *Old Buryat Painting* [*Staroburyatskaya zhivopis*] (Moscow: Iskusstvo, 1977).

I cite those of Gumilyov's books published in recent years which are of a scientific nature: *Ancient Rus and the Great Steppe* [*Drevnyaya Rus i velikaya step*] (Moscow, 1989); *Ethnogenesis and the Earth's Biosphere* [*Etnogenez i biosfera Zemli*] went into three editions (the latest is Leningrad, 1990) and two books on religious themes: *Lest the Candle be Extinguished* [*Chtoby svecha ne pogasla*] and, with A. Panchenko, *The Holy Bible* [*Zakon Bozhiy*] (Leningrad, 1990).

When telling me about her efforts to save her son, Anna Andreevna mentioned the writer L. Seyfullina's name with particular gratitude; at various times she also mentioned the following scholars: M. I. Artamonov,

A. P. Okladnikov, V. V. Struve; after Stalin's death, as far as I remember, she conducted her efforts with the help of the writers A. Surkov, A. Fadeev, I. Erenburg, the Orientalist N. I. Konrad and the architect L. V. Rudnev.

A constant help to Anna Andreevna in these efforts was E. G. Gershteyn. In 1976, she published a special work about events leading up to the release of Lev Gumilyov. (See "Memoirs and Facts" in the journal *Russian Literature Triquarterly* (no. 13, Ann Arbor: Ardis) – also published in Russia in 1989 (*Gorizont*, no. 6).

Matvey Petrovich Bronshteyn (1906–38): theoretical physicist, worked for the Leningrad Physico-Technical Institute (now the A. F. Ioffe Institute), Doctor of Sciences of Leningrad University, author of scientific works in the field of gravitational theory, cosmology, astrophysics and relativistic quantum theory. However, Bronshteyn's contribution to science is not limited to this: he is also the author of other works, particularly articles on nuclear physics and the theory of semi-conductors.

M. P. Bronshteyn's works started to appear in print in 1925. They were published in *Zhurnal Fiziko-khimicheskogo obshchestva*, in *Physikalische Zeitschrift*, in *Zhurnal geofiziki i meteorologii*, in *Nauchnoe Slovo* and many others.

In November 1935, M. P. Bronshteyn defended his doctoral dissertation on the subject of "The Quantization of Gravitational Waves". The results of this were published in 1936, in volume VI of *Zhurnal eksperimentalnoy i teoreticheskoy fiziki*, and in 1979, part of the 1936 article was reprinted, this time in the collection *Albert Einstein and the Theory of Gravity* [*Albert Eynshteyn i teoriya gravitatsii*] (Moscow: Mir).

A few foreign books dealing with various branches of physics came out in translation, edited and with a foreword by M. P. Bronshteyn (e.g. in 1937, P.A.M. Dirac's book *The Principles of Quantum Mechanics* [*Osnovy kvantovoy mekhaniki*], published by ONTI).

Apart from purely scientific works (more than 30 in total), M. P. Bronshteyn wrote popular articles in magazines, as well as popular science books and literary science works: thus, in 1935, ONTI published two of his popular books: *The Structure of Matter* and *Atoms, Electrons, Nuclei* [*Stroenie veshchestva* and *Atomy, elektrony, yadra*]; in 1936, Detgiz published the first of his popular science books: *Solar Matter* [*Solnechnoe veshchestvo*]; in 1937, they also published *X-Rays* and *The Inventors of the Radio-Telegraph* [*Luchi Iks* and *Izobretateli radiotelegrafa*]. In Russia science fiction is a branch of popular science literature. S. Ya Marshak promoted this genre through his editorial activities at Detgiz. *The Inventors of the Radio-Telegraph* came out at the time of Matvey Petrovich's arrest, and all copies of it were destroyed. Only the first version was published in the journal *Kostyor* (no. 4–5, 1936).

For more about M. P. Bronshteyn's role in the development of theoretical physics, popular and scientific literature, see, in particular:

The Big Soviet Encyclopaedia [*BSE*]. 3rd ed., vol. 4, M. S. Sominsky. Abram Fyodorovich Ioffe (Moscow and Leningrad: Nauka, 1964);

V. Ya. Frenkel, *Yakov Ilich Frenkel* (Moscow and Leningrad, 1966);

S. Ya. Marshak, "The Tale of a Discovery". *God XVIII: Almanakh.* No. 8, ed. A. M. Gorky (Moscow);

Lydia Chukovskaya, "On Books Forgotten or Unnoticed". *Voprosy literatury*. No. 2, 1958;

L. Landau, "A Few Words about this Book": Introduction to *Solar Matter* [*Solnechnoe veshchestvo*], 2nd ed. (Moscow, 1959);

D. Danin, "The Thirst for Clarity" *Novy mir*, no. 3, 1960;

G. E. Gorelik, "The First Steps in Quantum Gravitation and Planckian Quantities". *The Einstein Collection* [*Eynshteynovsky sbornik*]. 1978–79 (Moscow: Nauka, 1983);

G. E. Gorelik, V. Ya. Frenkel, "M. P. Bronshteyn and his Role in the Formation of the Quantum Theory of Gravity". *Eynshteynovsky sbornik*, 1980–81 (Moscow: Nauka, 1985);

A. D. Sakharov, *Memoirs* [*Vospominaniya*] (New York: Chekhov Publishing House, 1990), p. 165, and the journal *Znamya*, no. 11, 1990, p. 147.

In 1989, Nauka published *Matvey Petrovich Bronshteyn* by G. E. Gorelik and V. Ya. Frenkel; in 1990, a volume of general scientific works by M. Bronshteyn, *Solar Matter* [*Solnechnoe veshchestvo*], came out.

M. P. Bronshteyn was arrested in August 1937. Only 20 years later, in 1957, did I receive official notification about the death of my husband and his rehabilitation "in the absence of incriminating evidence". By comparing the date of his "death" given in one notification, with the date of sentencing in another, it is evident that he was "tried" on 18 February 1938 and "died" – i.e. was shot – on the same day. In February 1938, they came for me too, but by chance did not find me at home.

The following physicists participated in efforts to free M. P. Bronshteyn: S. I Vavilov, A. F. Ioffe, L. I. Mandelshtam, I. E. Tamm and V. A. Fok; as did the writers: S. Marshak and K. Chukovsky.

A Note on the Fate of My Journals

My *Akhmatova Journals* did not have an ordinary fate. Some copies which managed to find their way into the Soviet Union from abroad became the property not only of the readers, not only of honest researchers, in the habit of acknowledging their sources, but some were also appropriated by witting and unwitting predators, with no reference to the *Akhmatova Journals*. In one article or book or another about Akhmatova I would read Anna Andreevna's words (or even my own!), which the author had made his own. My name was banned for 16 years – whoever wanted could take whatever he wanted! Now the ban on my name has been lifted. And still articles and memoirs by strangers are just as full of quotations as before, with no reference to my work. It is as if this book was born out of nowhere, and has no master. I know for certain that Akhmatova did not speak only to me, and that when talking about the same subject she often repeated herself. But I maintain that where I have put her words in quotation marks, I wrote them down without translating them into the language of another generation (as did many of those she spoke to). I did not paraphrase, but reproduced them word for word . . . Under photographs of Anna Akhmatova the name of the photographer usually appears. His work is respected. So why is it that my work, the work of a writer over many years, is not accorded the same respect or protection? I used to go and see Akhmatova without a microphone, but equipped with other apparatus, no less powerful: my memory, which I put to use constantly throughout my childhood, teens and young adult life, a memory for words, poetry and prose.

5 March 1993

Behind the Scenes
(facts, people, books, documents)

I am deeply grateful to my friends who have never failed to help me in my work: E. G. Gershteyn, N. N. Glen, the late V. M. Zhirmunsky, V. V. Ivanov, V. N. Kornilov, A. G. Nayman, the late N. A. Olshevskaya, Evg. B. and E. B. Pasternak, and the late M. S. Petrovykh.

I am also grateful to Zh. O. Khavkina, an irreplaceable helper over many years of work, and E. Ts. Chukovskaya. I wish, particularly, to express my appreciation of E. B. Efimov, who has enriched my work with diverse bibliographical and archival information.

May I warn the reader that in the footnotes and in the numbered notes I have used information drawn from books and articles which were published no later than 1992. Immediately following the journal entries is a selection of those poems by Anna Akhmatova without which our conversations cannot be understood.

The section "... But strong are the bolts of prison gates" contains information on Anna Andreevna's son (L. N. Gumilyov) and my husband (M. P. Bronshteyn), with whose prison fates we were then preoccupied.

The footnotes supply only the most essential information: either the very briefest information on facts and people or bibliographical references to Akhmatova's works and excerpts from Akhmatova's texts.

All additional explanatory material has been arranged according to the dates in my diary and can be found in the numbered notes that follow.

*　　　*　　　*

The titles which occur most frequently in the footnotes and numbered notes have been abbreviated as follows:

FSB – Anna Akhmatova, *From Six Books* [*Iz shesti knig*] (Leningrad: Sovetskiy pisatel, 1940).

FT – Anna Akhmatova, *The Flight of Time* [*Beg vremeni*] (Moscow and Leningrad: Sovetskiy pisatel, 1965).

Works – Anna Akhmatova, *Works* [*Sochineniya*]. Jointly edited by G. P. Struve and B. A. Filippov (Washington: Mezhdunarodnoe literaturnoe sodruzhestvo). Vol. 1, 1967 (2nd edition revised and extended); vol. 2, 1968.

In Memory A.A. – Anna Akhmatova. Poems in the collection: *In Memory of Anna Akhmatova* [*Pamyati Anny Akhmatovoy*] (Paris: YMCA-Press, 1974).

BPL–A – Anna Akhmatova, *Lyric and Narrative Poems* [*Stikhotvoreniya i poemy*]. Compiled, edited and annotated by V. M. Zhirmunsky (Leningrad: Sovetskiy pisatel, 1976). (Poet's Library, big series.)

Articles – Anna Akhmatova, *Articles and Pieces* [*Stati i zametki*]. Compiled and annotated, with an afterword by E. G. Gershteyn. 3rd edition, revised. (Moscow: Kniga, 1989).

My Voice – Anna Akhmatova, *They Will Recognize My Voice . . . Lyrics Poems. Narrative Poems. Prose. The Poet's Image* [*Uznayut golos moy . . . Stikhotvoreniya. Poemy. Proza. Obraz poeta.*] Compiled by N. N. Glen, L. A. Ozerov (Moscow: Pedagogika, 1989).

Akhmatova. Ardis – Anna Akhmatova, *Poems, Letters, Memoirs, Iconography* [*Stikhi, perepiska, vospominaniya, ikonografiya*]. Compiled by E. Proffer (Ann Arbor: Ardis, 1977).

Journals, vol. 2 – Lydia Chukovskaya, *The Akhmatova Journals* [*Zapiski ob Anne Akhmatovy*]. Vol. 2, 1952–62 (Paris: YMCA-Press, 1980); *Neva*, no. 4, nos. 5–6, nos. 7–9, 1993.

Memoirs A.A. – the collection: *Memoirs about Anna Akhmatova* [*Vospominaniya ob Anne Akhmatovoy*]. Compiled by V. I. Vilenkin and V. A. Chernykh. Annotated by A. V. Kurt and K. M. Polivanov (Moscow: Sovetskiy pisatel, 1991).

Meetings – P. N. Luknitsky, *Meetings with Anna Akhmatova* [*Vstrechi s Annoy Akhmatovoy*]. Vol. 1, 1924–25. Paris: YMCA-Press, 1991.

Papers on A.A. – *Papers on Akhmatova* [*Akhmatovskiye chteniya*]. In the collection *Secrets of the Craft* [*Tayny remesla*]. Issue no. 2 (Moscow: Nasledie, 1992).

BPL–P – Boris Pasternak, *Lyric and Narrative Poems* [*Stikhotvoreniya i poemy*] (Moscow and Leningrad: Sovetskiy pisatel, 1965). (Poet's Library, big series.)

BPL–M – Osip. Mandelstam, *Lyric Poems* [*Stikhotvoreniya*] (Leningrad: Sovetskiy pisatel, 1973). (Poet's Library, big series.)

Faces – the collection *Faces* [*Litsa*]. A biographical almanac, 1st edition. Compiled by A. V. Lavrov (Moscow and St Petersburg: Feniks-Atheneum, 1992).

*   *   *

1938

1. Nikolay Nikolaevich Punin (1888–1953): art historian and critic, author of the books *Japanese Engravings* [*Yaponskaya gravyura*] (1915), *Andrey Rublyov* (1916), *Tatlin* (1921). In 1920, N. Punin's book *Contemporary Art* [*Sovremennoe iskusstvo*] (a series of lectures) came out; in 1927–28, *New Directions in Russian Art* [*Noveyshie techeniya v russkom iskusstve*]; and in 1940, the textbook *The History of West European Art* [*Istoriya zapadnoevropeyskogo iskusstva*]. In 1976, many years after Punin's death and rehabilitation, the publishers Sovetskiy Khudozhnik published a collection of selected articles by him: N. N. Punin, *Russian and Soviet Art* [*Russkoe i sovetskoe iskusstvo*].

   Before the Revolution (from 1913 to 1916), N. N. Punin worked for the journal *Apollon*; after the Revolution, he was a commissar attached to the Russian Museum and the Leningrad State Hermitage; he was deputy to A. V. Lunacharsky, People's Commissar of Enlightenment, for museums and the preservation of monuments, and he taught at institutions of higher education.

   Punin was arrested twice; he was released the first time, but the second time he died in prison.

   Many of Akhmatova's poems are dedicated to Punin. For example, "The fantastic autumn constructed a high cupola" (*FT, Anno Domini*); "And you'll forgive me" (*BPL–A*, p. 288); "They led you away at daybreak" (*My Voice*, p. 295); "From you I hid my heart", No. 21; "Not for weeks, not for months – but for years", "And as always happens in days of severance", "I drink to my ruined home" (*FT, The Reed*). After N. N. Punin's death Akhmatova dedicated the poem "And that heart will no longer show a response" (*FT, Seventh Book*) to him.

   One of the "Northern Elegies" ("So here it is – that autumnal landscape") is also addressed to Punin; judging by the lines

   > Fifteen years that seemed as though they were
   > Fifteen pretended centuries of granite

Anna Andreevna's marriage to Punin lasted 15 years (from 1923 to 1938). Subsequently Akhmatova placed an epigraph from Pushkin at the start of the entire "Northern Elegies" cycle "All a sacrifice in memory to you". It is very possible that she is referring to Punin with these words. On their relationship in the first years of their marriage see a piece by I. N. Punina in the almanac *Faces*, "From Nikolay Nikolaevich Punin's Archives" – a piece in which the correspondence between Anna Andreevna and Nikolay Nikolaevich is given, in particular, from the time when he went to Japan on business in 1927. N. N. Punin's daughter, Irina Nikolaevna, is also the author of a biographical sketch on him – see volume 2 of *Papers on A.A.*, p. 271.

2. Vasily Vasilievich Knyazev (1887–1937, shot): poet; a satirist before the

Revolution, author of *The Red Gospel* [*Krasnoye evangelie*]; *The Song of the Red Bell-Ringer* [*Pesni krasnogo zvonarya*]; after the Revolution *Red Bells and Songs* [*Krasnye zvony i pesni*]; permanent employee at *Krasnaya gazeta*. In 1937, Knyazev was arrested and shot.

Prince Dmitry Petrovich Svyatopolk-Mirsky (1890–1939): specialist on Russian and English literature; he emigrated to England in 1922, where he compiled anthologies of Russian poetry, wrote on Russian literature and taught Russian literature at the University of London; in 1932, already a member of the Communist Party of Great Britain, he returned to the Soviet Union; there he published articles on Eliot, Joyce, Smollett, Huxley (some in journals, some as prefaces to books) and compiled an anthology of English poetry. In 1937, D. P. Svyatopolk-Mirsky was arrested; he died in a labour camp in 1939.

1939

3. A.A. recited: "You have not died yet, you are not yet alone" and "As along the streets of Kiev-Viy" – see: *BPL–M*, pp. 187 and 200.

4. Evidently, I took Anna Andreevna's claim regarding her illness to be a medically established fact and immediately informed Korney Ivanovich of this misfortune. I recently learnt that the following document, addressed to A. A. Fadeev and written in Korney Ivanovich's hand, is kept in TsGALI:

> Dear Aleksandr Aleksandrovich,
> In a few days, on 25 or 26 February, Anna Akhmatova will be coming to Moscow. She has cancer. The cancer is external – on her forehead – so she can still be saved. She will stay at Nikolay Iv. Khardzhiev's. [Telephone] K 4–21-90. We heartily beg you to take most decisive measures to get her urgent medical and financial help.
>
> F. Panfyorov   S. Marshak
> K. Chukovsky   Olga Forsh
> Vera Inber

In the margin, on the right, a note: "According to N. I. Khardzhiev, A. Akhmatova does not, at present, need medical or material help. 27.2.39" (TsGALI, f[archive].631, SP [Writers' Union] SSSR [USSR] contents 15, unit 407, p. 96.)

5. *Nikolay Ivanovich Khardzhiev* (b. 1903): prose writer, art historian, poetry specialist. He has written stories about Fedotov, Baranshchikov, Polzunov, as well as numerous articles on innovations in fine art, and also on poetry. See, for example, his article "Mayakovsky and Painting" [Mayakovsky i zhivopis] (Moscow, 1940). N. Khardzhiev co-edited the first volume of the first posthumous *Complete Works of V. Mayakovsky* [*Polnoe sobranie sochineniy V. Mayakovskogo*] with V. Trenin (Moscow, 1935); with T. Grits he co-edited the book *Unpublished Works of Velimir Khlebnikov* [*Neizdannye proizvedeniya Velimira Khlebnikova*] (Moscow, 1940); he prepared for publication and annotated a selection of poems by O. Mandelstam for the Poet's Library, big series (*BPL–M*).

N. I. Khardzhiev was a close friend of Akhmatova's and Mandelstam's.

A.A. and Nikolay Ivanovich met in Leningrad in 1930; from then on it became Akhmatova's practice to consult Nikolay Ivanovich about her poems, translations and prose. When completing her memoirs on Amedeo Modigliani, A.A. supplemented it with N. Khardzhiev's brief analysis, in which he maintains, in particular, that Modigliani's drawing of Akhmatova "has an affinity with the figure in one of the most famous architectural-sculptural structures of the 16th century": with the allegorical figure "Night" by Michelangelo on the lid of Giuliano de Medici's sarcophagus. (See the Moscow almanac *Day of Poetry* [*Den poezii*], 1967.)

In 1989, in the journal *Voprosy literatury*, no. 6, E. Babaev published Anna Akhmatova's letters to N. I. Khardzhiev; the same material was published in a greatly extended version in the second volume of *Papers on A.A.*, (p. 198, 1992).

6. *I know the Fontanka inside out*: A.A. lived on the Fontanka embankment, as far as I know, in various years in these houses: 1921–22 in house no. 18, in courtyard 4; in 1924 on the corner of the former Frantsuzskaya (now Kutuzovskaya) embankment, at 2, Fontanka; she spent about 30 years in the celebrated "Fontanny palace" (34, Fontanka), i.e. in the annexe of the former palace of the Sheremetev princes.

Olya – Olga Afanasevna Glebova-Sudeykina (1885–1945): stage actress, singer, dancer, a close friend of Anna Andreevna's. About her and her place in the life and poetry of Akhmatova see V. Zhirmunsky's commentary in *BPL–A*, pp. 457 and 513; apart from vol. 1 of my *Journals*, see also vol. 2.

Artur Lourié's memoirs ("Olga Afanasevna Glebova-Sudeykina") have been published in the almanac *Aerial Ways* [*Vozdushnye puti*] (New York, 1967, vol. 5, p. 139). In 1972, in France, a whole book devoted to her was published, about her life, about people close to her, about her work in the theatre, about the dolls she made, her embroidery, her designs on porcelain. See: Elaine Moch-Bickert. *Olga Glebova-Soudeikina – amie et inspiratrice des poètes*. Thèse présenté devant l'Université de Paris IV, Lille.

7. Mikhail Leonidovich Lozinsky (1886–1955): poet, member of the Poets' Guild, translator, editor of translations, a devoted friend, for over four decades, to Anna Akhmatova. It is not without reason that Akhmatova gives her famous definition of friendship in precisely the poem addressed to Lozinsky:

> ... over the seasons of the year,
> Indestructible and faithful,
> The lofty freedom of the soul,
> That bears the name of friendship ...

and in her "A Word about Lozinsky" she also stresses his devotion to his friends as the main trait of the departed.

In 1912, Mikhail Lozinsky dedicated his poem "She Who Did Not Forget" to Anna Andreevna (in 1916 it was included in the collection *Mountain Spring* [*Gornyy klyuch*]; Akhmatova addressed poems to Lozinsky from 1913 until 1940: "We shall not drink from the same glass" (1913; *FT, Rosary*); "The heavy amber day drags on for ever" (1913; *FT, Rosary*); "They are flying, they are still on their way" (1916; *FT, White Flock*); "Inscription in a book" (1940; *FT, Reed*). V. M. Zhirmunsky suggests also (see *BPL–A*, p. 457) that, apart from the aforementioned, two more of Akhmatova's poems of 1913 are addressed to Lozinsky: "The sun came

flooding into the room" and "You have come to comfort me, my darling!"
(*BPL-A*, p. 72).

Before the Revolution M. L. Lozinsky was secretary of the journal
Apollon and owned the publishing house Hyperborean. After the Revolution he was in charge of translations from Italian at the publishing house
Vsemirnaya literatura, where he was on the editorial board. From the '20s
onwards, translation became the main thing in Mikhail Leonidovich's life.
He translated Dante, Benvenuto Cellini; Lope de Vega, Tirso de Molina;
Goethe, Schiller; Shakespeare, John Fletcher, Kipling; Corneille, Leconte
de Lisle, Molière, Romain Rolland. Lozinsky also translated the Armenian
poet Sayat Nova and the Georgian N. Baratashvili; he worked on the
translation of Firdausi's *Shah-nama* and the Armenian epic *David Sasunsky*.

"... In the difficult and noble art of translation," writes Akhmatova
(see "A Word about Lozinsky"), "Lozinsky was to the 20th century what
Zhukovsky was to the 19th ... I met Mikhail Leonidovich Lozinsky in
1911, when he came to one of the first meetings of the Poets' Guild. That
was also the first time I heard him recite his poetry."

On M. L. Lozinsky see Ivan Tolstoy's essay "Sharply to the Wind!"
(*Leningrad Panorama* [*Leningradskaya panorama*], Leningrad: Sovetskiy pisa-
tel, 1988, p. 436) and memoirs by Elizaveta Miller "Mikhail Leonidovich
Lozinsky" (*Russkaya mysl*, 6 April 1990).

On M. L. Lozinsky see also *Journals*, vols. 2 and 3.

8. Dmitry Nikolaevich Zhuravlyov (1900–91): first a student, later an actor
    at the Vakhtangov Theatre. In 1931, D. N. Zhuravlyov developed an
    enthusiasm for "literary recital" and began giving public performances;
    his repertoire contained the most diverse works of Russian and West
    European poetry and prose: Pushkin, Gogol, Blok, Mayakovsky, Akhma-
    tova, Merimée, Maupassant.

    A.A. met Dmitry Nikolaevich in 1938 or 1939: it happened after Akhma-
    tova had heard him recite *The Queen of Spades*. There is a reference to his
    recital of "The Overcoat" – see *Journals*, vol. 2.

    D. N. Zhuravlyov is the author of memoirs on Akhmatova, published in
    his book *Life, Art, Meetings* [*Zhizn, iskusstvo, vstrechi*] (Moscow: VTO, 1985).

9. The words are from a short story by Chekhov. In this case A.A. calls men
    "the inferior race". However, in Chekhov's "The Lady with the Lapdog",
    these same words are spoken by the protagonist Dmitry Dmitrievich
    Gurov, and refer not to men, but to women.

10. In 1937, at the time of the rout of the Leningrad branch of Detizdat, headed
    by S. Ya. Marshak, Aleksandra Iosifovna Lyubarskaya, a member of staff
    at this publishing house, was arrested. At the investigation she was charged
    with spying for Japan, and sabotage. She was released on 14 January 1939,
    and when we met, she told me about the beatings she had endured while
    under interrogation. We were old friends: even before we worked together
    on the editorial staff, we had studied together in the Department of Phil-
    ology at the state courses attached to the Institute of Art History. (About
    the rout of the "Leningrad editorial staff" see Lydia Chukovskaya. *V
    laboratorii redaktora*. 2nd ed. Moscow: Iskusstvo, 1963, p. 322; A. Lyubar-
    skaya "Worse than Nothing". *Neva*, no. 1, 1989; A. Lyubarskaya "How
    it was". *Neva*, no. 7, 1990, and also *Journals*, vol. 2.)

    A. I. Lyubarskaya (b. 1908): editor and folklorist. Many folk and literary tales appeared and continue to appear adapted by her. She adapted tales of the peoples of the Soviet Union – first under the title of *The Magic Well* [*Volshebny Kolodets*] (1945), and later *In a Thrice Nine Kingdom, Beyond Thrice Ten Lands* [*V Tridevyatom Tsarstve, v Tridesyatom Gosudarstve*] (1966 and 1971). She wrote a prose version of the Karelo-Finnish epic *The Kalevala*, which has been published many times. A. Lyubarskaya, together with T. Gabbe, prepared for publication a collection *In the Footsteps of the Folk Tale* [*Po dorogam skazki*]; together with Z. Zadunayskaya, the famous book by Selma Lagerlöf *The Wonderful Adventures of Nils*; she also retold and adapted tales such as *The Fairy Tales of Topelius*, Asbjornsen's fairy tales and many others.

11. *Gesha* – Gersh Isaakovich Yegudin (1908–84): mathematician, Mitya's and my friend. It was he who saved me in February 1938: he rang Moscow from Leningrad and gave the people who were sheltering me to understand that they had come for me to my Leningrad flat with a warrant for my arrest. (See "Instead of a Foreword".)

12. The most precise demands of the Futurists, regarding the layout of lines and punctuation in poetry, were expressed by Mayakovsky in the article "How Are Verses Made" (1926).
     "Begone – rather ashamed am I ..."
     Mayakovsky then explains why in his poem "To Sergey Esenin" he doesn't put a full stop or an exclamation mark between the words "Infinity ... Fly", but breaks the line up into parts:

Infinity . . .
               You fly,
                         and make the stars shine brighter.

[Translation taken from Vladimir Mayakovsky. *How Are Verses Made?* Translated with an introduction and notes by George Hyde. Bristol: Bristol Classical Press, 1990.]

13. Boris Pasternak, *Safe Conduct* (Leningrad: Sovetskiy pisatel, 1931, p. 15). [Translation taken from *Safe Conduct* in *Boris Pasternak: The Voice of Prose* edited by Christopher Barnes. Edinburgh: Polygon Books, 1986.]

14. *I only like one story [of Maupassant's] – the one where the man goes mad*: let me remind you: the man loses his mind in the story "The Horla" (1886). I reread it recently. The story is written in the form of a diary of a mentally ill person, suffering from something like persecution mania. It seems to the hero that an invisible but terrible and powerful monster (which he calls the "Horla") has settled next to him, under the same roof, in his own house. The monster influences him by its powers of suggestion, and at night it sucks the life out of his closed lips. The hero conducts many experiments to check if the Horla really exists: for example, he leaves bread, carafes of water, milk, wine on the table in the evening, and in the morning he discovers that the water and milk have been drunk. At first, the hero considers the Horla as a figment of his disturbed imagination, but gradually he convinces himself of the reality of its presence and tries to destroy it by burning it.
     I don't know which year Akhmatova read the story for the first time. But when I reread it now against the background of my entries on Akhmatova, I couldn't help remembering many things: for instance, Vladimir Georgiev-

ich's words (spoken to me on 9 July 1940): Anna Andreevna "saw Sreznevskaya ill and . . . is looking for the same symptoms within herself"; I can't
help recalling the constant arguments between Anna Andreevna and those
around her: did they or did they not search her room in her absence? and,
finally, many, many poems – for example "The Northern Elegy" of 1921,
addressed to Gumilyov:

> In that house it was terrifying to live
> [...]
> And would leave a tiny drop of wine
> And crumbs of bread for him who by night
> Would scratch at the door like a dog
> Or peer through the narrow little window
> [...]
> Now you are there, where all is known – Tell me:
> What lived in that house apart from us?

Isn't it the same feeling which engulfs the hero of Maupassant's story:
somebody invisible is constantly watching me and, maybe, even living
under the same roof as me?

It seems to me that Akhmatova continually repeated to herself, like an
incantation, Pushkin's "God forbid I should go mad". Her mind was sober,
clear and perceptive. And that's exactly why her consciousness was so
filled with horror at what was happening (which others did not see) and
horror at the possibility of losing her mind. Akhmatova sensed things
more clearly than others and perceived what was happening; the reality
was monstrous; peering into the cellar of memory, she exclaimed:

> But where is my home and where my *reason*?

– or, creating her "Requiem":

> Already *madness* with its wing
> Has spread itself over half my soul . . .

. . . These are the kind of thoughts which rereading my *Journals* and
Maupassant's story, the one Akhmatova had mentioned about "a man who
is losing his mind", provoked in me quite spontaneously.

15.   . . . *a figurine by Danko*: a porcelain figurine made, in 1923, by the sculptor
Natalya Yakovlevna Danko, who worked in ceramics at the State Porcelain
Factory. In addition to this figurine, Natalya Danko (1892–1942) also
made a bust of Akhmatova, cast in bronze. Photographs of these two
pieces can be found in V. Vilenkin's book *In the Hundred-and-First Looking
Glass* [*V sto pervom zerkale*] (2nd ed., corrected and extended. Moscow:
Sovetskiy pisatel, 1990).

The porcelain figurine by Natalya Danko was painted by her sister
Elena Yakovlevna, who worked at the same factory for a time. (Then the
State Factory, since 1925 named after M. Lomonosov). Elena Yakovlevna
Danko (1898–1942) was not only a painter, but also a writer, poet,
memoirist and playwright. As well as memoirs on F. Sologub, she is the
author of several plays for the puppet theatre and several children's books,
the most famous of which is the book on the history of the porcelain
factory in Russia called *The Chinese Secret* [*Kitayskiy sekret*] (Moscow and
Leningrad, 1929).

Talking about her journey to Moscow, to visit the Mandelstams, on the eve of Osip Mandelstam's arrest in 1934, Akhmatova says that she didn't have enough money for the ticket and had to sell A. Remizov's book *The Order of Merit – Federation of Apes* [*Ordenskiy znak – Obezyaney palaty*] and Danko's figurine. "They were bought by S. Tolstaya for the Writers' Union Museum," says Akhmatova. (See Anna Akhmatova. *Works in Two Volumes* [*Sochineniya v dvukh tomakh*], vol. 2., Moscow: Khudozhestvennaya literatura, 1990, p. 214.)

Photographs of numerous works by Natalya Danko, which she made at the porcelain factory, have been displayed by Yu. M. Ovsyanikov in the collection *Panorama iskusstv*, no. 6 (Moscow, 1983). Among these are sculpted images of Novikov, Pushkin, Anna Pavlova and also figurines of a militiaman, a partisan and of a young woman embroidering a red banner, as well as a mustard pot, an ink pot, a mug and a powder box. For Elena Danko's selected poems and her memoirs on Fyodor Sologub, with a foreword by M. M. Pavlova, see the almanac *Faces*.

Akhmatova was friends with the Danko sisters. They both died during the war when, in 1942, they were evacuated, half dead, from the besieged city [of Leningrad] to the Urals. Elena Yakovlevna died in transit, on the train, and Natalya Yakovlevna soon after reaching their destination in Irbit.

16. *She asked whether I had heard of Pallada*: I will cite in full the lines dedicated to Pallada Olimpievna Gross by the literary scholars R. D. Timenchik and A. E. Parnis:

> Gross (Starynkevich, Bogdanova-Belskaya, Countess Berg, Deryuzhinskaya, Peddi-Kabetskaya) Pallada Olimpievna (1887–1968): poetess, author of the volume *Amulets* [*Amulety*] (Petrograd, 1915), graduate of the drama studio run by N. Evreinov. She was the prototype for Polina in Kuzmin's novel *The Sailor-Voyagers* [*Plavayushchie-puteshestvuyushchie*]. Petrograd poets dedicated many poems to her, which were compiled to form the album "Palladae" [*Pallada*], which was famous in literary circles. Some of those have been published, for example: M. Gartveld, "Nocturnal Seductions" [*Nochnye soblazny*] (St Petersburg, 1913, p. 55); B. A. Sadovskoy, "Death's Dwelling Place" [*Obitel smerti*] (Moscow, 1917, p. 25); V. Kurdyumov, "A Powdered Heart" [*Pudrennoe serdtse*], (St Petersburg, 1913, pp. 51–2). She appears under the name Diana Olimpievna in O. Morozov's story "A Fate" [*Odna sudba*] (Leningrad, 1972), and under the name Pallada Skuratova in V. Milashevsky's book *Yesterday and the Day Before. Memoirs of an Artist* [*Vchera, pozavchera. Vospominaniya khudozhnika*] (Leningrad, 1972, p. 85). (See: *Academy of Science Yearbook, 1983* [*Ezhegodnik AN SSR na 1983 . . .*], Leningrad: Nauka, 1985, p. 253.)

I cite also a passage from Pallada Gross' letter to Anna Akhmatova, written not long before Anna Andreevna's death, and two years before her own:

> I will probably die soon, therefore I very much want to see and hear you – I am now a shadow of the reckless Pallada. A terrible shadow, of no use to anyone. Whereas life bustles and leaps so fascinatingly . . . Thank God you ride along with it; as your contemporary, I am boundlessly happy for you and proud of you. I am

writing my memoirs . . . I have been writing them slowly and more often than not lying down.

(See the collection: *On Anna Akhmatova: Poems, Essays, Memoirs, Letters* [*Ob Anne Akhmatovoy: Stikhi. Esse. Vospominaniya. Pisma*], Leningrad: Lenizdat, 1990, p. 550.)

17. *Volodya* – Vladimir Kazimirovich Shileyko (1891–1930): Assyriologist, specialist in the ancient cultures of Middle Eastern Asia, an expert in dead cuneiform languages; he also wrote poetry. His principal work is *Votive Inscriptions of the Sumerian Rulers* [*Votivnye nadpisi shumeriyskikh praviteley*], with an essay on the history of Sumer (1915). Vladimir Kazimirovich was Akhmatova's second husband. They married in 1918 and separated in 1921. For a while they lived in Moscow.

When compiling her collection *FT* (see typed copy, stored in TsGALI), Anna Akhmatova created a special cycle, addressed to Shileyko: "Black Dream". The cycle consisted of six poems. However, the editors of the Leningrad branch of the publishing house Sovetskiy pisatel felt it necessary to destroy the cycle and they published only one of the six poems: "Third Zachatevsky". About her work on the collection *FT*, in which I participated, see *Journals*, vol. 3.

On V. K. Shileyko see: Vyach. Vs. Ivanov's "Dressed in Clothes of Wings" in the book *The Shoots of Eternity* [*Vskhody vechnosti*]. Assyro-Babylonian poetry translated by V. K. Shileyko. Moscow, 1987. See also: Tamara Shileyko's "Legends, Myths and Poetry", *Novy mir*, no. 4, 1986.

18. *Olga Nikolaevna* – Vysotskaya (1885–1966): an actress with the Starinny Theatre and with the Meyerhold Studio. In 1912, while working at the Alexandrinsky Theatre, V. Meyerhold dedicated his directorial work on F. Sologub's *Hostages of Life* [*Zalozhniki zhizni*] to her. (See V. E. Meyerhold, *Essays, Letters, Speeches, Conversations* [*Stati, pisma, rechi, besedy*], vol. 1, Moscow: Iskusstvo, 1968, p. 235.)

19. Zoya Moiseevna Zadunayskaya (1903–83): she, like A. I. Lyubarskaya, T. G. Gabbe and I, first studied in the Department of Philology at the state courses attached to the Institute of Art History, and later she became one of the editors at the Leningrad branch of Detizdat. Of the members of the main core of "the Leningrad editorial staff" at the time of the rout, only the two of us were not arrested: Zoya Moiseevna and I. I was fired first; then Z. Zadunayskaya was dismissed "for links with enemies of the people", that is for her friendship with Lyubarskaya and Gabbe. She and I together wrote a letter to Ezhov which we cunningly managed to deliver to him personally (through his ex-wife's doctor). In this letter we maintained the innocence of our colleagues and asked to be included in the case and for our testimonies to be heard. The letter had no effect whatsoever. At the time we were composing it and organizing its personal delivery we were not yet aware that no letters at all were taken into account, nor were spoken or written statements. The difference between spoken and written statements was merely that written ones, although of no help to those arrested, were seldom harmful to their writers. Whereas when a person stood up at a meeting and stated publicly that the arrested was innocent, that person was certain to be arrested himself (if he was a member of the party) or (if not a party member) he would be deprived of work for years.

However, it was not clear to us how the Big House operated, all the more since the details were in constant flux.

Zoya Moiseevna Zadunayskaya, in collaboration with T. Gabbe, adapted T. B. Aldrich's book *The Story of a Bad Boy* (1932); and in collaboration with A. Lyubarskaya *The Wonderful Adventures of Nils* by Selma Lagerlöf (1940). In subsequent years Z. Zadunayskaya developed an interest in folklore. Later she adapted *Folk Tales of the Baltic Peoples* [*Skazki narodov Pribaltiki*], Chinese folk tales and, with N. Gesse, Italian fairy tales, Moldavian ones and many others.

20.   . . . *I started telling her . . . about Mishkevich's provocations, about his tricks with my Mayakovsky*: prior to the rout of the editorial staff, the poet and critic Miron Levin and I were assigned by S. Ya. Marshak to prepare a one-volume edition of Mayakovsky's poetry for publication (edited jointly by L. Yu. and O. M. Brik). G. Mishkevich, who had become "editor-in-chief" at Lendetizdat in 1937, accused me of sabotage and attempted to prove my involvement with the machinations of the "enemies of the people" who had been arrested. At a meeting, as proof, he produced deliberate misquotations from Levin's and my notes for the Mayakovsky volume.

As a result of his slander, this book, like many others, fell through. If only it had just been books! Either following orders from above, or on his own initiative, G. I. Mishkevich, in an effort to come up with evidence of "sabotage by Marshak's group", fabricated political accusations against M. P. Bronshteyn, A. I. Lyubarskaya, T. G. Gabbe, and he falsified proofs, etc. (Regarding Mayakovsky, the book was published in 1938, by the Leningrad branch of Detizdat, with the designation "edited by G. Mishkevich".) In 1937, after the arrests, he issued a wall newspaper, in which he called the editors and writers who had been arrested spies, wreckers and saboteurs. (For more about this issue of the wall newspaper see *Journals*, vol. 2.)

Either in 1949, or in 1951, G. I. Mishkevich was himself arrested; however, not on account of his pogrom against the editorial staff, but on some completely fictitious, nonexistent charge.

21.   M. P. Bronshteyn, *Solar Matter* [*Solnechnoe Veshchestvo*] (Leningrad: Detskaya Literatura, 1936).

22.   *That was the only monument in Leningrad which Mayakovsky celebrated*: A.A. is referring to the following lines of Mayakovsky's poem "Man":

> The streetlights were again located
> in the middle of the street.
> The houses were the same.
> Likewise,
> from a niche
> the sculpture of a horse's head.

> – Pedestrian,
> Is this Zhukovsky Street?

> He looks at me
> as a child looks at a skeleton,
> eyes this big,
> tries to get by.

"It's been Mayakovsky Street for thousands of years:
He shot himself here at the door of his loved one."

[Translation by Garry Wiggins from *The Ardis Anthology of
Russian Futurism*. Edited by Ellendea Proffer and Carl R. Proffer.
Ann Arbor: Ardis, 1980, p. 59.]

23. *Miron Pavlovich Levin* (1917–40): critic and poet; when he first appeared
on our editorial staff he was not yet 19 – as a joke we all addressed him
formally by name and patronymic: "Miron Pavlovich." M. Levin: author
of the articles: "S. Marshak" and "Mayakovsky and Children" (see the
journal *Detskaya literatura*, no. 4, 1939), as well as numerous poems which
were never published in his lifetime.

At that time Miron Levin was dying of tuberculosis of the throat, in the
Crimean sanatorium, Dolosy. He used to send me his poems in letters. I
quote here those I recited to Anna Andreevna then:

The voice quietly disappears,
And leaves one on one's own.
That is how comrades abandon
The body of a friend.

———

Words we utter which are cheerful,
But this life of ours is dead, is dead, is dead.
And only in the ringing valour of jests
Does life appear before us as a fine deed.

———

Let us think up, my dear, for luck
A simple, a simple number.
That we if but a tiny bit, if but
In part, but for a moment,
Should have good luck.

———

Once more approaches
The usual finale:
It's four o'clock,
Veronal has not helped.

The person can't sleep
And can't fall asleep.
And so he sets out
On a long journey.

Ascends the veranda,
Sits down in the dark.
In hospital overalls,
With a fag in his teeth.

He sees in the distance,
Closing his eyes,

His city, beloved,
On the river, far off.

———————

Mikhailovsky Castle by the Summer Garden,
Chestnuts and circus, and Mikhailovsky Garden.
That's all that I need. I need no more.
Give me my city and castle back!

In 1991, in the journal *Ogonyok* (no. 34), I. Kuznetsov published a few
poems by Miron Levin; in 1992, in the Paris newspaper *Russkaya mysl* of
28 August, Sofya Polyakova published a few more of his poems with a
short introduction.

24. *He* [Kolya], *clearly, was a nice person, thoughtful, brave . . .* – Nikolay Sergeevich Davidenkov (1915–50?): biologist and writer, son of an Honoured
Scientist, the famous neuropathologist S. N. Davidenkov. He was a friend
of Lev Gumilyov's, arrested and in prison at the same as Gumilyov; but
in the unpredictable year of 1939, in contrast to Lyova, Kolya, together
with a whole group of students, was brought to trial before an ordinary
court, was acquitted and released.

Kolya and I soon struck up a friendship, and I became the editor of a
popular book on Darwin, which Davidenkov was writing for the House
of Entertaining Science.

N. Davidenkov's fate was complicated and horrible: in spite of having
been acquitted by the court he was not reinstated at the university. Because
of that, he was liable for conscription into the army, and in early 1941,
this did indeed happen. Davidenkov served with our troops in Poland,
from where he occasionally wrote to me. Then the letters ceased – Hitler
had attacked the Soviet Union; near Minsk, Davidenkov, badly wounded,
was taken prisoner. He later escaped from a German prison camp and
published a book in the West (or possibly several books?) about 1937,
then he fought the Germans in one of the Allied units on the Western
front, then he was captured by the Soviets and ended up in a labour camp
where he was shot.

This is only one of the versions of the military and prison camp biography of N. S. Davidenkov which I have come across by chance. True, in
May 1950, I received a letter from him in his own hand, written in the
labour camp – a farewell letter – but, it goes without saying, Kolya could
hardly put anything about himself in it. A few poems were enclosed in
the letter. He did say one particular thing in the letter: "Prose, not poetry,
has turned out to be what is most important for me. It has been my life
(in every sense) for these four years, interrupted only by the war – and
now here I am launching into a biography; God preserve us from such a
biography."

In the '50s and '60s, only unsubstantiated rumours, and varying ones
at that, reached me about Kolya's end. A detailed account of N. Davidenkov's fate is given in A. Solzhenitsyn's book *The Gulag Archipelago*.

According to A.A., Kolya visited her frequently before his arrest and,
after his release, recited his poetry to her and knew her "Requiem" by
heart.

25. Anna Evgenevna Arens (1892–1943): First wife of N. N. Punin; by profession a specialist in internal diseases. Anna Evgenevna married Nikolay Nikolaevich in 1917, and after their separation she continued to live in the same flat.

26. V. G. Benediktov, *Poems [Stikhotvoreniya]*. Introduced, edited and annotated by L. Ya. Ginzburg (Leningrad, 1939 [Poet's Library, big series]).

27. Rakhil Aronovna Braude (1901–71): my friend and neighbour; until '37, she was the secretary on our editorial staff, but after the editors' and writers' arrests she was advised that it was obligatory for her to hand in her "voluntary" resignation. Living on Rubinshteyn Street, right opposite me, she took great care of me after Matvey Petrovich's arrest; she even used to take my place in prison queues at night.

28. *. . . I don't like his* [V. Bryusov's] *poetry, or his prose*: In her early youth Akhmatova had a different attitude to Valery Bryusov: she liked and knew his poems by heart. Evidence of this is in her letters to S. V. Shteyn, published and annotated by E. G. Gershteyn – see *Novy mir*, no. 9, 1986, p. 196.

29. Here is an excerpt from Gumilyov's letter to Bryusov which Anna Andreevna mentioned:

> [11 May 1909, Tsarskoe Selo]
> You have probably heard already about the lectures Vyacheslav Ivanovich is giving to a few young poets, me included. And it seems to me that only now am I beginning to understand what poetry is.
> (N. S. Gumilyov, *Unpublished Poems and Letters [Neizdannye stikhi i pisma]*, Paris: YMCA-Press, 1980, p. 61).

30. *You can see from his diary what a nasty man he was. [. . .] "Pretending to give my brother a massage I twisted his arms"*: Speaking about Bryusov's "diary", Akhmatova is referring to Valery Bryusov's book *From My Life, My Youth [Iz moey zhizni. Moya yunost]* (1927). I quote the genuine text: "My brother was terminally ill; he was dying slowly in bed, he had gone blind and had lost his mind. My heart was filled with pity for him. But rationally I was convinced that pity, like any other sentimentality, is stupid, and I decisively overcame this feeling within myself. [. . .] At times he had convulsions and then he would have his arms and legs massaged. One evening I took part in this massaging together with his sick-nurse, who used to be his wet-nurse. She was massaging his legs, I his arms. But instead of massaging, I started to squeeze them any-old-how, to twist his arms, trying to cause him even more pain. He tried to wrest himself away, he groaned even louder, but I persisted.'

Valery Bryusov's brother, Nikolay (1877–87), died of a brain tumour.

31. Anna Andreevna had two brothers: the elder, Andrey (1886–1920) and the younger, Viktor (1896–1976). Here (and further on, see p. 74) A.A. is speaking of Andrey. About their mother, Inna Erazmovna, née Stogova (1856–1930); about their father, Andrey Antonovich Gorenko (1848–1915), a naval engineer; and about the entire family, her sisters, Irina (c. 1888–c. 1892), Inna (1883–1905), Iya (1894–1922). See Amanda Haight, *Anna Akhmatova: A Poetic Pilgrimage* (New York and London:

Oxford University Press, 1976; now published in Russia as A. Kheyt, *Anna Akhmatova. Poeticheskoe stranstvie*, Moscow, 1991), and also an interview with Viktor Andreevich Gorenko, published in *Akhmatova. Ardis.*

32. *Literaturny sovremennik*, no. 1, 1937, was dedicated entirely to Pushkin; evidently A.A. was interested in an article by B. Kazansky, "Foreigners on the Duel and Death of Pushkin".

33. *Tsezar* – Tsezar Samoylovich Volpe (1904–41): a researcher and critic of Russian literature. In his youth he attended a seminar which was given in the early '20s by Vyacheslav Ivanov at the University of Baku. Tsezar Volpe wrote articles on V. Bryusov and Andrey Bely; works on Zhukovsky and I. Kozlov; he participated in assembling an anthology, *Russian Poets of the 18th and 19th Centuries* [*Russkie poety XVIII–XIX vv*] (1940, 1941), and also compiled (jointly with O. Nemirovskaya) the documentary book *Blok's Fate* [*Sudba Bloka*] (Leningrad, 1930). Volpe also wrote articles about our contemporaries: for example, about M. Zoshchenko and Boris Zhitkov. In 1991 Sovetskiy pisatel published a collection of his works under the title *The Art of Dissimilarity* [*Iskusstvo nepokhozhesti*].

Tsezar Samoylovich Volpe: my first husband, Lyusha's father. A.A. was asking me "what Tsezar, on his return from Moscow, says" about Nikolay Ivanovich, because Volpe and Khardzhiev were great friends.

34. Sergey Nikolaevich Davidenkov (1880–1961): Kolya's father, since 1934, an Honourable Scientist of the RSFSR, one of Leningrad's greatest neuropathologists. From 1932, and until the end of his life, S. N. Davidenkov was head of the department of nervous disorders at the Leningrad Institute for advanced medical studies. During the war years he was Chief Neuropathologist at the Leningrad front, and from 1945, a full member of the Academy of Medical Sciences of the USSR. His principal works are devoted to neurological traumas, hereditary illnesses and neuroses.

Vasily Gavrilovich Baranov (1899–1988): endocrinologist, specialist on diabetes; chairman of the Leningrad branch of the All-Union Society of Endocrinologists; since 1960 full member of the USSR Academy of Medical Sciences. In the '30s V. G. Baranov taught at the First Medical Institute and at the Erisman Hospital (i.e. V. G. Garshin's place of work) he was head of the Department of Endocrinology.

35. Vera Nikolaevna Anikieva (1894–1942): art critic and museum guide; specialist in contemporary art. From 1920 until 1934 Vera Nikolaevna worked in the Russian Museum; later on in the All-Russian Academy of Arts.

I'll mention two of her research projects: on V. Lebedev and on A. Pakhomov. Her work on Lebedev is published only in part and only in the German translation (see the journal *Die Bildenden Künste in der UdSSR*, 1934), but an entire book was published on Pakhomov: *A. F. Pakhomov* (Leningrad, 1935).

Vera Nikolaevna died of hunger during the blockade.

36. Aleksandr Nikolaevich Tikhonov (A. Serebrov, 1880–1956): author of memoirs covering the seven years 1898–1905, on Chekhov, Savva Morozov and Komissarzhevskaya. Before the publication of this book (*Time and People* [*Vremya i lyudi*]. Moscow: Sovetskiy pisatel, 1949), A. N. Tikhonov was known in literary circles mainly as a friend and assistant of Gorky's, as an organizer, publisher and editor; A. N. Tikhonov played a large role

in the publishing house Vsemirnaya literatura, founded by Gorky after the Revolution, and also in the journal *Russkiy sovremennik*, in which M. Gorky, Evg. Zamyatin, L. Dobychin, B. Pilnyak, Abr. Efros, Yu. Tynyanov, K. Chukovsky and the poets Boris Pasternak, Marina Tsvetaeva, Anna Akhmatova were published. A. N. Tikhonov later worked in the publishing houses Federatsya and Academia, and during the war in the publishing house Sovetskiy pisatel, which published the book *Anna Akhmatova: Selected Works: Poems [Anna Akhmatova: Izbrannoe: Stikhy]*. Tashkent, 1943.

37. Emma Grigorievna Gershteyn (b. 1903): a close friend of Anna Andreevna's, literary historian, specialist on Lermontov, author of numerous studies on Lermontov and of the book *Lermontov's Fate [Sudba Lermontova]* (Moscow, 1964). Akhmatova wrote a review of this book (*Notes in the Margin [Zametki na polyakh]*), which was published in *Literaturnaya gazeta*, 16 March 1965. This book, substantially expanded, was reissued in 1986.

   For more on E. G. Gershteyn, on her historico-literary works, her efforts on behalf of Lev Nikolaevich Gumilyov, her part in Anna Akhmatova's scholarly research on Pushkin, see vols. 2 and 3 of my *Journals*. A.A. and Emma Grigorievna met in 1934, in Moscow at the Mandelstams'.

   Anna Andreevna's letters to Emma Grigorievna were published in the journal *Voprosy literatury* (no. 6, 1989). An essay by E. G. Gershteyn, "The Thirties", about her acquaintance and friendship with Akhmatova, was also published there. See also her book *New Material on Mandelstam [Novoe o Mandelshtame]* (Paris, Atheneum, 1986) and articles in the collection *Memoirs [Vospominaniya]*.

38. Lidiya Yakovlevna Ginzburg (1902–90): prose writer, writer of memoirs, literary historian and theorist, specialist on Vyazemsky, Lermontov, Herzen. In 1929, she was preparing for publication and annotating P. A. Vyazemsky's *An Old Notebook [Staraya zapisnaya knizhka]*; she also edited several editions of his poems.

   In 1940, L. Ginzburg published a book *Lermontov's Creative Path [Tvorcheskiy put Lermontova]*. In the first half of the '50s L. Ya. Ginzburg worked on the Herzen-Ogaryov volumes of *Literary Heritage [Literaturnoe nasledstvo]*, and in 1957, her book on *My Past and Thoughts* was published.

   L. Ginzburg's later works are: books – *On Lyric Poetry [O lirike]* (Moscow and Leningrad, 1964 and Leningrad, 1974); *On Psychological Prose [O psikhologicheskoy proze]* (Leningrad, 1979); *On Old and New Topics [O starom i novom]* (Leningrad, 1982); *Literature in Search of Reality [Literatura v poiskakh realnosti]* (Leningrad, 1987); *A Person at the Writing Desk [Chelovek za pismennym stolom]* (Leningrad, 1989). Almost all Lidiya Ginzburg's unpublished prose works were included in the latter book: memoirs, essays and other writings.*

   Lidiya Ginzburg's memoirs on poets also include reminiscences about Anna Akhmatova. They met at the house of G. A. Gukovsky with whose wife, Natalya Viktorovna Rykova, A.A. was very friendly. (The poem "Everything is ravaged, bartered, betrayed" – *FT, Anno Domini*, is dedicated to her.) Through Natalya Viktorovna, Lidiya Yakolevna passed on to

---

*   *Chelovek za pismennym stolom* will be published in an English translation by Alan Myers under the title *Behind the Lines, Notes, Memoirs, Narratives 1920–80* by Harvill in 1995.·

Anna Andreevna the reprint of her article on Vyazemsky. She liked the article.

"The article is very good," said Anna Andreevna. – "This was the first sentence I heard from Anna Andreevna, and I was very proud of it," relates L. Ya. Ginzburg in her memoirs.

"From then onwards we saw each other throughout the next 40 years, until the very end. Often – during the '30s and after the war, in the second half of the '40s; less often in the '50s and '60s, when Anna Andreevna used to spend long periods in Moscow." (See: Lidiya Ginzburg, "Akhmatova", in the collection *The Day of Poetry* [Akhmatova *Den poezii*], Moscow, 1977 [and the collection *Behind the Lines*].)

39.   Yakov Semyonovich Kiselyov (1896–1984): a Leningrad lawyer, famous advocate (see Ya. S. Kiselyov, *Judicial Speeches* [*Sudebnye rechi*]. Leningrad, 1967; Voronezh, 1971).

As is common knowledge, in the '30s as a rule lawyers and advocates were not permitted to take on the cases of those arrested under Article 58. Thus, no lawyer was allowed to touch the case of M. P. Bronshteyn, sentenced by the Military College of the Supreme Court (why by this particular body, and not by any other, is unknown). Nevertheless, Korney Ivanovich and I, while writing official letters and petitions seeking reconsideration of the case, made use of Ya. S. Kiselyov's good advice on more than one occasion.

1940

40.   *It turns out . . . the Acmeists had merit . . . How kind, don't you think?*: coming from the mouth of the critic Valery Pavlovich Druzin (1903–80), a member of LAPP, this remark about the Acmeists really did sound tolerant, even courteous. In 1929, in the book *The Style of Contemporary Literature* [*Stil sovremennoy literatury*], Druzin wrote: "Inimical to the revolution, [Acmeism] was devoid of alimentary juices." In 1936, in the newspaper *Literaturny Leningrad* he wrote: "The greatest masters of Soviet poetry . . . each one in his own way in his creative growth, in his struggle for realism had to *rid himself of the legacy of Acmeism* and Futurism . . . The Symbolist tradition of disdain for the authentic depiction of reality and the traditions of *Acmeist props*, each in their different ways *prevents one from seeing* the world . . . How *poor* Balmont's or *Akhmatova's* landscape is beside the richness of colours of Pushkin's and Nekrasov's. [*Italics all mine. – L. Ch.*]

Akhmatova's world appeared poor to Druzin; but, then again, later he would express a high regard for the richness of the visual world not only in Pushkin's and Nekrasov's works, but also in Vs. Kochetov's (1955, 1961, 1962), Firsov's (1966, 1972) and Gribachyov's (1971).

Druzin was always vilifying those whom, at that given moment, the authorities wanted vilified: it was no accident that after the 1946 Resolution, Druzin was the one appointed to "reinforce" the editorial staff of the journal *Zvezda*, after the rout. During the anti-Semitic campaign of 1948–53 Druzin published articles under such expressive titles as: "Expose the Remnants of Bourgeois Cosmopolitism and Aestheticism" (*Zvezda*, no. 2, 1948) and "Hangers-On of an Anti-Patriotic Group . . ." (*Sovetskoe iskusstvo*, 12 February 1949).

Of course, in 1940 Akhmatova didn't yet know Druzin's article of the late '40s and all the subsequent ones, but his anti-literary and, in particular, his anti-Acmeist activities were already well known to her.

41. *Aleksandra Osipovna, née Rosset, married name Smirnova* (1809–82): at one time, in her youth, lady-in-waiting at the Imperial court, celebrated beauty, salon hostess; later, hostess of a salon in Kaluga, where her husband, N. M. Smirnov, in the mid-1840s, became a governor. Rosset-Smirnova entered the history of Russian literature not as a writer of memoirs, but mainly for her conversations and correspondence with famous writers. Almost all the poets of her time dedicated some poems to her. "None of them passed by without bestowing their poetic offerings upon her," writes L. V. Krestova, referring to poems dedicated to Rosset-Smirnova by Zhukovsky, Pushkin, Lermontov, Vyazemsky, Khomyakov and Tumansky. A. O. Rosset-Smirnova was friends with the Karamzin family, and later with Gogol and Aksakov. It is to Smirnova – the governor of Kaluga's wife – that many letters from Gogol's book *Selected Passages from Correspondence with Friends* [*Vybrannye mesta iz perepiski s druzyami*] are addressed.

About Smirnova's memoirs which A.A. mentions, see A. Smirnova, *Notes, Diary, Memoirs, Letters* [*Zapiski, dnevnik, vospominaniya, pisma*]: with articles and annotations by L. V. Krestova. Edited by M. A. Tsyavlovsky (Moscow, 1929).

42. *We went on to talk about Krandievskaya's memoirs . . .* Natalya Vasilievna Krandievskaya (1888–1963): second wife of A. N. Tolstoy; poetess, author of memoirs about Kuprin, Esenin, Aleksey Tolstoy.

43. *There is no maiden sweeter-scented than I!*: the last line of Marietta Shaginyan's poem "The Full Moon". It begins: "Whoever you are – come in, passer-by . . .", and ends with the lines:

This night – from the Caspian to the Nile . . .
There is no maiden sweeter-scented than I!

This poem was first published in M. Shaginyan's book *Orientalia* [*Orientalia*] (Moscow: Altsiona, 1913).

44. I didn't get the passage from *Fallen Leaves* quite right. See V. Rozanov, *Fallen Leaves, The First Basket* [*Opavshie listya, korob pervyy*] (St Petersburg, 1913, p. 499).

45. Anatoly Andreevich Volkov (1909–81): critic, literary historian, about whom the *Short Literary Encyclopaedia* [*KLE*] says that his works "are primarily of a compilatory nature". However, Volkov's works on the Acmeists could more accurately be described as pogrom-like. Here is the title of a 1933 article: "Acmeism and the Imperialist War" (*Znamya*, no. 7); the title of a 1935 book: *The Poetry of Russian Imperialism* [*Poeziya russkogo imperializma*].

I will cite a few lines from these works: ". . . Acmeism is not merely chronologically linked with the Imperialist war, but, in the full sense of the word, is its true ideological offspring. [. . .] The Stolypinist bloc, which consisted of Black Hundred landlords and the bourgeoisie, strengthened the police-bureaucratic regime, set the conditions for the aggression of Russian Imperialism. It is in Gumilyov's works that the aggressive intentions of this bloc found their fullest expression [. . .] Akhmatova felt and expressed fully in her poetry the ideological 'creak' which accompanied the Stolypinist-bourgeois break-up of the gentry's feudal estates."

Inspired by the 1946 Resolution, A. Volkov published an article on "the theory and poetry of Acmeism", entitled "The Flag-Bearers of an Ideological Vacuum" (*Zvezda*, no. 1, 1947), and in the '50s in *The History of Russian Literature* [*Istoriya Russkoy Literatury*] he called Akhmatova a petit-bourgeois poetess.

"Volkov, in a rather gentler way," wrote Akhmatova, "in some or other 4th edition, continues to rant on about a link between the Acmeists and the bourgeoisie . . ." (See "Anna Akhmatova, Autobiographical Prose" in *Literaturnoe obozrenie*, no. 5, 1989, p. 7, and *Journals*, vol. 2.)

46. Aleksandr Nikolaevich Boldyrev (b. 1909): specialist on Iranian philology. From 1936 until 1942, A. N. Boldyrev worked in the Hermitage, in the Oriental department. When, during the war, a substantial part of the Hermitage collection was evacuated to Sverdlovsk, Boldyrev was appointed curator of the Oriental manuscripts remaining in Leningrad.

In the '50s, A. N. Boldyrev became a professor at Leningrad University, head of the Iranian philology department.

47. My novella *Sofia Petrovna* was picked up by Samizdat 17 years later, then abroad 25 years later. It was published under its proper title in New York in 1966, in *Novy zhurnal* (in nos. 83 and 84), and under the wrong title – as a separate book – in 1965, in Paris (*The Deserted House* [*Opustely dom*], Pyat Kontinentov Press). From the Paris publisher's foreword it appears that he completely misunderstood the story: he takes the heroine's interior monologue to be the author's voice, identifying the heroine's consciousness with the author's. In fact, although the author does sympathize with Sofia Petrovna, in contrast to her, she understands what is happening and tries to expose the reality around her; whereas Sofia Petrovna is blind.

Indeed, the story was written about this very blindness of society.

The novella has been translated (unfortunately not from the *Novy zhurnal* text, but from the distorted Pyat Kontinentov Press text) into French, English, German, Dutch, Swedish and Danish. I have given the history of the battle for publication of *Sofia Petrovna* in its homeland in volume 2 of my *Journals*, and also in a separate book *The Process of Expulsion* [*Protsess isklyucheniya*] (Paris: YMCA-Press, 1979; and Moscow: Mezhdunarodnaya assotsiatsiya deyateley kultury *Novoe vremya* and the journal *Gorizont*, 1990).

At last, after almost half a century, the novella has been published at home, and more than once. See the journal *Neva*, no. 2, 1988; in my book *Stories* [*Povesti*] (1988) and in several collections (*The Top Floor* [*Posledniy etazh*] 1989; in the book containing almost all my works, *The Process of Expulsion*, 1990; in the collection *Difficult Stories* [*Trudnye povesti*] 1992, and others). It has also been published in English in a translation based on the corrected *Neva* text as *Sofia Petrovna* (London: Harvill, 1989).

48. A.A. is talking about volume 6 of the *Complete Works of N. A. Dobrolyubov* [*Polnoe sobranie sochineniy N. A. Dobrolyubova*], which came out in 1939: it is in volume 6 that his poems, stories and diary have been published. The introduction and commentary to this volume are by B. Ya. Bukhshtab.

49. A. Lyubarskaya, L. Chukovskaya. "On the [Russian] Classics and Their Commentators." *Literaturny kritik*, no. 2, 1940.

50. The reference is undoubtedly to Pasternak's ballad which begins with the words: "It happens like a messenger on a swift steed" – see: *BPL–P*, p. 96.

51 Aleksandr Aleksandrovich Osmyorkin (1892–1953): artist, painter of landscapes, still lifes, portraits, theatre sets. Before the Revolution Osmyorkin
took part in exhibitions by the Jack of Diamonds group (1913, 1915) and
the World of Art (1916, 1917); after the Revolution he worked closely with
Konchalovsky, Lentulov and Mashkov; he took part in many exhibitions,
including international ones. Ilya Erenburg, characterizing the artist's
paintings after his death, wrote: "Osmyorkin saw a link between the
human face and surrounding objects, between still-lifes and landscapes."
(See the introduction to the catalogue *Exhibition of Works of A. A. Osmyorkin*
[*Vystavki proizvedeniy* . . .] Moscow, 1959).

   Osmyorkin was also a teacher. In the '30s, his teaching activities "gained
him fame as one of the most talented pedagogues, and one of the most
loved by the young, at the Soviet school of art" (see the collection: *One
Hundred Memorable Dates* [*Sto pamyatnykh dat*]. Moscow: Sovetskiy
khudozhnik, 1967, p. 246). Osmyorkin taught at the Surikov State Art
Institute in Moscow and at the Repin All-Russian Academy of Arts in
Leningrad.

   As I mention in my *Journals* a few lines later, "Soon I. arrived". This
was Ioganson; during those years Osmyorkin and Ioganson were friends
and were often seen together.

   Boris Vladimirovich Ioganson (1893–1973): artist (he painted numerous
pictures "about Soviet reality"); during those years he was teaching at the
same place as Osmyorkin. In time their paths, artistic and human, diverged
sharply: Osmyorkin remained a master, a creator, a pedagogue, a true
man of art, whereas Ioganson excelled as an administrator: he was vice-
president of the USSR Academy of Arts (1953–58) and then president
(1958–62), and later he was first secretary of the USSR Artists' Union
Board (1965–67). When, in 1948, the purge of literature, and later of
music, spread to fine arts, Osmyorkin also started being persecuted for
"formalism" and for "toadying to the bourgeois West", and he was later
expelled from the Academy. Ioganson, so the story goes, was among his
persecutors, and Osmyorkin called him "my friend *Iago*nson".

   At a session of the Academy of Arts in May 1948 it was declared that "the
education of the young was in the hands of inexperienced, under-qualified
pedagogues, people with clearly expressed formalist tendencies . . . modernists, apologists for non-ideological, decadent, Western art" (*Pravda*, 29
May 1948). These accusations were made against two of the best and most
popular teachers at the art institutes – the painter A. Osmyorkin and the
sculptor A. Matveev. Osmyorkin was hounded, forbidden to teach, and
that led to the beginning of his fatal illness.

   Akhmatova and Osmyorkin met, apparently, at the end of the '20s or
at the beginning of the '30s. On 28 March 1937, A.A. attended the Gorky
Bolshoy Dramatic Theatre's Pushkin anniversary production (*The Little
Tragedies*, directed by A. P. Diky, designed by A. A. Osmyorkin). The sets
appealed to her, and she congratulated the artist on his great success.
(Aleksandr Aleksandrovich was a poetry lover; he had a thorough knowledge of Pushkin and esteemed Akhmatova.)

   Anna Andreevna's portrait, which Osmyorkin was painting during the
white nights in Leningrad, was completed in 1939, and is now in the State
Literary Museum in Moscow. It is called "The White Night". It may, of
course, have been given this title merely because Osmyorkin was fasci-

nated by the special light characteristic of the northern night, but it could
also be that there is an echo, in the title, of Pasternak's lines:

> Sometimes the eye is sharp in sundry ways,
> Sometimes in sundry ways an image is exact.
> But the mixture of most frightening strength
> *Is nocturnal distance beneath the gaze of white nights.*

> Thus I see your countenance and glance.
> (To Anna Akhmatova – *BPL–P*, p. 200.)

52. *Lotta* – Rakhil Moiseevna Khay (1906–49): specialist on 17th-century
Dutch painting, who worked for the West European art section of the
Hermitage. During the war R. M. Khay was the executive curator of the
Hermitage collection which had been evacuated to Sverdlovsk. Her
scholarly works were published mainly in *Studies of the West European
Arts Section of the State Hermitage* [*Trudy Otdela zapadnoevropeyskogo iskusstva
Gosudarstvennogo Ermitazha*]: see years 1940, 1941 and 1949.

53. *Nina* – Nina Antonovna Olshevskaya (1908–91): actress, director, close
friend of Anna Andreevna's, wife of the writer V. E. Ardov. Olshevskaya
and Akhmatova met in 1934 in Moscow at the Mandelstams'. For more
on N. A. Olshevskaya see also E. G. Gershteyn, "Conversations with
N. A. Olshevskaya-Ardova – Memoirs" and *Journals*, vol. 2.

   When she came to Moscow, more often than not, A.A. would stay –
sometimes for weeks, sometimes even for months – "at the Ardovs'
on Ordynka" (Ordynka, 17, flat 13), that is with Nina Antonovna's
family.

54. A.A. is referring to the following words from Mandelstam's article "Notes
on Poetry": "Russian Symbolists were truly pillars of style: they had no
more than 500 words between them ... But at least they were ascetics,
stoics. They used rough-hewn logs as a pedestal. Whereas Akhmatova
has a piece of parquet for hers – which amounts to being a stylite on a
pillar of parquet." (*Russkoe iskusstvo*, book 2/3, 1923, p. 69.)

   Stolpnichestvo [the life of a stylite] means religious asceticism, first prac-
tised by the Christian ascetic Simeon (356–459) – Simeon Stolpnik. Simeon
spent about 40 years on top of a high pillar, on which a place to sit and
one to stand had been arranged, without coming down to earth. For more
details see *Brokgauz and Efron's Encyclopaedia* [*Entsiklopedicheskiy slovar F. A.
Brokgauza i I. A. Efrona*], vol. 58.

55. *He didn't like my poetry*: A.A. was completely mistaken. Subsequently, in
conversation with me, on 11 May 1957 (see vol. 2 of my *Journals*), she
proudly read out to me some of Mandelstam's lines, discovered by Nadezhda Yakovlevna Mandelstam amongst his papers. Analyzing Akhmatova's poetry, Mandelstam finished his review thus: "At present her poetry
is close to becoming one of the symbols of Russia's grandeur." This review
(for *The Muses' Almanac* [*Almanakh Myz*], 1916) was not published at the
time and only appeared in 1968 in *Voprosy literatury*, no. 4.

56. *. . . our dear Tanya*: that is Tatyana Yevseevna Gurevich (c. 1905–41),
who, for several years, worked on the editorial staff of the journals *Chizh*
and *Yozh*. During the rout of the Leningrad editorial staff she proclaimed

at a meeting that she did not believe that the editors who had been arrested were saboteurs, and for that she was dismissed. Tatyana Evseevna struggled a long time without any work; then the Sovetskiy pisatel gave her a job. She was killed in the autumn of 1941: as a result of a direct hit by a high-explosive bomb on Gostinyy Dvor, where the publishing house was then situated. At that time, to avoid the bombing, Anna Andreevna lived in the janitor's room at the writers' house on the Griboedov canal, where B. V. Tomashevsky had taken her and settled her in, considering it a safer place. (For more details see *Journals*, vol. 2. Olga Berggolts says of Akhmatova, in her Blockade diary (in the entry for 24 September 1941), "She sits in pitch blackness, she can't even read, she sits as if in a cell for the condemned. She cried about Tanya Gurevich (everyone remembers and pities Tanya today) and put it so well: 'I hate, hate Hitler, I hate Stalin, I hate those who are bombing Leningrad and Berlin, all those who're leading this war, this shameful, terrible war...'" (*Almanach Aprel*, no. 4, 1991, p. 139).

57. *Tusya* – Tamara Grigorievna Gabbe (1903–60): member of the "Marshak editorial staff" which was routed in 1937; playwright and folklorist. Her children's plays, published as individual little books, brought her the highest acclaim; they were staged repeatedly in Moscow and other theatres across the country with great success: *The Town of Master Craftsmen or The Tale of Two Hunchbacks* [*Gorod masterov ili Skazka o dvukh gorbunakh*]; *The Crystal Slipper* [*Khrustalnyy bashmachok*]; *Avdotya Ryazanochka* [*Avdotya Ryazanochka*].

The most significant of her works on folklore – the book *Fact and Fable. A Collection of Russian Folk Tales, Legends and Parables* [*Byl i nebyl. Sbornik russkikh skazok, legend i pritch*] – was published posthumously (Novosibirsk, 1966) with two afterwords – by S. Marshak and V. Smirnova; before that, but also posthumously, an anthology was published *In the Footsteps of the Folk Tale* [*Po dorogam skazki*] (coauthored by A. Lyubarskaya, Moscow, 1962). In Tamara Grigorievna's lifetime a number of translations and adaptations by her, of French popular tales, Perrault's fairy tales, Andersen's fairy tales, the Brothers Grimm and others, were published.

All her life, even after leaving the State Publishing House, she remained an editor, a mentor to writers. My book *In the Editor's Laboratory* [*V laboratorii redaktora*] is with good reason dedicated to her.

Her main literary talent remained undisclosed: she was one of the most sensitive specialists on Russian poetry I ever met in my entire life.

For more about T. G. Gabbe see also *Journals*, vol. 2.

58. The discussion concerns Daniil Kharms (1905–42): poet and prose writer who belonged to the Oberiu group. I call him "ours" because in the late '20s, S. Ya. Marshak involved the group, Kharms in particular, in writing books for children. In a few years, Kharms had become one of the most significant children's poets; in spite of continual attacks by bureaucratic pedagogical critics, the Leningrad branch of Gosizdat managed to publish a considerable number of poems and stories by Kharms: *How Papa Shot Me a Polecat* [*O Tom, kak papa zastrelil mne khorka*]; *Ivan Ivanych Samovar* [*Ivan Ivanych Samovar*]; *The Game* [*Igra*]; *How Kolka Pankin Flew to Brazil...* [*O Tom, kak Kolka Pankin letal v Braziliyu*] and others. He was also permanently employed by the magazines *Yozh* and *Chizh*.

Daniil Kharms was first arrested in December 1931, and exiled to Kursk, but his exile didn't last long, and by November 1932 Kharms had already returned to Leningrad.

Kharms survived the rout of the Leningrad editorial staff (1937–38). But during the war, in besieged Leningrad, they "got" him all the same, and he died in prison. After his rehabilitation the Moscow publishing house Detskiy mir commissioned me to compile a collection of his poems; the collection was published in 1962 under the title *The Game*. My name should have appeared on the title page as compiler, but, due to carelessness, the publishers omitted it.

The long-unpublished poet's book was attacked immediately by those very same bureaucratic pedagogical critics, and in addition by the journal *Krokodil* (no. 4, 1963). In defence of the book S. Marshak, S. Mikhalkov and K. Chukovsky wrote an open letter, which was published in one of the next issues of that very same *Krokodil*. At the same time, I, as compiler of this collection, and taking full responsibility for the selection of the poems, wrote an article on the essence and importance of Kharms' poetry. But they refused to publish it and it has not been published to this day.

A Kharms collection "for children" called *What Was That?* [*Chto eto bylo?*], which was wider-ranging than mine, was published in Moscow in 1967 edited by N. Khardzhiev.

... Approximately 30 years after my discussion with Anna Andreevna about Kharms, and after approximately the same time since the poet's death, collections of his poems and articles on his work started appearing abroad. See, for example, *Selected Works* [*Izbrannoe*], compiled by G. Gibian, published in Würzburg in 1974. Later, in Bremen, 1978–88, the four volume *Collected Works of D. Kharms* [*Sobranie proizvedeniy D. Kharmsa*], edited by M. Meylakh and V. Erl, was published. In Russia, Kharms' books started being returned to us more than 40 years after that conversation with Akhmatova: in 1988, in Leningrad, a collection of poetry, prose, plays and letters edited by A. Aleksandrov, called *Flight to the Heavens* [*Polyot v nebesa*] appeared; in Moscow two collections compiled by Vladimir Glotser: *Incidents* [*Sluchai*] (1989) and *The Old Woman* [*Starukha*] (1991). In 1992, in *Novy mir*, no. 2, Vladimir Glotser published the notebooks, letters and diaries of D. Kharms, and in the same year, in the almanac *Minuvshee*, no. 11, A. Ustinov and A. Kobrinsky published "Daniil Kharms' Diary Entries". Amongst the works on Kharms' biography I cite: V. I. Glotser, "Towards the History of Daniil Kharms' Last Arrest and Death", *Russkaya literatura*, no. 1, 1991; I. Malskiy, "The Rout of the Oberiu: Materials from the Investigation", *Oktyabr*, no. 11, 1992.

59. Viktor Shklovsky. *On Mayakovsky* [*O Mayakovskom*] (Moscow: Sovetskiy pisatel, 1940).

60. Vitaly Markovich Primakov (1897–1937): a major military figure. During the Civil War he was Commander of a Red Cossacks cavalry corps. From 1935, he was Deputy Commander of the Leningrad military district. Shot in 1937.

61. Nikolay Leonidovich Stepanov (1902–72): literary scholar who wrote mainly on Khlebnikov and Mayakovsky. See such works of his as: "The Works of V. Khlebnikov" (in vol. 1 of *The Collected Works of Velimir Khlebnikov* [*Sobraniye proizvedeniy Velimira Khlebnikova*], 1928); the introduction to

an edition of Khlebnikov's poems in the Poet's Library, small series (1940); the introduction and notes to the 3-volume *V. Mayakovsky* in the same series (1941) and others.

62. Zhenya Lunts (Evgeniya Natanovna, married name Gornshteyn, 1908–71): a school friend of mine. First we shared a desk at Tagantseva secondary school, then at Tenishev College. Zhenya was the sister of the writer Lev Lunts, a member of the Serapion Brotherhood, critic and playwright (1901–24). In 1921, her parents took Zhenya abroad and we never saw each other again.

63. Tanya: Lyusha's coeval, daughter of Z. M. Zadunayskaya and V. I. Valov; we often arranged joint entertainment for the girls; besides that, in the summer months Zoya Moiseevna and I would usually rent a dacha together and take turns wih the girls. Tanya's father, the writer Vasily Ignatevich Valov (b. 1902), died of starvation in 1941, during the Leningrad blockade.

64. Actually it was "The Affected" (see *Zavety*. St Petersburg, no. 5, 1914, pp. 47–51).

65. Unfortunately, I don't know which poem was meant. I was only able to see a few issues of the almanac *The Siren* [*Sirena*] (a proletarian weekly. Voronezh, nos. 1–3, 1918; nos. 4–5, 1919) which do not contain any poems by K. Balmont.

66. *Katya likes the article . . . if women have a profession, a job, they let themselves become blinkered by it*: I don't know which journal's editorial staff E. R. Malkina was working on at the time, or which work so absorbed her; I do know she had close friends on the editorial staff of the journal *Literaturny kritik*. Ekaterina Romanovna could have shown Akhmatova the article she was editing unofficially, simply at the author's request. Her circle of literary acquaintances was very wide.

   Ekaterina Romanovna Malkina (1899–1945): by training a classicist and philologist, specialist in Russian literature, and also a translator. In her youth, as far as I remember, she attended the translators' studio run by World Literature and the House of Arts, where Gumilyov, amongst others, taught; she was friends with Mikhail Leonidovich Lozinsky; she translated Grillparzer's play *Woe to Liars* [*Weh dem, der Lügt*] for the publishing house World Literature, and it was thanks to this translation that she got to know Blok; from 1924, until the early '30s, she worked at the Hermitage, in the Department of Hellenic and Scythian Antiquities; at the Hermitage she met Punin and, through him, Anna Andreevna. In the early '40s, Ekaterina Romanovna worked at Pushkin House.

   She spent the war years and the period of the blockade in Leningrad. A week before the defence of her doctoral dissertation in January 1945, she was killed by some boys – trainee electricians, who were repairing the wiring in her flat. Currently E. R. Malkina's archive is held in the manuscript department of Pushkin House.

   An obituary, which appeared in *Literaturnaya gazeta* on 27 January 1945, gives a detailed account of her fate and literary legacy. It was signed by many people, including Anna Akhmatova, M. L. Lozinsky, Olga Forsh and Olga Berggolts. I quote:

> Ekaterina Romanovna Malkina has died tragically in Leningrad. She was well known in literary and scholarly circles as a talented scholar

and critic, as an active member of the Writers' Union and a remarkable person.

Throughout the blockade E.R. lived in Leningrad, and it was there
that the strength and purity of her soul manifested itself fully. Her
conduct was truly heroic. She endured all her deprivations, dangers
and heavy personal losses selflessly and simply, without any affectation. She worked ceaselessly: she conducted a wide range of literary
and editorial work at the Leningrad radio committee, she worked
at the Writers' Union, she lectured in lecture halls and hospitals.
During the blockade years she completed a major scholarly work –
the book *The Plays of Blok* [*Dramaturgiya A. Bloka*]. In 1938, she
defended her dissertation for the Candidate of Philological Science
degree: "A. Blok in the Years of Reaction". She was due to defend
her new book as a doctoral dissertation.

We will never forget the radiant image of E. R. Malkina – Katya
Malkina, as everybody called her. And we must ensure that her
wonderful book on Blok is published.

67. Elga Moiseevna Kaminskaya (1894–1975): actress; she recited Russian
poetry on stage, both the classics and contemporary works. I don't know
if the evening of Blok and Akhmatova's poetry took place; I assume not.

However, Elga Kaminskaya (in the '20s, at any rate) frequently
demanded Anna Andreevna's permission to recite her poetry on stage and
A.A. was reluctantly obliged to consent. On this see *Meetings*, pp. 149–
53.

68. *Yakubovich . . . all his life he adored Tomashevsky:* Dmitry Petrovich Yakubovich (1897–1940): literary historian, specialist on Pushkin, who dealt mainly
with studies of Pushkin's prose, and also with the links between Pushkin's
works and classical literature, Ovid and English literature – Shakespeare
and Walter Scott. He worked on a dictionary of Pushkin's classical termin-
ology, on the monograph *Pushkin and Walter Scott* [*Pushkin i Valter Skott*]
and helped edit the complete academic collected works of Pushkin (it was
this work which brought about his friendship with B. V. Tomashevsky).

In 1933, Dmitry Petrovich became academic secretary of the Pushkin
Commission, and after 1936, its chairman. Soon after the Commission
began to publish its *Annals* [*Vremennik*], and Yakubovich was made executive editor of this special publication.

When Yakubovich died on 30 May 1940, Tomashevsky delivered the
speech at his funeral Akhmatova tells me about, and later published a
long article in the *Annals* in which he gives a detailed analysis of D. P.
Yakubovich's studies of Pushkin in their entirety. This (the 6th) volume
of the *Annals* opens with a portrait of Dmitry Petrovich, and also contains
a complete list of his works.

May I remind the reader that A.A. was a member of the Pushkin Commission and was in constant contact with B. V. Tomashevsky and other
Pushkin scholars.

D. P. Yakubovich was the author of two poems addressed to Akhmatova. See R. D. Timenchik's article "Anna Akhmatova and Pushkin House"
in the collection *Pushkin House* [*Pushkinskiy Dom*] (Leningrad: Nauka, 1982,
pp. 114–15).

69. *I saw him at Blokh's . . . .:* that is, at Yakov Noevich Blokh's (1892–1968):

owner of the publishing house Petropolis. This publishing house managed to exist in Petrograd from 1918 until 1922, and during that time published quite a number of poetry collections: amongst these, in 1922, a collection by Fyodor Sologub, *The Reed-Pipe. Russian Shepherdesses* [*Svirel. Russkie berzherety*]. Blokh also managed to publish collections of poetry by Gumilyov, Akhmatova, Mandelstam and Kuzmin.

70. I cite a poem by Igor Severyanin condemning Akhmatova's poetry. It was written in 1918, at the height of Akhmatova's fame, when readers knew her poems by heart, when the collection *Rosary* had already been published five times, and *White Flock*, twice. Severyanin's poems were published in his book *The Nightingale* [*Solovey*] (Moscow–Berlin: Nakanune, 1923).

Verses to Akhmatova

Akhmatova's verses are considered
In good taste and tone (*comme il faut*)
A yawn or two and they are read
Nothing lingering in the mind! . . .

"Does not the heart of modern woman,
Much in demand, lie in them?" – So they say
And with a show of secret boredom
Some quotes are cited.

I do not agree, I am offended
For the modern age: can it be
The spirit of woman is so humbled
That dull tears are an aim in themselves?

After all, that is Nadson's way,
And does she not come close to him?
What a creaking "little bed"!
What creeping *ennui*!

When upon the stage she declaims
Her verses, I feel so awkward:
How stylish sounds her high-flown wailing
In lifeless Petrograd! . . .

And just as heavy on the ear
Is the poet (what do they call him?!).
Ah, I recall: "a fly in marble"
And he is Osip Mandelstam.

If in Lokhvitskaya "backwardness",
And "Gipsy song style" have some "meaning",
Then in Akhmatova her "weariness"
Means nothing whatsoever.

Subsequently, as is evident from the poem Severyanin wrote in 1923, he drastically revised his opinion of Akhmatova as a nonentity. See Igor

Severyanin, *Medallions: Sonnets and Variations on Poets, Writers and Composers*
[*Medalony: Sonety i variatsii o poetakh, pisatelyakh i kompozitorakh*] (Belgrade:
published by the author, 1934, p. 8), and also in the book: *To Akhmatova*
[*Posvyashchaetsya Akhmatovoy*] edited by Pamela Davidson and Isia Musty
(Tenafly, New Jersey: Ermitazh, 1991, p. 35).

71. Akhmatova's opinion regarding the huge significance of Annensky's work
for Russian 20th-century poetry, was unshakeably firm. She was to repeat
it even a quarter of a century later, in 1965: in Moscow, talking to the
critic E. Osetrov, and in Paris talking to the literary scholar N. A. Struve.
Here is an excerpt from her conversation with E. Osetrov:

> "Lately," [Osetrov recounts Akhmatova's words. – *L.Ch.*] "some-
> how, there have been particularly strong echoes of Innokenty
> Annensky's poetry. I find that quite natural. Remember what Alek-
> sandr Blok wrote to the author of *The Cypress Chest* [*Kiparisoviy larets*],
> quoting lines from *Quiet Songs* [*Tikhie pesni*]: 'This will be for ever
> in one's memory. Part of the soul remains in it.' I am convinced
> that Annensky should have exactly the same honourable place in
> our poetry as Baratynsky, Tyutchev and Fet."
> "Do you consider Annensky to be your teacher?"
> "It's not only me who does. Innokenty Annensky was not Paster-
> nak's, Mandelstam's and Gumilyov's teacher because they imitated
> him, no, there can be no question of imitation. But the aforemen-
> tioned poets were already 'contained' in Annensky. Remember, for
> example, Annensky's poems from "The Farcical Trefoil" [*Trilistnik
> balagannyy*]:

>> Come and buy, folks, come and buy some balloons!
>> Hey, you in the fox fur, if there's money to spare,
>> Don't be mean with your kopecks:
>> I'll let them fly up to the sky
>> Then – for two hours just keep your eyes skinned!

> "Compare 'Children's Balloons' with the poems of the young Mayakov-
> sky, published in the journal *Satirikon*, deliberately filled with emphati-
> cally vernacular vocabulary . . .
> "If you recite

>> Clattering, chattering
>> Clattering, chattering . . .

> to an uninitiated person he will think that these are poems by Velimir
> Khlebnikov. However, what I recited was Annensky's 'Harness Bells'.
> We wouldn't be wrong if we were to say that a seed was planted in
> 'Harness Bells', from which Khlebnikov's poetry later grew.
> "Pasternak's generous downpours are already beating down on the
> pages of *The Cypress Chest*. The roots of Nikolay Gumilyov's poetry lie
> not in the poems of the French Parnassian poets, as is generally thought,
> but in Annensky.
> "I trace my beginnings back to Annensky's poetry. His work, in my
> opinion, is notable for its tragic character, for its sincerity and artistic
> integrity . . ."

(E. Osetrov, "The Future, which Ripened in the Past", *Voprosy literatury*, no. 4, 1965, pp. 186–187).

A.A. expressed the same thoughts about these same poets in a conversation with N. A. Struve (see N. Struve, "Eight Hours with Anna Akhmatova" in *Works*, vol. 2, p. 339); *Zvezda*, no. 6, 1989, p. 123.

It is remarkable that already in 1910, in one of his reviews, published in the May–June issue of the journal *Apollon*, Gumilyov called Innokenty Annensky's poetry a "banner" for "seekers of new paths".

In a poem in memory of Annensky (1945), entitled "Teacher", Akhmatova wrote:

> And he whom I consider as my master,
> Passed like a shadow and left no shadow,
> Imbibed all the poison, drank up all this torpor.
> He waited for fame, but waited in vain,
> He, who was a portent, a presage,
> Had pity for all, inspired languor in all –
> And then expired . . .
> *FT, Seventh Book*

Akhmatova, it appears, considered Annensky to be a prophetic phenomenon not only in poetry. Here is a line, omitted from the final version of *FT* and *BPL–A*:

> He, who was a portent, a presage,
> *Of all that was to befall us thereafter* . . .

That "all" refers to more than just poetry.

Akhmatova mentions *The Cypress Chest* in "Ode to Tsarskoe Selo" (*FT, Seventh Book*) and indisputably means Annensky (even though she does not refer to him by name) in her lines on Tsarskoe Selo: "Here so many lyres are hanging on the branches" (see the concluding quatrain of the poem "All the souls of those I have loved are on distant stars", no. 34. – *FT, Seventh Book*).

72. Vsevolod Nikolaevich Petrov (1912–78): art historian, expert on late 18th- and mid-19th-century Russian art, author of scholarly works, "covering" – in his words, taken from an autobiographical statement – "the entire history of Russian sculpture of the classical period, from the last quarter of 18th century up until 1850 – from Kozlovsky to Klodt." (See his autobiography in the book *Essays and Studies* [*Ocherki i issledovaniya*]. Moscow: Sovetskiy khudozhnik, 1978, p. 291.) Vs. N. Petrov also concerned himself with the World of Art group and with major Soviet artists: he wrote about N. Altman, N. Tyrsa, V. Konashevich, A. Pakhomov, V. Kurdov, Yu. Vasnetsov and T. Shishmaryova.

From 1934 until 1949, Vsevolod Nikolaevich worked at the Russian Museum: first in the graphics department, later in the sculpture department. In the '50s Petrov was involved in editing the publication *The History of Russian Art* [*Istoriya russkogo iskusstva*] (Moscow: Akademiya Nauk USSR; vols. 6, 8 and 10).

Petrov considered himself Punin's disciple. He met Anna Andreevna through Nikolay Nikolaevich. In 1953, N. N. Punin died in a labour camp, and after the Twentieth Party Congress he was rehabilitated; and in 1976, the publishers Sovetskiy khudozhnik brought out his book which contained, amongst other things, an article by Vs. N. Petrov: "N. N. Punin and His Work on the History of Art." See note 1.

73. *The Rybakovs*: Lidiya Yakovlevna (1885–1953) and her daughter, Olga: long-standing acquaintances of Anna Andreevna's, family of the lawyer I. I. Rybakov, who perished in 1938. In the circle of artists and writers Iosif Izrailevich Rybakov (1880–1938) was known as a collector of works of art: paintings, sculptures, antique icons, antique and contemporary porcelain, rare books and manuscripts. This collection also contained gifts from Anna Akhmatova.

A.A. met Rybakov in late 1922 or early 1923, when she was married to V. K. Shileyko and lived in the Marble Palace.

74. In spring 1914, Akhmatova wrote the poem "The Reply", which opens with the lines: "What strange words/ A quiet day brought me in April" (*FT, White Flock*). This was a reply to Count V. A. Komarovsky's poem addressed to Akhmatova. It ended thus:

> This is the day of glory. Skilfully or
> Painfully that which has been taken
> With pious hand or given with unfeeling
> Hand has been smashed to pieces before people.

Vasily Alekseevich committed suicide on 21 September 1914. Both poems – Komarovsky's to Akhmatova and Akhmatova's to Komarovsky – were published only after his death, both in the journal *Apollon* in 1916, Akhmatova's in no. 4/5, Komarovsky's in no. 8.

Count Vasily Alekseevich Komarovsky (1881–1914): poet; from the late 1890s he lived in Tsarskoe Selo; he was first published in 1912; his first book of poems, which also happened to be his last, *The First Jetty* [*Pervaya pristan*], was published in 1913. The following year N. Gumilyov responded to this book with warm approval (and with reproaches directed at its critics). He called *The First Jetty* a book of "the fruit of ten years of creative work by an indisputable poet". "Beneath many of the poems," wrote Gumilyov, "the words 'Tsarskoe Selo' appear, and beneath many others one can infer them. [...] A little town [...] consecrated to the memory of Pushkin, Zhukovsky and lately Innokenty Annensky, it fascinates the poet and he has given us not only the landscape particular to Tsarskoe Selo, but also the Tsarskoe Selo sphere of ideas." Characterizing Komarovsky's poetry, Gumilyov compares it on one hand to the poetry of Innokenty Annensky, on the other to that of Henri de Régnier. (See N. Gumilyov, *Letters on Russian Poetry* [*Pisma o russkoy poeẓii*]. Petrograd: Mysl, 1923, pp. 180–1.)

V. N. Toporov, author of the article on Komarovsky in *KLE* (vol. 9), finds that "pre-Acmeist traits" in Komarovsky's poetry influenced Akhmatova and Mandelstam: "A combination of tranquil, 'measured' classical forms (the cult of A. S. Pushkin, the alexandrine) and a content of internal tragedy, of the historical and the personal and the biographical . . ."

75. The efforts to get Akhmatova a special pension and new living quarters were undertaken by the Praesidium of the Soviet Writers' Union most energetically, persistently and "at a very high level." In November 1939 the Praesidium referred Akhmatova's case to the commission for the

allocation of special pensions at Sovnarkom, to the Vice Chairman of Sovnarkom, A. Ya. Vyshinsky, and also to the Leningrad City Council. The documents for this case are stored at TsGALI.

From a letter written on 15 November 1939 by Konstantin Aleksandrovich Fedin to Mikhail Mikhailovich Zoshchenko, it appears that Mikhail Mikhailovich was asked to pass the Praesidium's decision on to the Chairman of the Leningrad City Council (p. 5), P. S. Popkov. He did pass it on, but it had no effect. Then a whole group of writers, N. Aseev, V. Lebedev-Kumach, Anna Karavaeva, K. Fedin, approached Vyshinsky: ". . . Akhmatova's achievements in Russian poetry," they wrote, and "her literary significance are great." When this letter had no effect either, Vyshinsky was approached by a member of the Central Committee, Aleksandr Aleksandrovich Fadeev:

> The celebrated poetess AKHMATOVA is living in Leningrad, in dire financial straits and extremely bad conditions [he wrote]. I hardly need to tell you how unjust it is towards AKHMATOVA herself, who, despite all the incongruities of her poetic gift with our time, was, and remains, nonetheless, the greatest poet of the pre-Revolutionary period. And I don't have to tell you what an unfavourable impression this makes, not only on the old poetic intelligentsia, but also on the young people who have learnt much from AKHMATOVA.
>
> Up till now, AKHMATOVA has not had a single metre of living space of her own. She lives in the room of her ex-husband, from whom she has long been divorced. I don't have to explain how humiliating this is for her.

After Fadeev's letter, Vyshinsky himself gave Popkov instructions. (TsGALI, f. [Archive] 631, SP SSSR [Writer's Union, USSR] contents 15, unit 508, pp. 5–8, and also unit 413 (1), pp. 64–5).

What happened afterwards, and why all these efforts and instructions had no success, I do not know.

76. The collections of M. Kuzmin's poetry mentioned in this conversation are: *The Trout Breaks through the Ice* [*Forel razbivaet lyod*], Leningrad, 1929; *Nets* [*Seti*] Moscow, 1908; *The Guide* [*Vozhaty*], St Petersburg, 1918. The individual poems mentioned ("Tsarevich Dimitry" and "The wind from the lake is piercing") were published in the collection *The Guide* (see pp. 55 and 41).

77. N. Gumilyov, *Letters on Russian Poetry* (Petrograd: Mysl, 1923, p. 157).
    "The poetry of M. Kuzmin is primarily 'salon' poetry – not that the poetry isn't genuine or beautiful; on the contrary, its 'salon quality' gives it something extra, which makes it unlike the rest."
    Autumn Lakes [*Osennie ozera*], M. Kuzmin's second book of poetry, was published in Moscow (Skorpion, 1912).

78. *He couldn't stand me. Anna Dmitrievna reigned in his salon*: as is known, M. Kuzmin wrote a foreword to the Anna Akhmatova's first collection, *Evening* (1912). However, he subsequently started to measure Akhmatova's poetry against that of another poetess, Anna Dmitrievna Radlova (1891–1949). In Petrograd, one after another, three of her collections of poetry were published: *The Honeycomb* [*Soty*] (Fiametta, 1918); *Ships* [*Korabli*] (Alkonost,

1920); and *The Winged Guest* [*Krylati gost*] (Petropolis, 1922). In his review of Radlova's poetry, Kuzmin called her "a genuine, remarkable poet with a wide range and horizon", and her literary debut "an event in poetry." (I am quoting from the collection *Faces*, p. 275.) But I think it was not this literary rivalry that enraged Akhmatova. She herself was already extremely famous by the time Radlova's poetry was published, her books had been printed and reprinted. She considered M. Kuzmin to be the personification of evil, and his salon to be a breeding ground of depravity. It is not by chance that in "Poem without a Hero", the line "Who does not know, what the conscience means . . ." refers to him, as well as the whole stanza ending with these lines:

> Darling and mocker of us all –
> Against him the most loathsome sinner
> Is divine grace personified . . .

O. N. Gildebrant (Arbenina) in her memoirs, in the same collection *Faces*, published her angry response to this characterization of Kuzmin and Akhmatova's words, slandering Radlova.

Radlova's fate was difficult, tormented and complex. Her life ended in one of the camps of the Gulag. A. D. Radlova was the wife of Sergey Ernestovich Radlov (1892–1958), a director, a pupil of Meyerhold and in the '30s, head of an independent theatre studio ("the Radlov theatre"), which was renamed the Lensovet Theatre in '39.

Anna Radlova's literary activities were closely linked to Kuzmin's: in 1923 their joint declaration of a new direction in art, "The Declaration of Emotionalism", was published in the collection *Abraksas*. It had four signatures: M. Kuzmin, Anna Radlova, Sergey Radlov and Yur. Yurkun.

During the war, in March 1942, Anna Radlova and Sergey Radlov were evacuated from besieged Leningrad, with the theatre, to Pyatigorsk. In August, the Germans entered the city. The Radlovs didn't wish to (or didn't manage to) leave the city and (willingly or unwillingly) remained in Pyatigorsk. The theatre kept on working. Then in September '43 the Germans transferred the theatre to Berlin. It continued to work in Germany and later, briefly, in France. From here, willingly or unwillingly (?), in February 1945, the Radlovs returned to the Soviet Union. There both were arrested. However, they were not separated; they were allowed to continue various dramatic activities, and even to go on tour. Anna Dmitrievna died in the camps in 1949, and Sergey Ernestovich in 1959, five years after his early release.

For more details see Valeriy Gaydaburg's article in the journal *Teatr*, no. 10, 1992.

79. Three poems by K. Simonov were published in *Literaturny sovremennik* of 1940, in no. 5/6: "Homeland", "The Muscovite", "Friendship", and five poems by N. Braun: "Irpen", "Mother", "The Ravine", "We shall say goodbye and we shall part", "How hard it is for the heart, not loving!"

80. For more on the hoax played by Maksimilian Voloshin and Elizaveta

Vasilieva (they composed poems in the name of the nonexistent poetess Cherubina de Gabriak); on correspondence between the editor-in-chief of the journal *Apollon*, Sergey Makovsky, and Innokenty Annensky (whose poems Makovsky postponed, in order to urgently publish Cherubina's poems) concerning this; on Annensky's poem "My Anguish" – see A. V. Lavrov and R. D. Timenchik's publication in the *Manuscript Department of Pushkin House Yearbook for 1976* [*Ezhegodnik Rukopisnogo otdela Pushkinskogo doma na 1976 god*] (Leningrad, 1978, p. 240).

I, however, will quote only the beginning of Annensky's letter in that publication, about which Akhmatova was telling me:

> 12 November 1909
> Dear Sergey Konstantinovich,
> I was, of course, very disappointed by the fact that my poems will not appear in *Apollon*. From your letter I understood that there were serious reasons for this. I'm only sorry that you choose to see caprice in my wish to have my poems published specifically in no. 2. I do not deny that this may be a motive for my actions and wishes in general. But in this case there were various other reasons, and I am very, very annoyed that the publication has fallen through. Well, let's not talk about it and let's try not to think about it . . .

That very same day Annensky also wrote "*one of his terrifying poems about anguish*" – "My Anguish". This poem turned out to be his last. (See his collection *The Cypress Chest*, which appeared in 1910, published by Grif, when I. Annensky was already dead).

In A. Lavrov and R. Timenchik's publication they say that in the '30s Akhmatova wrote a whole article about the episode described above; the article was called "Annensky's Last Tragedy."

In 1988, in the journal *Novy mir*, no. 12, an important work by Vladimir Glotser, "Elis. Vasilieva . . .", was published. This work contains the poetess' autobiography, her poems and letters. The reader will find a great deal of new material on the duel between N. Gumilyov and M. Voloshin here, and also on the editor of the journal *Apollon*, S. Makovsky.

In 1989, a book by Cherubina de Gabriak was published in Moscow, which had been compiled by E. Ya. Arkhipov back in 1927: *Autobiography. Selected Poems* [*Avtobiografia. Izbrannye stikhotvoreniya*].

81. "To the Blue Star": a cycle of poetry by Gumilyov, which he wrote in the album of a young girl, Elena Dubuchet, whom he met in Paris in 1917. These are poems

> Of the unhappy love of Gumilyov
> In the final year of the world war.

Many poems from this cycle, amongst others, were published post-humously, in the collection *To the Blue Star* [*K siney zvezde*] (Berlin: Petropolis, 1923; and in 1988 in the book *Nikolay Gumilyov. Lyric and Narrative Poems.* [*Nikolay Gumilyov. Stikhotvoreniya i poemy*] (Leningrad: Sovetskiy pisatel [Poet's Library, big series]).

The poem "Ezbekkiya" (which is actually not about "a forest", as I say, but about a garden in Cairo) has nothing to do with "To the blue star", it is "a reminiscence about Akhmatova":

At that time I was tormented by a woman.

82. A.A. quotes it quite accurately. See: Aleksandr Blok. *Collected Works* [*Sobranie sochineniy*]. In 8 vols., vol. 8, 1963, p. 328.

83. The lines referred to are from two poems by Blok: "Black Blood" (1) and "With its bitter tears".

84. In spite of her harsh reaction to "The Snow Mask" [Snezhnaya maska], in the early '20s A.A. collaborated with the composer A. S. Lourié and wrote a libretto based on motifs from it. This work is mentioned by Akhmatova in the "lost" list. In fact, judging by the entry for 24 December 1921 in K. Chukovsky's *Diary*, Akhmatova had, by that time, already written a substantial part of it. Korney Ivanovich writes:

> . . . She [Akhmatova] was lying on the bed in her coat – she put her hand under the plaid and took out some large sheets of paper rolled into a tube. "This is the ballet *The Snow Mask* based on Blok. Listen and don't get at me about the style. I can't write prose." And she started to read her libretto, which I found so touching as a splendid, subtle commentary on "The Snow Mask". I do not know whether it is a good ballet, but the analysis of "The Snow Mask" is excellent. "I haven't yet worked out the death scene in Act III. I am writing this ballet for Artur Sergeevich. He asked me to. Maybe Diaghilev will put it on in Paris."
> (*K. Chukovsky. Diary 1901–29 [Dnevnik. 1901–29]*. Moscow: Sovetskiy pisatel, 1991, p. 184).

References to this libretto can be found not only in K. Chukovsky's *Diary*. As B. Kats and R. Timenchik point out in the book *Anna Akhmatova and Music [Anna Akhmatova i muzyka]* (Leningrad, 1989), A.A. read it to V. Khodasevich and I. Gruzdev. Moreover, in the Riga newspaper *Novy put*, of 10 July 1921, there was an announcement about the ballet *The Snow Mask*.

May I remind readers of the lines in the draft of "Poem without a Hero": "I was writing a libretto for Artur,/ so it seemed to me in my sleep."

Artur – Artur Sergeevich Lourié (1891–1966): composer, author of numerous articles on music, a close friend of Anna Akhmatova's and Olga Glebova Sudeykina's. His own musical works and his articles on music aroused great interest in Petersburg artistic circles of the 1910s. In particular, he set Anna Akhmatova's poems to music, for example "I won't start drinking wine with you", "The sky's dark blue lacquer has dimmed", "Somewhere there is a simple life and a world", "You gave me a difficult youth", "Since Agrafena-Kupalnitsa's" and many, many others.

In 1922, Lourié left Russia for good and settled first in Europe (in Berlin, in Paris), then in 1941 in the USA. During the years he continued to work on the Akhmatova cycle: he set the poems "Willow", "The Shade" and fragments of "Poem without a Hero" to music. In emigration A. S. Lourié created two operas based on texts by Pushkin: *Feast in the Time of Plague* and *The Blackamoor of Peter the Great*.

In my archives I have a copy of Lourié's letter to Akhmatova, dated 11 January 1960. The copy was given to me by Vladimir Bronislavovich Sosinsky. (On V. B. Sosinsky see *Journals*, vol. 2, note 247.) The letter mentions Akhmatova's prophetic lines about the fate of Russian émigrés, in particular the line "Like wormwood smells the bread of strangers" (from the poem "I am not with those who abandoned their land") and the lines from "Poem without a Hero" ("Your dubious reputation,/ Which has lain twenty years in the ditch").

As if in reply, Lourié writes:

> . . . What can I tell you about myself? My "reputation" has also lain 20 years in the ditch, i.e. since the time I came to this country . . . Here nobody needs anything and a foreigner has no road open to him. You foresaw all this already 40 years ago: "Like wormwood smells the bread of strangers". All your photographs look at me all day long . . .

In another letter, addressed to V. B. Sosinsky (from 20 January 1962):

> I heard recently that A.A. seems to be ill, that she had a heart attack and that she's in hospital. Is it true? Please let me know. This news upsets me greatly. For she is a close and old friend of mine. We two are the last shadows of her masquerade here on this earth.

I think that several of Akhmatova's love poems are addressed to A. S. Lourié, and not only the one that V. M. Zhirmunsky points out: "Yes, I loved them, those nightly gatherings" (*BPL–A*, p. 475). Thus, for example, "On Not Sending the Poem" (*FT, Seventh Book*) and "You were right, not to take me along" (*BPL–A*, p. 305). The latter was printed with an error in *BPL–A*: it should say "perpetual" [*skvoznoy*] and not "nocturnal" [*nochnoy*] insomnia. P. N. Luknitsky points out in his diary, with reference to Anna Andreevna's words, that the poem "Somehow we've managed to part" is also addressed to Artur Lourié. (See *Meetings*, p. 46.)

85. Tatyana Aleksandrovna Bogdanovich (1872–1942): writer, author of history books for children; my godmother.

86. Vladimir Stepanovich Chernyavsky (1889–1948): master of dramatic recitals. He performed works by Chekhov, Blok, Romain Rolland, but mainly by Pushkin. For his stage recitations of Pushkin's poems, Chernyavsky devised several programmes: a "Friendship" cycle, a "Southern" cycle, a "Country" cycle and so on. He also performed *Eugene Onegin* and *Mozart and Salieri* and "The Shot". Chernyavsky also wrote some theoretical articles on methods of stage performance of Pushkin's prose and poetry (see the collection *Pushkin Through the Spoken Word* [*Pushkin v zvuchashchem slove*]. Leningrad, 1936, p. 45).

I don't know whether Chernyavsky performed any of Anna Akhmatova's poems.

87. Anna Andreevna had in mind an article by S. Nagorny entitled "The Next Issue". The article is devoted to an analysis of volume 8–9 of the journal *Literaturny sovremennik*, 1940. In an article published in this volume, the critic I. Grinberg justifiably wrote:

> . . . Akhmatova's "intimate" quality is not really so simple [. . .] in the poems which seem totally "intimate" there is a sense of time, a sense of memory of the wide world. It is this very memory of the world, this sense of the epoch, which lends such power to the lyric

poems of great poets, which makes these poems so intense, capable
of alluring, captivating the reader (p. 213).

S. Nagorny retorted: ". . . Akhmatova's poems are deeply alien to the very
spirit of Soviet society" (*Literaturnaya gazeta*, 29 September 1940).

88. The unfinished poem "February" (1933) was included in the section "Posthumous Poems" on pp. 290–312 of the collection: E. Bagritsky, *Lyric
Poems* [*Stikhotvoreniya*]. Introduction by I. Grinberg (Leningrad: Sovetskiy
pisatel [Poet's Library, small series], 1940).

89. I did write this article "Zoshchenko for Children" and sent it off to the
editors of the journal *Detskaya literatura*. The editors lost it. I subsequently
used some thoughts from this article in my book *In the Editor's Laboratory*
(see the 2nd ed., Moscow: Iskusstvo, 1963).

90. Valeriya Sergeevna Sreznevskaya (née Tyulpanova, c. 1887–1964): wife
of psychiatrist Vyacheslav Vyacheslavovich Sreznevsky, senior consultant
at the psychiatric clinic in the Vyborg District of Petersburg.

Valeriya Sergeevna – "Valya" – was a school friend of Akhmatova's;
they met when they were still children, in 1896, and a few years later,
when the Tyulpanov family rented a floor in the same house as the Gorenko family (in E. I. Shukhardina's house, near the railway station, on
Shirokaya Street), the girls became friends: they went to school together,
went swimming together, read books, went skating, etc. Through Valya
Tyulpanova "Anya Gorenko" met "Kolya Gumilyov".

V. S. Sreznevskaya is the author of memoirs about Gumilyov and
Akhmatova, "Daphnis and Chloë". See the journal *Zvezda*, no. 6, 1989,
and also the collection *Memoirs* [*Vospominaniya*]. It is well known that
A.A. edited Valeriya Sergeevna's memoirs. On this see Anatoly Nayman,
Remembering Anna Akhmatova [*Rasskazy o Anne Akhmatovoy*] (Moscow: Khu-
dozh. Lit., 1989, p. 89).

Akhmatova dedicated two poems to her: "Instead of wisdom – experience" (*FT, White Flock*) and "In memory of V. S. Sreznevskaya" (*FT,
Seventh Book*).

91. Erikh Fyodorovich Gollerbakh (1895–1945): art historian, poet and liter-
ary scholar; bibliophile, bibliographer; author of the books *V. V. Rozanov.
His Life and Work* [*V. V. Rozanov. Zhizn i tvorchestvo.*] (1922), *The Portrait in
Russia* [*Portretnaya Zhivopis v Rossii*] (1923), *The History of Engraving and
Lithograph in Russia* [*Istoriya Gravyury i Litografii v Rossii*] (1923) and many
others.

A large part of the specialist works on art and literature by E. Gollerbakh
(born in Tsarskoe Selo) is devoted to portraits and biographies of poets,
whose works are connected with Tsarskoe; for example, the book *The City
of Muses* [*Gorod Muz*], in which he discusses not only Pushkin, Zhukovsky
and Vyazemsky, but also Innokenty Annensky, N. Gumilyov, V. A. Komarovsky, Anna Akhmatova; or the book *Akhmatova's Image* [*Obraz Akhmatovoy*], a collection consisting of poems dedicated to her by contemporaries
– Blok, Gumilyov, Komarovsky, Mandelstam, Sologub, Kuzmin – and a
photograph of a statuette by Natalya Danko; he also published a book
called *Tsarskoe Selo in Poetry* [*Tsarskoe Selo v poezii*], in which Akhmatova's
poems on Tsarskoe, in particular, are reprinted.

Evidently, Akhmatova was annoyed by E. Gollerbakh's attempts to popularize, to make more widely accessible, a theme dear to her – the memory of youth, of Tsarskoe Selo, of Gumilyov's death, of her love for Nedobrovo – in a word, the very personal theme of Tsarskoe Selo, which comes through in her poetry with such refined austerity.

In Leningrad in 1990 a special book on Gollerbakh by O. S. Ostraya and L. I. Yuniverg was published, *Erikh Fyodorovich Gollerbakh as Collector and Publisher* [*Erikh Fyodorovich Gollerbakh kak kollektsioner i izdatel*].

92. Mariya Yakovlevna Varshavskaya (1905–83): worked at the Hermitage, author of many scholarly works, at one time head of the painting section in the West European Art department; for many years curator of Flemish painting. M. Ya. Varshavskaya's main works are devoted to two painters: *Van Dyck: Paintings in the Hermitage* [*Van Deyk: Kartiny v Ermitazhe*] (Leningrad, 1963) and *Rubens: Paintings in the Hermitage* [*Kartiny Rubensa v Ermitazhe*] (Leningrad, 1975).

93. ... *She told me indignantly about Maximov's speculations*: A.A. was referring to pages from the book *The Poetry of Valery Bryusov* [*Poeziya Valeriya Bryusova*], which was published in 1940. Dmitry Evgenevich Maksimov (1904–87): professor at Leningrad University, historian of Russian poetry, author of books on Lermontov, Blok and Bryusov. (Much later, in 1966, his books *The Poetry of Lermontov* [*Poeziya Lermontova*] and, in 1975, *The Poetry and Prose of Al. Blok* [*Poeziya i proza Al. Bloka*] were published). Anna Andreevna's indignation was aroused by one of D. E. Maksimov's early works: in the above-mentioned book on Bryusov, he claims that Gumilyov's attitude to Bryusov was that of a "respectful pupil". He based his convictions on articles by Gumilyov (see, for example, N. Gumilyov's review in the newspaper *Rech*, 29 May 1908) and on the inscriptions, which Nikolay Stepanovich wrote in those volumes of his poetry which he gave to Bryusov. (May I also mention that the first edition of Gumilyov's *The Pearls* [*Zhemchuga*] had the direct dedication "To my teacher Valery Bryusov").

After reading Anna Andreevna's angry remark in my *Journals* (published 1976), D. E. Maksimov wrote to me in 1978:

> In your memoirs ... a "Maksimov" is mentioned, whom A.A. scolded for an excessively literal interpretation of some letters ... Obviously, or most likely, that "Maksimov" is me and the reference is to the highly respectful letters from Nikolay Stepanovich to Bryusov. If my memory serves me well, I took this respect at face value (Gumilyov was *very young* at the time, and such an attitude on his part seemed more than possible). A.A. did not agree with me. She, naturally, didn't want to admit that even the young N(ikolay) S(tepanovich) had admired V. Ya. Bryusov.

D. E. Maksimov writes about Anna Andreevna's displeasure: "That was the very *beginning* of my long and warm acquaintance with Anna Andreevna."

Further on D. E. Maksimov writes to me that in subsequent years A.A. was sympathetically attentive to him and his work and he gives much proof of this: friendly inscriptions on books and the request to make the introductory speech at her recital of "Poem without a Hero" and many more such things.

D. E. Maksimov was the author of memoirs on Anna Akhmatova. See the collection *Memoirs A. A.*

In 1969, after Akhmatova's death, D. Maksimov's book *Bryusov: Poetry and Stance* [*Bryusov: Poeziya i pozitsiya*] was published (Leningrad: Sovetskiy pisatel). On p. 119, he says:

> ... one should not exaggerate the measure of closeness between Bryusov's poetry and the Acmeists' lyric poetry ... Bryusov did not get on with the Acmeists on a personal level either, he was sharply critical of their theoretical programme and soon parted ways with them completely.

On Gumilyov's attitude to Bryusov see his letters in the book *N. S. Gumilyov. Unpublished Poems and Letters* [*N. S. Gumilyov. Neizdannye stikhi i pisma*] (Paris: YMCA-Press, 1980). See also: Nikita Struve: "Eight hours with Anna Akhmatova" (*Works*, vol. 2, p. 341), and that same "Eight hours ..." in the journal *Zvezda*, no. 6, 1989, p. 124. And on Anna Andreevna's own attitude to Bryusov see pp. 38–39 of this volume.

94. This refers to three poems by V. Khlebnikov: "The Refusal", "The Solitary Actor" – see: *The Collected Works of Velimir Khlebnikov, 1928–33* [*Sobranie Sochineniy Velimira Khlebnikova, 1928–33*], vol. 3 – and "But I ..." – ibid., vol. 5.

95. Without commenting on Pasternak's letter to Akhmatova, I quote an excerpt from it, to which Anna Andreevna drew my attention:

> [11 November 1940]
> Dear, dear Anna Andreevna!
> Is there anything I can do to cheer you up at least a little and interest you in existing in this darkness which has fallen upon us again, the shadow of which I feel upon me daily, with a shudder. How can I remind you enough that to live and to want to live (not just any way, but only your way) is your obligation to the living, because the meaning of life is easily destroyed and rarely maintained by anyone, and you are its principal creator.
> Dear friend and unattainable example, I should have said all this to you on that grey, August day, when we last saw each other, and you made me remember how absolutely dear you are to me. And yet I missed opportunities to see you, I went to Moscow, day after day, to meet the extra, unscheduled train from the Crimea, carrying pupils and Zina with her sick son, who needed to be hospitalized, without even knowing *the day* of its arrival ...
> (*Literary Heritage* [*Literaturnoe nasledstvo*], vol. 93. *The History of Soviet Literature in the 1920s and 1930s* [*Iz istorii sovetskoy literatury 1920–30-kh godov*]. Moscow: Nauka, 1983, pp. 662–4).

96. Boris Pasternak, *Selected Translations* [*Izbrannye perevody*] (Moscow: Sovetskiy pisatel, 1940).

97. See B. Pasternak's inscription, reproduced exactly and fully in the catalogue *Books and Manuscripts from the Collection of M. S. Lesman* [*Knigi i rukopisi v Sobranii M. S. Lesmana*] (Moscow: Kniga, 1989, p. 383).

98. L. Ya. Ginzburg, *Lermontov's Creative Path* (Leningrad: GIKHL, 1940).

99. *Mayoshka*: a folklore character, something in the nature of the Russian Petrushka, which came to Russia from France. "Mayyo" ("Mayeux" in French) is an "embittered hunchback, a clever wit, a cynic who keeps falling in love, a popular character in countless cartoons, mainly by Charles Traviés, and a whole series of French novels of 1830–1848." In the 1830s, Lermontov was given this nickname by those who mocked him: the jokers made fun of the poet's shortness and his big head, finding an external likeness between him and the French Mayeux. (See *M. Yu. Lermontov. Complete Collected Works* [*M. Yu. Lermontov. Polnoe sobranie sochineniy*] 5 vols. Edited and annotated by B. M. Eykhenbaum. Moscow and Leningrad: Academia, 1935–37, vol. 3, p. 664.)

1941

100. I arrived in Chistopol on the same steamer, on the same day – 6 August 1941 – as the Shneyder couple, Mikhail Yakovlevich Shneyder and Tatyana Alekseevna Arbuzova. In Chistopol we turned out to be neighbours. I knew Mikhail Yakovlevich from before; I met and immediately befriended Tatyana Yakovlevna on the steamer, on the voyage. Mikhail Yakovlevich was then in the final stage of tuberculosis, Tatyana Alekseevna fought with great self-sacrifice for his life. I knew (from personal experience) that both of them were kind, benevolent people.

Mikhail Yakovlevich Shneyder (1891–1945): specialist in script-writing, author of critical articles on screenplays and compiler of screenplay anthologies. His wife, *Tatyana Alekseevna Arbuzova* (1903–1978), a pupil at Meyerhold's studio in her youth. (After Shneyder's death she married K. G. Paustovsky.)

The Shneyders warmly welcomed Marina Ivanovna into their little home. They immediately started looking for a room for her not far from their own.

On Tsvetaeva's last day in Chistopol before her return to Elabuga, see: Lydia Chukovskaya's "On the Threshold of Death" [Predsmertie] (in the journal *Sobesednik*, no. 3, 1988) and Tatyana Arbuzova's "Extract from a Diary" (see the collection *They Felled the Rowan Tree* ... [*Ryabinu rubili...*]. Moscow: Vozvrashchenie, 1992).

101. *Lev Moiseevich Kvitko* (c. 1890–1952): a Jewish poet who wrote in Yiddish; he became part of Russian poetry thanks to Korney Chukovsky's support, but mainly through translations by S. Marshak, E. Blaginina, M. Svetlov and later also Anna Akhmatova. During the war Kvitko was a member of the Jewish anti-fascist committee. At the time of the "struggle against cosmopolitanism" he was arrested and shot together with other Jewish literary figures such as: I. Fefer, D. Bergelson and Perets Markish.

102. *... the greatest anguish in my life is Iosif –* Iosif Izrailevich Ginzburg (1901–45): engineer, husband of Tamara Grigorievna, was arrested for expressing indignation, in the presence of colleagues, at the pact between the USSR and fascist Germany. This was before Hitler attacked the Soviet Union. But the fascist attack on the USSR changed nothing in the fate of this man, arrested for anti-fascism. He remained in the labour camp and died near Karaganda, while working on a dam during a flood.

PUBLISHER'S GLOSSARY

This glossary of miscellaneous information is provided for the benefit of readers who may not be entirely familiar with Russian nomenclature, literature or institutions. It does not pretend to be exhaustive and is offered merely as a supplement to the author's own detailed notes.

Acmeism: A literary movement that grew out of the Poets' Guild in opposition to the Symbolists. Its main figures were Nikolay Gumilyov, Anna Akhmatova and Osip Mandelstam. Whereas the Symbolists tended to regard the poet almost as a mystic, a seer who recorded visions of some underlying eternal metaphysical truth, in which words often had little objective reality but, as Mandelstam complained in his essay "Concerning the Nature of the Word", "the rose is an image for the sun, the sun an image for the rose, the dove is an image for the girl, the girl is an image for the dove", the Acmeists were interested in form, objective precision and clarity in poetry. See Robert Tracy's introduction to *Stone* by Osip Mandelstam (London: Harvill, 1991) for a fuller discussion of Acmeism.

Acts: The Acts of the Apostles.

Aldington, Richard (1892–1962): A founder member of the Imagist movement in London (1913), husband of H.D., with whom he translated from Greek and Latin, and editor of first the *Egoist*, and later, with Wyndham Lewis and Ezra Pound, of *Blast*. *Death of a Hero* (1929), his novel of the 1914–18 war, in which he fought, was a bestseller in the USSR.

Aleksandr Nikolaevich (p. 56): Boldyrev. See note 46.

Aleksandr Nikolaevich: Tikhonov. See note 36.

Aleksandra Iosifovna: Lyubarskaya. See note 10.

Anna Dimitrievna: Radlova. See note 78.

Anna Evgenevna: Arens. Punin's first wife.

Annensky, Innokenty Fyodorovich (1856–1909): A poet, playwright and classical scholar, who was out of sympathy with the dominant Symbolist movement. His influence on Akhmatova and some of the other Acmeists was profound. See also notes 71, 74 and 80.

Apollon: A leading literary and art journal, founded by Nikolay Gumilyov and Sergey Makovsky and published in St Petersburg (1909–17). From 1912 it became the official journal of the Acmeists.

Art Theatre: See Moscow Art Theatre.

Aseev, Nikolay Nikolaevich (1889–1963): A poet of the same Futurist group as Mayakovsky, and co-founder of the journal *LEF*. He was awarded a Stalin prize in 1941, and wrote patriotic verses during the war (1941–45) and anti-American verses after it.

Balmont, Konstantin Dmitrievich (1867–1942): One of the most famous and popular of Symbolist poets. He had an extraordinary gift for languages, translating many poets into Russian. He emigrated in 1920 and died in Paris in extreme poverty.

Baranov, Vasily Gavrilovich: See note 34.

Baratynsky, Evgeny Abramovich (1800–44): One of the great Russian poets of the 19th century, whose work, especially his philosophical poems, of which "Autumn" is a prime example, is highly regarded. "Baratynsky is unique among us, for he thinks," remarked Pushkin of his admired contemporary; and Joseph Brodsky has commented that Baratynsky is "the most analytical lyric poet Russia has had".

Barclay de Tolly (1716–1818): The Russian field marshal, who was commander in chief against Napoleon in 1812.

Belinsky, Vissarion Grigorievich (1811–48): An influential critic of his time, who was later regarded as the founder of Soviet criticism.

Bely, Andrey (pseud. Boris Nikolaevich Bugaev) (1880–1934): A leading Symbolist poet and novelist, whose most celebrated work is the novel *Petersburg* (1916, 1922).

Berggolts, Olga Fyodorovna (1910–75): A writer whose first works were for children or collections of journalism. Her first volumes of poetry appeared in the 1930s. She was married to the poet Boris Kornilov, who was shot in 1938. Her diaries were confiscated at her death, although excerpts appeared in the West in 1980. Her most important work is her *Leningrad Notebook* (1944), referred to here as her "Blockade diary", an account of the siege of Leningrad.

Blaginina, Elena Aleksandrovna (1903–89): A poet, who also wrote for children.

Blok, Aleksandr Aleksandrovich (1880–1921): The leading poet of Russian Symbolism – also a playwright and essayist – whose influence on 20th-century Russian poetry was colossal. For Zhirmunsky he was "the last Romantic poet" and for Akhmatova "a monument to the beginning of the century".

Blokh, Yakov Noevich (1892–1968): see note 69.

Boldyrev, Aleksandr Nikolaevich (1909–1990?): See note 46.

Bondi, Sergey Mikhaylovich (1891–1983): A leading Pushkin scholar.

Boris Leonidovich: Pasternak.

Boris Mikhailovich: See Eykhenbaum.

Braun, Nikolay Leopoldovich (1902–75): A poet whose early work was influenced by Pasternak, Mandelstam and Tikhonov; later it became more narrative, realistic and reflective.

Brik, Liliya (Lily) Yurevna (1891–1978): The sister of Elsa Triolet, she was married to Osip Brik, through whom she met Mayakovsky. She became the poet's lover and muse; the Briks' home was the Futurist salon.

Brik, Osip Maksimovich (1888–1945): A leading Formalist literary critic and theoretician and one of the founders of OPOYAZ (Society for the Study of Poetic Language). With Mayakovsky and others he was co-founder of the Futurist journals *LEF* (1927–8) and *Novy LEF* (1928–9).

Bryusov, Valery Yakovlevich (1873–1924): A poet and critic. He was the founder of Russian Symbolist poetry and editor of the Symbolist journal *Vesy*, which published the work of all the major Symbolists, including Blok, Bely, Sologub, Gippius, Balmont and Vyacheslav Ivanov. See also note 93.

Bunin, Ivan Alekseevich (1870–1953): A major Russian writer of stories and novellas, whose often lyrical celebrations of the Russian countryside had established his reputation by the turn of the century. He was deeply opposed to the Revolution and left Russia for France in 1920. He was awarded the Nobel Prize in 1933.

Busy Buzzer (Mukha-Tsokotukha): A very popular illustrated children's book by Korney Chukovsky about the short busy life of a fly.

Capella: A concert hall in Leningrad.

Charskaya, Lidiya Alekseevna (1875–1937): A Romantic novelist.

Cheka: The secret police, known at different stages in the history of the USSR as the Cheka, NKVD, MGB, KGB.

Chukovsky, Korney Ivanovich (1882–1969): A critic and influential man of letters and one of Russia's best-loved writers for children. He was awarded a doctorate by Oxford University in 1962.

Circus: The home of the Leningrad State Circus.

cranes of Ibycus . . . talking reed: "The Cranes of Ibycus" (1797) is a ballad by Schiller; the "talking reed" is an Eastern Legend. Each has the inevitability of revenge as its theme, and in each case the natural world is the only witness to a murder and later speaks out against it, bringing about the exposure of the perpetrators.

Dadon: Herzen called Nicholas I Dadon after a comical and belligerent Tsar in Pushkin's poem "The Golden Cockerel".

Delmas, Lyubov Aleksandrovna (1879–1969): A singer and one of Blok's lovers, to whom he dedicated the verse cycle "Carmen".

D'Anthès, Georges (1812–95): The officer, rumoured to have been having an affair with Pushkin's wife, Natalya Goncharova, who killed Pushkin in a duel in 1837.

Detizdat: The State Publishing House for Children's Literature (literary and popular scientific), which had offices in Moscow and Leningrad. See also notes 10, 19 and 20.

Detskoe: Formerly Tsarskoe Selo, the town outside St Petersburg where Akhmatova grew up and attended the Gymnasium.

Dobrolyubov, Nikolay Aleksandrovich (1836–61): An influential 19th-century critic.

Eabany: The companion of the eponymous hero of the Sumerian epic, *Gilgamesh*, on whose behalf Gilgamesh descended into hell with the hope of returning his friend to life. The name "Eabany" in the old translation of the epic (Leningrad, 1919) is the result of an inaccurate reading of the cuneiform script. Today the name is transcribed as "Enkidu". (See *The Epic of Gilgamesh*, translated by I. S. Dyakonov, Leningrad, 1961. See also *BPL–A*, p. 449.)

embankment: The embankment of the Neva river in Leningrad.

Engineers' Castle: Formerly the Mikhailovsky Castle, it was built between 1797 and 1800. The castle was the last residence of Paul I, and the site of his murder in 1801.

Esenin, Sergey Aleksandrovich (1895–1925): A popular poet noted for his lyric descriptions of the Russian countryside. He married Isadora Duncan in 1922 and travelled to Western Europe and the USA with her. In the 1920s his popularity was rivalled only by Mayakovsky. He hanged himself in a Leningrad hotel in 1925.

ewig weiblich: Eternally feminine.

Eykhenbaum, Boris Mikhailovich (1886–1959): A literary historian and leading Formalist critic.

Ezhov, Nikolay Ivanovich (1894–1939): A member of the Central Committee from 1934 and chief of the NKVD (1936–8) during the Terror.

Fadeev, Aleksandr Aleksandrovich (1901–56): A Soviet novelist whose books include *The Rout* (1927) and *The Young Guard* (1945), both of which were held up in the Stalin years as models of Socialist Realism. He was Secretary General of the Union of Soviet Writers (1946–53). He committed suicide in 1956.

Fedin, Konstantin Aleksandrovich (1892–1977): A member of the Serapion Brethren, leading Fellow-Traveller and, later, veteran Soviet novelist whose best-known books are *Cities and Years* (1924) and *The Bonfire* (1961). He was Pasternak's next-door neighbour in Peredelkino.

Filosofov, Dmitry Vladimirovich (1872–1940): A critic and publicist, who wrote for *The World of Art*.

Fink, Viktor Grigorievich (1888–1973): A critic, publicist and memoirist.

Fyodor Kuzmich: See Sologub.

Fontanka: One of the three main canals crossing Nevsky Prospekt in Leningrad, on the banks of which stood Fontanny House, formerly the Sheremetev Palace. See also note 6.

Gippius, Zinaida Nikolaevna (1869–1945): A poet, prose-writer, playwright, essayist and critic. She was active in the religious and philosophical societies of St Petersburg at the turn of the century. She emigrated with her hsuband Dmitry Sergeevich Merezhovsky in 1919 and became prominent in émigré life in Paris.

Golenischev-Kutuzov, Count Arseny Arkadievich (1848–1913): A minor lyrical poet and literary critic.

Gollerbakh, Erich Fyodorovich: See note 91.

Goncharov, Ivan Aleksandrovich (1812–91): An important realist writer whose best-known novel is *Oblomov* (1859).

Gorenko, Anna: Real name of Anna Akhmatova:

Goslitizdat: State Literary Publishing House, and effectively the main censor; it was also known as Gosizdat and Goslit.

Ira: See Irina Nikolaevna Punina.

Gosizdat: Abbreviation for Goslitizdat (see above).

Guild: See Poets' Guild.

House of Creativity: Each artistic union had, and has to this day, a House of Creativity, where writers, artists and musicians could rent rooms in which to work and rest.

House of Entertaining Science: Occupying part of the Sheremetev Palace, the House of Entertaining Science was home to a publishing house, a reference library and several science clubs.

Ivanov, Vyacheslav Ivanovich (1866–1949): A poet and leading figure of the Symbolist movement. Ivanov's fifth-floor appartment in Petersburg, known as the Tower, was the most famous literary salon in Russia. He emigrated in 1924.

Izmaylov, Nikolay Vasilievich (1893–1981): A scholar who worked at Pushkin House (q.v.).

Khardzhiev, Nikolay Ivanovich: see note 5.

Khlebnikov, Velimir (pseud. Viktor Vladimirovich) (1885–1922): A Futurist poet and theoretician noted for his linguistic experimentation. He died of malnutrition in 1922, his work neglected.

Koktebel: See Voloshin.

Kolya: Nikolay Davidenkov. See note 24.

Korney Ivanovich: See Chukovsky.

Kruchyonykh, Aleksey Eliseevich (1886–1968): Futurist poet and theoretician noted for his extreme linguistic experiments; a member of LEF.

Kseniya Grigorievna: Davidenkova. See footnote on p. 62.

Kukriniksy: The collective pseudonym of three painters who worked together – Mikhail Kupryanov, Porfiry Krylov and Nikolay Sokolov.

Kuzmin, Mikhail Alekseevich (1875–1936): A major 20th-century Russian poet, whose work – he published a seminal essay "On Clarity" in 1910 – to some extent prefigured Acmeism. He was excluded from literary life from 1924 and published nothing after 1929; he died destitute.

Kvitko, Lev Moiseevich: See note 101.

LAPP: Leningrad Association of Proletarian Writers.

Leningrad: A literary journal published in Leningrad.

Lermontov, Mikhail Yurevich (1814–41): One of Russia's greatest Romantic poets and novelists, author of *A Hero of Our Time*. A contemporary of Pushkin, he too was killed in a duel.

Levin, Miron Pavlovich: see notes 20 and 29.

Lidiya Yakovlevna: Ginzburg. See note 38.

Lifshits, Benedikt Konstantinovich (1886–1938): A poet associated with the Futurists; also a translator of French prose and poetry, particularly the work of the French Symbolists.

Literatura i iskusstvo (Literature and Art): A bi-monthly journal.

Literaturnaya gazeta (Literary Gazette): The weekly paper of the Writers' Union.

Literaturny Sovremmenik (Literary Contemporary): A monthly literary journal, the organ of the Leningrad branch of the Writers' Union, published from 1933 to 1941.

Litfond (Literary fund): An organization set up in 1859 in St Petersburg in order to help writers and their families who were in need. It closed down during the Civil War, but was revived in 1927.

Lotta: Rakhil Moiseevna Khay (1906–49). See note 52.

Lozinsky, Mikhail Leonidovich (1886–1955): Regarded as one of the greatest translators of poetry and prose in Russian Literature. See also note 7.

Lycée period: Akhmatova is referring to Pushkin's time (1812–17) at the Lycée in Tsarskoe Selo, which marked the beginning of his extraordinary career as a poet. There he began to read widely and to write poetry in a variety of forms and to gain an entrée to literary circles in the capital.

Lyubov Dmitrievna: Blok's wife.

Lyonechka: Leonid Borisovich Pasternak (1938–1976). Pasternak's son by Zinaida Nikolaevna.

Lyusha (also Lyushenka): Elena Tsezarevna Chukovskaya – the author's daughter.

Maecenas: Gaius Maecenas (c. 70–8 BC). A Roman statesman, who was an adviser to Augustus and renowned as a patron of Horace and Virgil. Here "Maecenas" is ironically intended, referring to NKVD informers. Usually in Russian *Metsenat* means patron.

Makovsky, Sergey Konstantinovich (1877–1962): A poet, critic, art theorist and writer of memoirs, who founded the leading art journal *Apollon* with Nikolay Gumilyov and was its editor (1909–13).

Marble Palace: An example of early classical architecture in Russia, the palace was built 1768–85.

Marina Ivanovna: Tsvetaeva.

Marshak, Samuil Yakovlevich (1887–1964): Translator, poet and children's writer, who was head of Detizdat until 1937, the State Publishing House for Children's Literature.

Matvey Petrovich (Mitya): Bronshteyn. See ". . . But strong are the bolts of prison gates" p. 243.

Max: See Voloshin.

Mayakovsky, Vladimir Vladimirovich (1893–1930): The leading figure in Russian Futurism, who came to prominence with the publication of the manifesto *A Slap in the Face of Public Taste* (1912). His verse tragedy *Vladimir Mayakovsky* was produced as part of a Futurist event in Luna Park, St Petersburg, in December 1913. He committed suicide in 1930.

Maykov, Apollon Nikolaevich (1821–97): A well-known 19th-century poet; a contemporary of Tyutchev.

Mendeleevs: The family of Blok's wife, Lyubov Dmitrievna; her father was the celebrated chemist D. I. Mendeleev.

Ménière's disease: A disorder of the inner ear characterized by a ringing or buzzing in the ear, dizziness, and impaired hearing.

Merezhkovskys: Merezhkovsky, Dmitry Sergeevich (1866–1941): writer and philosopher, husband of Zinaida Gippius (see above). Merezhkovsky emigrated with his wife first to Poland, then to Paris where he died, an opponent of the Communist régime to the end.

Mickiewicz, Adam (1798–1855): Poland's national poet.

Mikhail Alekseevich: See Kuzmin.

Mikhail Leonidovich: See Lozinsky.

Modzalevsky, Boris Lvovich (1874–28): A philologist, literary scholar, publisher and Senior Curator of Pushkin House, whose commentaries on Pushkin were a by-word for excellence. His son, Lev Borisovich (1902–48), was also a literary scholar, who produced important academic descriptions of Pushkin's manuscripts.

Moscow Art Theatre: Theatre founded by Vladimir Nemirovich-Danchenko and Konstantin Stanislavsky, which introduced to the theatre the works of Chekhov, Gorky, etc.

Nadya: Nadezhda Yakovlevna Mandelstam (1899–1980). Wife of the poet Mandelstam and the author of *Hope against Hope* and *Hope Abandoned*.

Nedobrovo, Nikolay Vladimirovich (1882–1919): A philologist and literary critic, who had studied in St Petersburg, and was the author of an important article about Akhmatova (1915). A close friend of Akhmatova (1914–17); she addressed many poems to him.

Nekrasov, Nikolay Alekseevich (1821–78): One of the great poets of the generation that followed Pushkin and Lermontov whose work was more civic and realist than personal and Romantic.

Nevsky: Nevsky Prospekt; one of the main boulevards in Leningrad.

Neygaus, Genrikh Gustavovich (1888–1964): A celebrated pianist and teacher of music. Pasternak fell in love with his wife, Zinaida Nikolaevna, in 1931, and later married her; despite this the two men remained friends.

Nikolay Ivanovich: Khardzhiev (1903–). See note 5.

Nikolay Nikolaevich: Punin. See note 1.

Nikolay Stepanovich (Kolya): Gumilyov. Akhmatova's first husband.

Nina: Nina Antonovna Olshevskaya. See note 53.

NKO: People's Commissariat of Defence.

Novy mir (New World): Moscow literary and political monthly journal, organ of the Union of Soviet Writers, founded in 1925.

Obllit (*Obl*astnaya *lit*eratura): Regional Office of Literary Censorship.

Ogonyok (Little Flame): A weekly social–political and artistic, illustrated magazine, published in Moscow since 1923.

Oktyabr (October): Soviet political and cultural monthly journal, organ of the RSFSR Union of Writers, founded in 1924.

Olga Nikolaevna: Vysotskaya. See note 18.

Olya: Olga Afanasevna Glebova-Sudeykina (1885–1945). See note 6.

Orbeli, Iosif Abgarovich (1887–1961): Orientalist, Academician, Director of the Hermitage (1934–51).

Orlov, Vladimir (1908–85): A prominent Soviet literary critic and winner of the USSR State Prize (1950); he devoted 50 years of his life to studying Blok.

Osip: Osip Emilevich Mandestam (1892–1938).

Osmyorkin, Aleksandr Aleksandrovich (1892–1953). See note 51.

Ostroumova-Lebedeva, Anna Petrovna (1851–1955): An engraver, portraitist and water-colourist.

Penaty: The artist Repin's residence not far from Petersburg.

People's Will: A populist revolutionary organization formed in 1879, responsible for the assassination of Alexander II in 1881.

Peredelkino: The colony of Litfond dachas outside Moscow which were let to writers, and where Pasternak, Korney Chukovsky, Fedin and others lived.

Peredvizhniki (The Wanderers [literally the Brotherhood of Travelling Exhibitions]): A group of artists founded in 1871 by Ivan Kramskoy, Vasily Perov, Nikolay Ge, Ivan Shishkin and other former students of the Petersburg Academy of Arts. They were soon joined by such major painters as Ilya Repin and Vasily Surikov. Their work was central to the development of Russian art in the late 19th century, and their commitment to "Nationality and Realism" and hostility to West European developments in art became the foundation stone of Socialist Realism.

Pisarevism: Dmitry Ivanovich Pisarev (1840–68) was a philosopher and revolutionary democrat who preached socialism through industrialization.

Poets' Guild: A group of poets, including Gumilyov and Nikolay Gorodetsky, who in 1911 broke away from and set up in opposition to the Symbolist poet Vyacheslav Ivanov's Academy of Verse. Out of this group grew the Acmeists, who included Akhmatova and Mandelstam amongst their number.

Poet's Library (Biblioteka Poeta): The Poet's Library (big series [*bolshaya seriya*]/ small series [*malaya seriya*]) is the standard edition for Russian poets and was edited by Yury Tynyanov from 1931 until his death in 1943.

Pravda (Truth): The main newspaper of the Communist Party of the USSR.

Printer's sheets: A printer's sheet was one signature of a book. In Russia at that time a typical signature comprised 24 pages. Thus Akhmatova was warning Chukovskaya that she was taking on the proof-reading of a book of some 264 pages.

Prival Komediantov: The name under which the Stray Dog "cabaret" (q.v.) was reopened after it had been closed by the police in 1915.

Punin, Nikolay Nikolaevich: Akhmatova's third husband. See note 1.

Punina, Irina Nikolaevna: N. N. Punin's daughter by Anna Evgenevna Arens. See also note 1.

Pushkin House: Founded in St Petersburg (1905) as an archive and museum of Russian Literature, it later became part of the Russian Academy of Sciences (1918), and under A. Lunacharsky (People's Commissionar of Education) was merged (1931) with the Institute of Russian Literature.

Pushkin's notebooks: These were the originals on loan from Pushkin House.

Rachel: Famous French classical actress of the late 19th century.

Radlov, Sergey Ernestovich (1892–1958): A leading soviet producer who in the early '20s organized mass Revolutionary spectacles in Leningrad. After an association with Meyerhold he became well known in the '30s for his original productions of Shakespeare. See also note 78.

Radlova, Anna Dmitrievna (1891–1949): Poet and translator, particularly noted for her versions of Shakespeare. See also footnote on p. 46 and note 78.

Raskolnikov, Fyodor Fyodorovich (1892–1939): Deputy People's Commissar for the Navy (1918); Soviet Ambassador to Afghanistan (1922–3); Soviet Ambassador to Bulgaria 1937; committed suicide in Paris in 1939.

Razlyv: A town on the Baltic, one of the stops on the Finland railway.

Red Arrow: the Moscow–Leningrad express.

Repin, Ilya (1844–1930): One of the great Russian painters of the 19th and 20th centuries.

Reysner, Larisa Mikhailovna (1897–1928): A Bolshevik heroine of the Russian Revolution, author of *The Front* (1922); wife of Fyodor Raskolnikov, whom she divorced in 1922. According to Trotsky, she had "the beauty of an Olympian goddess, a subtle mind and the courage of a warrior".

Rozhdestvensky, Vsevolod Aleksandrovich (1895–1977): A poet influenced by Acmeism.

Rozanov, Vasily Vasilievich (1856–1919): A writer, literary critic, philosopher and political journalist, who wrote freely about sexuality and gender at a time when these subjects were a source of embarrassment and tended to be overlooked, as they continued to be under the Communist régime. Regarded as one of the great writers (of non-fiction), his works include an influential essay on Dostoevsky's *Brothers Karamazov* (1894), *Fallen Leaves* (1913–15, discussed on p. 55) and *The Apocalypse of Our Times* (1917–18).

Ruslan and Lyudmila: Puhskin's first narrative poem, a folktale epic, begun in 1817 and completed in March 1820.

Russian Women: A long narrative poem by Nikolay Nekrasov.

Rybakovs: See note 73.

St Isaac's: One of St Petersburg's two main cathedrals, which stands in the centre of the city.

Saltykov-Schedrin, Mikhail Evgrafovich (pseud. N. Shchedrin) (1826–89): A polemicist and novelist, who is now considered the greatest satirist of 19th-century Russia. *A Contemporary Idyll* (1877–83) was one of a number of novels he published which satirized Russian life and institutions.

Samuil Yakovlevich: See Marshak

Schmidt: Pasternak's "historical epic" poem *Lieutenant Schmidt*, which was first published in serial form in 1926.

Shchyogolev, Pavel Eliseevich (1877–1931): A Pushkin specialist, and husband of the actress Valentina Andreevna Shchyogoleva (1878–1931).

Sergey Konstantinovich: See Makovsky.

Severyanin, Igor Vasilievich (1887–1941): A poet noted for his flamboyance and verbal extravagance; leader of the Ego-Futurists, he emigrated to Estonia in 1919, and died there under German occupation during the Second World War.

Shaginyan, Marietta Sergeevna (1888–1982): Soviet novelist and (before the Revolution) a minor poet on the fringes of the Symbolist movement. During the 1920s she was known mainly for her attempt to write thrillers and detective fiction in Western style.

Shakalik (lit. little jackal): Akhmatova's next-door neighbour's son, Vladimir (Vova) Smirnov, brother of Valya.

Shefner, Vadim Sergeevich (1914–): A lyric poet whose poems were first collected under the title *The Bright Shore* (1940).

Shevchenko, Taras (1814–61): The greatest Ukrainian poet of the 19th century.

Shileyko, Vladimir Kazimirovich: Akhmatova's second husband. See note 17.

Shura: Aleksandra Iosifovna Lyubarskaya. See note 10.

Simeonov Bridge: A bridge over one of the Neva's tributaries.

Simonov, Konstantin Mikhailovich (1915–79): A popular Soviet author best known for his wartime lyrics and novels, such as *Days and Nights*, about the Battle for Stalingrad.

Slonimsky, Mikhail (Misha) Leonidovich (1897–1972): A member of the Serapion Brethren, who first published stories and later novels. He was a member of the board of the Writers Union (1934–54).

Smirnova, Tanya: Akhmatova's next-door neighbour in Fontanny House in Leningrad; mother of Vova (Shakalik) and Valya.

Sologub, Fyodor Kuzmich (1863–1927): A poet, novelist and playwright, and leading figure in the Symbolist movement, he is best known for his novel *The Petty Demon* (1907).

Sovetskiy pisatel (Soviet Writer): A Moscow literary publishing house founded in 1934.

Sovnarkom: Soviet of People's Commissars.

Spassky, Sergey Dmitrievich (1898–1956): A poet and prose-writer; at one time close to the Futurists, and a friend and correspondent of Boris Pasternak. Spassky was arrested in 1936 or '37, but was at liberty again by 1939. In 1949 he was arrested again and did not return from the camps until 1954.

Spektorsky: A novel in verse by Boris Pasternak, published in 1931.

Stray Dog: A famous literary "cabaret", where all the leading poets would recite their poems, and which before the Revolution was the favourite meeting place of the literary intellgentsia of St Petersburg. It was closed by the police in 1915.

Summer Garden: A large park in Leningrad, famous for its literary associations.

Sudeykina: Olga Afanasevna Glebova-Sudeykina. See note 6.

Tamara: Gabbe. See note 57.

Tanya: See Smirnova.

Tanya (Tanechka) pp. 84–6: Tatyana Evseevna Gurevich. See note 56.

Tatlin: Sculptor of the Soviet period.

Tishenka: Aleksandr Nikolaevich Tikhonov. See note 36.

Tower, The: Vyacheslav Ivanov's fifth-floor apartment, known as "The Tower", was the main meeting place for the Symbolists in St Petersburg until 1913 and the most renowned literary salon in the capital.

Tsarskoe Selo (lit. Tsar's Village): The imperial residence and estate just outside St Petersburg, where Pushkin attended the Lycée and where Akhmatova spent part of her childhood. Renamed Detskoe after the Revolution.

Tsentrifuga: A Futurist group founded in 1914, whose key figures were Nikolay Aseev, Sergey Bobrov and Boris Pasternak. It had its own publishing house and published a series of poetry almanacs.

Tsezar Samoylovich: See Volpe.

Tsyavlovsky, Mstislav Aleksandrovich (1883–1947): A scholar and a leading Pushkinist.

Tusya: Tamara Grigorievna Gabbe. See note 57.

Tynyanov, Yury Nikolaevich (1896–1943): A literary scholar, university professor and novelist, who was one of the leading figures in the Formalist school of criticism. For the last 12 years of his life he was editor of the Poet's Library (q.v.) in the publishing house Sovetskiy pisatel.

Tyrsa, Nikolay Andreevich (1887–1942): An engraver and artist.

Tyutchev, Fyodor Ivanovich (1803–73): A major 19th-century lyric poet, who is best-known for his poems addressed to the young love of his middle years, Elena Deniseva.

Vera (Verochka): Nikolaevna Anikieva. See note 35.

Veresaev, Vikenty Vikentevich (pseud. Smidovich) (1867–1945): A writer, scholar and literary biographer, who compiled lives of Pushkin and Gogol amongst others, and collaborated with Mikhail Bulgakov on plays for the Moscow Art Theatre in the 1930s.

Vesy (The Scales): The leading literary journal (1904–9) of the Symbolist movement.

Vladimir Georgievich (V.G.): see Garshin.

Volodya: Vladimir Kazimirovich Shileyko. See note 17.

Volokhova, A. A.: An actress and one of Blok's lovers, to whom he dedicated the verse cycle "Snow Mask".

Voloshin, Maksimilian Aleksandrovich (1877–1932): A poet, artist, translator and critic, who played an active role in the literary artistic life of pre-Revolutionary Russia. He was on the fringes of the Symbolist movement, and was involved with the journal *Apollon*, with the "World of Art" and with the publishing house, Musaget. In their house in Koktebel (Eastern Crimea), Voloshin and his mother, Elena (Pra) Ottobaldovna Voloshina, created a haven for the literary and artistic intelligentsia regardless of their politics. Their visitors included Mandelstam, Erenburg and Tsvetaeva.

Volpe, Tsezar Samoylovich (1904–41): A researcher and critic of Russian literature, who was dismissed as editor of the literary journal *Zvezda* for publishing Mandelstam's "Journey to Armenia" in 1932. See note 33.

Vova, Vovochka: See Smirnova.

VTEK: Labour Medical Board of Expertise.

Vyacheslav's: Ivanov's salon. See The Tower.

Vyazemsky, Prince Pyotr Andreevich (1792–1878): A critic, poet, translator and diarist. The son of an enlightened aristocrat and a contemporary of Pushkin, who delighted in polemic. He fought at the battle of Borodino (1812), squandered his fortune, lost a post in Warsaw because of his liberal sympathies (1821), and spent 20 years working in the Ministry of Finance. See also note 38.

Vyshinsky, Andrey Yanuarevich (1883–1954): Appointed Prosecutor General in 1935, he was thus the chief accuser during Terror.

Writers' Bookshop: A bookshop on Nevsky Prospekt reserved for writers.

Yakhontov, Vladimir Nikolaevich (1899–1945): An actor famous for his recitals of the Russian poets.

Year 1905, The: a narrative poem by Boris Pasternak about the 1905 Revolution, published in 1927.

Yury Nikolaevich (Yu. N.): See Tynyanov.

Zaum (zaumny yazyk – transrational language): An experimental language invented by the Futurists, who were concerned to transmit their message, which the reader or listener would intuit, by the sound rather than by the rational meaning of the words.

Zelinsky, Kornely Lyutsianovich (1896–1970): A critic and historian of literature, who was a founder-member of the literary Constructivists.

Zhenichka: A close friend of O. M. Brik.

Zhizn iskusstva (The Life of Art): An art journal.

Zhukovsky, Vasily Andreevich (1783–1852): A lyric poet, noted particularly for his translations of German Romantic poetry, and of Gray's "Elegy".

Zina: Zinaida Nikolaevna (Neygaus); Pasternak's second wife.

Zinaida Nikolaevna (pp. 61–2): See Gippius.

Zoshchenko, Mikhail Mikhailovich (1895–1958): A dazzling satirist and one of Soviet Russia's most popular writers in the 1920s. During the 1930s he came under increasing pressure to follow the party line, and in 1946, after the brief relaxation of artistic guide lines during the 1941–45 war, he was, with Akhmatova, subjected to a blistering attack by Stalin's close associate the Politburo member Zhdanov and expelled from the Writer's Union.

Zoya (Zoechka): Zoya Moiseevna Zadunayskaya. See note 19.

Zvezda (The Star): The monthly organ of the Leningrad branch of the Union of Soviet Writers, founded in 1924.

INDEX